RANDOM
HOUSE
LARGE
PRINT

Perfectly Clear

Perfectly Clear

Escaping Scientology and Fighting for the Woman I Love

MICHELLE LeCLAIR
AND ROBIN GABY FISHER

RANDOM HOUSE
LARGE PRINT

Cover photograph by Ross Oscar Knight Photography
Cover design by Katie Anderson

Penguin is committed to publishing works of quality and integrity. In that spirit, we are proud to offer this book to our readers; however, the story, the experiences and the words are the author's alone.

This book is the author's account of her experience leaving the Church of Scientology. Dates, places, titles and events are all factual, but the names and identifying characteristics of certain individuals have been changed.

The Library of Congress has established a Cataloging-in-Publication record for this title.

ISBN: 978-1-9848-2763-0

www.penguinrandomhouse.com/large-print-format-books

FIRST LARGE PRINT EDITION

Printed in the United States of America

10 9 8 7 6 5 4 3 2 1

This Large Print edition published in accord with the standards of the N.A.V.H.

This book is dedicated to the two greatest
loves of my life.

T, you are the one on whose shoulder I rest,
the one whose arms keep me protected,
the one whose heart has never stopped loving me
and the one whose soul opened mine
to the greatest gift that God could give . . .
the freedom to love.
I will love you for the rest of our lives and beyond.

To my children, Sage, Savannah, Jadon and London,
you gave me the strength to find freedom for us!
Your love, sweetness and resilience pushed me
to persevere when I didn't think
I had the strength to keep going.
Please, never forget, my sweet darlings, that truth,
love and family will always set you free.

There are only two answers for the handling of people from 2.0 down on the Tone Scale, neither one of which has anything to do with reasoning with them or listening to their justification of their acts. The first is to raise them on the Tone Scale by un-enturbulating some of their theta by any one of the three valid processes. The other is to dispose of them quietly and without sorrow.

—L. RON HUBBARD, **SCIENCE OF SURVIVAL**

In addition to violating and abusing its own members' civil rights, the organization [Scientology] over the years with its "Fair Game" doctrine has harassed and abused those persons not in the Church whom it perceives as enemies. The organization clearly is schizophrenic and paranoid, and the bizarre combination seems to be a reflection of its founder LRH [L. Ron Hubbard]. The evidence portrays a man who has been virtually a pathological liar when it comes to his history, background, and achievements. The writings and documents in evidence additionally reflect his egoism, greed, avarice, lust for power, and vindictiveness and aggressiveness against persons perceived by him to be disloyal or hostile. At the same time it appears that he is charismatic and highly capable of motivating, organizing, controlling, manipulating, and inspiring his adherents.

—SUPERIOR COURT JUDGE PAUL BRECKENRIDGE,
CHURCH OF SCIENTOLOGY OF CALIFORNIA
v. GERALD ARMSTRONG, JUNE 1984

CONTENTS

Perfectly
Clear

INTRODUCTION
The Raid

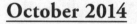

October 2014

I awaken with a jolt. My bedside clock says six forty-five a.m. I have overslept by almost an hour. I never oversleep! Why didn't I hear the alarm? I live in a cozy Spanish-style cottage nestled in the hills overlooking Pasadena with my partner, Charley, my kids and my mom. Charley is in bed beside me. The house is quiet. No one else is stirring. I have to get up. The kids have to be fed and dressed and gotten off to school and there isn't much time.

The sun won't be up for another twenty minutes. I throw off the covers, switch on the bedroom lamp and begin pulling on my workout clothes from the day before. I have one leg in my pants and am struggling with the other, but it doesn't want to cooperate. "C'mon!" I say, fighting with the stubborn pants leg.

I am finally making progress when I hear noises that don't belong. The hum of car engines? The squeak of the outside gate? I stop what I am doing for just a second, trying to make out the vague sounds outside. Suddenly, banging on my windows and doors shatters the morning quiet. The dogs bark frantically. What in God's name?

A man shouts, "Open the door!" My heart is hammering in my chest as I open my bedroom door. I am still only partially dressed. My knees are knocking together, threatening to buckle. Beams of light are streaming in the front windows and crisscrossing the living room. What the hell is going on?

I can't tell how many people are outside my house, but it sounds like an army of angry men. I hear the word "police." Surely they have the wrong house. "I'll handle this," Charley says.

My mom, still dressed in her pajamas, has crept upstairs from her bedroom and stands across from me, her palms up, her face contorted in confusion and fear. She mouths her words: **What's going on?**

Mom goes for the children, who are sleeping downstairs. I duck back into my bedroom. I straighten my clothes and grab a baseball cap to cover my slept-on hair. As I rush out of my room, I hear Charley. "Who are you and what do you want?" she asks, her voice firm and sure.

"Open up!" someone bellows.

Charley pulls the door open just enough for us to see a posse of scowling uniformed men on the other side. Some are wearing jackets with an LAPD insignia on the breast pocket. Some have holsters with guns. My God.

The pack storms past Charley into our home and I can smell their maleness. Testosterone mixed with sweat. The odor sickens me. A short, beefy officer with a buzz cut shows his badge and grunts, "Which one of you is Michelle Seward?"

"I am."

He hands me a paper that says "Search Warrant," cuing the forces to fan out. As they scatter, they remind me of worker ants crawling over an anthill.

My children appear on the stairs with my mother. My nine-year-old daughter is whimpering. My seven-year-old twin boys are wailing. I motion for my mother to take them back downstairs.

"Mommy is okay," I say. "Everything will be okay."

The team sets up shop in my tiny first-floor office. This is my sanctuary, the place where Charley and I drink tea by the fireplace and read the morning papers before the kids wake. I stand by helplessly as strangers rummage through my drawers, my file cabinets, and anything else they wish. The searchers make copies of innocuous documents: divorce papers, bill stubs, medical records, tax returns. They act as though they have no regard for my belongings—not my antique chairs, my favorite family photographs, the precious artifacts I have collected on trips to Africa.

While Charley watches the searchers, I step outside to call my attorney.

"The police are here and they're looking for something. I have no idea what . . ."

Steve Cooley is a celebrity on the Los Angeles legal scene, revered by both lawyers and cops. Before going into private practice, he spent forty years on the prosecutorial side of the California justice system. For the last twelve of those years, he headed the Los Angeles County District Attorney's Office, the very office that had ordered the raid on my home. He is familiar with my trouble with the church. He listens quietly as my words spill out.

"Who's the head deputy?" he asks. "Let me speak to him."

The deputy looks bewildered when I hand him the phone. He puts it to his ear. "Hello? . . . Hi, sir. How are you, sir? Yes, sir." The deputy reads the search warrant to my lawyer.

When he is finished speaking, he hands the phone back to me. I put it to my ear and Steve is already talking.

"Michelle, stay calm and cooperate with them," he says. "Be at my office as soon as the search is over."

After several hours of work, the officers finish turning my house upside down. The rooms are in disarray and muddy boot tracks stain the floor tiles. Before they leave, they confiscate my cell phone and my computer and search my car.

Huddled in the driveway is a clutch of people I recognize from the neighborhood. Our front gate is broken, and they're concerned that we've been robbed. An officer tells them not to worry, no one has been burglarized; this is a police search. I am humiliated.

Although I wish I could disappear, I force myself to stand up straight, pull my shoulders back. "What is this all about?" I ask again, more insistently than before.

The officer who handed me the search warrant finally speaks. "Ma'am," he says, dispassionately, "we have been informed that you have property in your possession that shows you've committed a felony."

❖

From the moment I decided to publicly leave the Church of Scientology, my life unspooled as if I were a character in a suspense novel. Strange cars idle at the curb outside my home at all hours of the day. Men wearing dark glasses follow me to the grocery store, the airport and my kids' school. My computer and my phone have been hacked. I have to be careful about everything I say, even in the privacy of my own home. I am under siege, but my stalker is slippery and elusive. I am fighting a ghost, an adversary I cannot see. I know, though, who is behind the crusade to destroy me.

Founder L. Ron Hubbard had explicit instructions for taking down anyone who threatened the church: "This is the correct procedure," Hubbard wrote in a 1967 policy memorandum. "Spot who is attacking us. Start investigating them promptly for felonies or worse using our own professionals, not outside agencies. Start feeding lurid, blood, sex, crime, actual evidence on the attackers to the press. Don't ever tamely submit to an investigation of us. Make it rough, rough on attackers all the way . . . There has never yet been an attacker who was not reeking with crime. All we had to do was look for it and murder would come out."

And so they watch, waiting for any misstep, searching for anything they can find, or twist, to use against me. Information is power, even when it is distorted. Especially when it's distorted.

———◆———

It is close to noon by the time I pull out of the driveway and head out to see my attorney. When I hit the freeway, I see that, as usual, it is choked with traffic. I merge into the right lane. Stop and go. Stop and go. I hate this about LA. No matter what time of day it is, you can't get anywhere on time. Will I ever get there? Adrenaline courses

through my veins. Fight or flight. I fight the urge
to jump out of the car by gripping the steering
wheel as vehemently as if my life depended on it.
Deep breath, I tell myself. **In, and out. In, and
out.**

I am trembling when I arrive at my attorney's
office. For a moment I sit in my car and try to
compose myself. I think of my children. I taste my
salty tears, tilt the rearview mirror toward me and
wipe my eyes.

Cooley is one of a stable of attorneys I have had
to employ since this nightmare began. He is an
imposing figure, a large, burly man and all business. "How are you?" he asks when I walk into
his office. The question sounds more like a polite
refrain than an expression of genuine concern, but
Cooley's eyes are sympathetic, betraying his hard
shell. I try not to cry. I know he doesn't do well
with tears.

Steve has invited a private investigator, Jon
Perkins, to join us. I collapse into a chair between
the two men. I can't help it; a loud sob racks my
body.

For four years, I have been the target of a witch
hunt by what could only have been the very people
I once trusted with my life: my fellow Scientologists. I foolishly believed my adversaries would
eventually tire of harassing me and move on to
the next "enemy," but false allegations from church
files landed anonymously on the desk of the Los

Angeles County District Attorney and I have been fighting to clear my name ever since.

What was happening to me was straight out of a Scientology book of dirty tricks, copied from a policy written in 1965 by L. Ron Hubbard that describes "anonymous third partying," a tactic of tipping off authorities to alleged unlawful activities or crimes committed by enemies of the church. "Show me any person who is critical of us and I'll show you crimes and intended crimes that would stand a magistrate's hair on end," Hubbard wrote.

In its "Third Party Law," the church defines "anonymous third parties" as instigators who quietly stir up trouble and stand by enjoying the shit show they cause. "The usually unsuspected and 'reasonable' third party, the bystander who denies any part of it, is the one that brought the conflict into existence in the first place," the law states. Parishioners are cautioned to be on the lookout for these phantom third parties, but the church itself instigated trouble and hid behind a veil of anonymity when it was in its own interests.

My troubles began when my Scientology mentor outed me in a report to the church Ethics Department, accusing me of questioning the legitimacy of some of the church's rules and beliefs: specifically, those that applied to homosexuality.

Parishioners routinely tattle on each other with written reports. I'd written them myself. Keeping each other in check was part of being a responsible member of the church. Hubbard, whose observations and beliefs inform church doctrine, explained the strategy of snitching in a 1982 church policy letter: "To succeed in this 'civilization' or any society, crude or sophisticated, one has to act continually to keep one's own environment under some control." I was well aware that, depending on the gravity of an allegation, a report to the church's Ethics Department often led to severe punishment and even expulsion.

Hubbard had declared homosexuals the lowest form of life—"perverted" and "dangerous" people who should be disdained as enemies of the church. Sixty years later, homophobia was still endemic in Scientology, but people were quieter about it.

I knew the rules, but I recklessly talked myself into believing that, because I was a top donor, contributing millions to the church, my relationship with a woman would be tolerated, or at least ignored. I couldn't have been more mistaken.

Perkins says my case mirrors every covert Scientology smear campaign he has ever uncovered during his career as an investigator. And, like the others, he says, it will be harder than hell to prove.

I knew how vindictive the church could be. I was aware they used the courts to bleed people dry with litigation, and that lying in the name of protecting the sanctity of the church was not only condoned but also encouraged. The ends justified the means, no matter how mean-spirited or outright dishonest the tactics used to win. Still, I hadn't been prepared for the force of their retaliation.

Now I was being accused of a felony?

Hadn't it been enough for church members to damage my good name and sabotage my business with their innuendo and lies? Now they wanted to see me dragged through the criminal justice system, headed for prison?

My thoughts ran wild. I knew of families, friends, marriages and careers torn apart by the church's shadowy actions. I had come to deeply regret that I participated in one of the church's covert campaigns to discredit a reporter from the BBC.

The BBC. Now that was a story. The church was really rattled to learn that journalists from the British news organization were investigating us for a television documentary. The church loathed journalists. L. Ron Hubbard called them "merchants of chaos." Media critics were targeted with "deflect and destroy" campaigns: Deflect bad press by destroying the credibility of the messenger. That was the plan for the BBC.

The group chosen by the church to participate in discrediting the BBC reporter was summoned to a confidential briefing at the executive offices in the Hollywood Guaranty Building. It was March 2007, long before I began having doubts about the church. The Guaranty Building is closed to the public, and even most Scientologists never get to see inside. It's the headquarters for the church's supersecretive Office of Special Affairs (OSA), the CIA of Scientology. Everyone who worked there at the time was dressed in uniform: navylike dress blues with gold buttons, service stripes and rank badges. Security was airtight. All guests' trips to the bathroom were escorted. All the church's covert operations are launched from there.

Our group included Kirstie Alley, Anne Archer, Leah Remini and a few other high-profile church members. A security detail ushered us upstairs and led us to a conference room a few steps from the elevator. Going beyond that boundary would have required a higher security clearance. The conference room was spacious and tastefully decorated with dark cherrywood tables and accents and bookcases filled with volumes of Scientology texts. A portrait of L. Ron Hubbard hung on the wall.

We sat around a large conference table and made small talk as we waited for the briefing to begin. I was starstruck. It was a real honor to be part of this prestigious group and showed that I was deeply trusted by the church.

After a few minutes, the conference room doors swung open and three of the top church executives strode in. Tommy Davis, the church's spokesman, who is also Anne Archer's son, did most of the talking. He said the BBC was filming a documentary and the church had chosen us for on-camera interviews. John Sweeney, the reporter, was hostile, so we needed to be briefed beforehand, he said.

Davis passed around the notorious Black PR Book, a thick loose-leaf binder with pictures and dossiers of enemies. Sweeney's page was dog-eared. We were each handed dossiers stamped "Confidential," with "intel" about Sweeney's alleged criminal activity and mental problems. Investigators from the OSA had dug up the information, Davis said. None of us questioned it. The word of the church was sacrosanct and we were honor-bound to never question a Scientologist.

For most of the afternoon, we were coached on how to conduct ourselves with Sweeney. Our job was to present a positive front for the camera, to show that we were successful, happy people whose lives had changed for the better because of Scientology. Should Sweeney challenge us with typical questions posed by cynical journalists—about brainwashing, and conspiracies, and physical abuse by church executives, or anything else negative—we were to be indignant and dismissive.

"You know what to do," Davis said. "Dead-agent all of his questions." "Dead-agenting" was church slang for "attacking the attacker." Our job was to deflect the questions and destroy the source.

The next morning, our group met at the Celebrity Centre in Hollywood, where the interview was scheduled to take place. We were served a sumptuous breakfast and given a quick refresher course before Tommy Davis announced that the television crew was setting up in a conference room upstairs. We finished our meal and filed up to a reception area adjacent to the room where the reporter was waiting. You could feel the electricity among us. Everyone knew that the "Get Sweeney" operation came from the top, and the team was ready to oblige our leader.

Anne Archer was first to be interviewed, and she gave a commanding performance. When the reporter asked her about the church's reputation for practicing mind control, she leaned in to him and asked angrily, "Do I look brainwashed to you? How dare you!" I caught a glimpse of Sweeney through a cracked door and felt a little sorry for him. He was about to be struck by the full force of the church's wrath. He wouldn't even know what hit him.

My moment of empathy quickly passed, though, and was replaced by another thought: This man was trying to hurt us. He had no interest in presenting a balanced report. He was our enemy and enemies had to be destroyed. When it was Kirstie's turn to sit in the chair opposite Sweeney, she taunted him for asking what she called his "inappropriate questions" about David Miscavige. "And I think that's probably why he wouldn't do an interview with you. Just like I wouldn't ask you if you're still molesting children." There was a lot of behind-the-scenes laughing and fist pumping after that one.

It pained me now to think about how we'd mocked Sweeney back then and did everything we could to diminish him. As he traveled between churches in Los Angeles and Clearwater, Florida, conducting his interviews, church members followed and goaded him. Davis was the lead soldier charged with getting under Sweeney's skin. He and others videotaped the reporter's every move. At one point, Davis and his entourage confronted Sweeney with a camera when he returned to his hotel at midnight. Sweeney had never said where he was staying. On another occasion, Davis's video crew ambushed the reporter while he was interviewing a former Scientologist in a parking garage. A third time, sensing that Sweeney's nerves were fraying, Davis stuck the camera in the reporter's face and shouted at him. As Scientology cameras rolled, the reporter lost his cool, exploding in a cringeworthy, red-faced rage. We rushed copies of the video to BBC bosses as proof of Sweeney's unprofessionalism and instability. And we posted them on YouTube, also, for its millions of viewers.

Sweeney was a seasoned journalist who had covered conflicts around the world, but it took the Church of Scientology to test his mettle. For months after the on-camera confrontation between Sweeney and Davis, the church played the video at meetings and events. Those of us who had participated boasted about our roles in the mission. The church later used the footage in its own documentary on the BBC's alleged prejudicial reporting tactics.

I knew how far the church would go to exact revenge. I had come to know a merciless church. Not even David Miscavige's closest allies were exempt from retribution if they were suspected of disloyalty—real or imagined. His top executives told of being punished with incarceration in a place called "The Hole," an ant-infested, sweltering set of double-wide trailers on the church's 520-acre compound in San Jacinto, California, where they were confined—for weeks or sometimes years—and forced to do hard labor, sleep on the floor, eat slop and undergo intense interrogation until they collapsed. Even worse, Miscavige's wife, Shelly, was banished to a California mountain compound more than a decade ago and still hasn't been seen in public, allegedly as punishment for displeasing her husband. If the leader's own wife and top commanders were subjected to such cruel and inhumane punishment, the poor BBC reporter never had a chance.

Sweeney's film **Scientology and Me** documented the church's campaign against him. He later wrote about his experience in the UK newspaper **The Independent**: "When I went to the wars for a living, I was gassed, shot at, shelled, bombed and had two sticks of dynamite shoved up my nose," he said. "But never did I feel such fear for my grip on reality as I did investigating the Church of Scientology."

Now they were coming after me. As Jon Perkins said, it would be hard as hell for me to prove it.

The idea of inevitable confrontations struck fear into my heart. It would be one woman—me—against the State of California and the mighty Church of Scientology, with its black heart and billion-dollar bank account. How could I possibly win that fight?

I looked from Jon to Steve, my eyes pleading for some consolation, waiting to hear how we would get out of this mess, that everything was going to be all right, as I'd promised my children hours before. But Steve didn't say anything like that. He was frowning and grim-faced.

"Look," he said. "The church may be behind this and they may not. But now we've got allegations of a crime committed. We need to focus on the accusations, not the church. And we need to bring in a criminal attorney."

"My God," I said. "This is never going to end. It just keeps getting worse. I don't know how much more I can take."

I felt a sense of doom as I left the meeting. Yesterday had been such a good day. No unfamiliar cars outside—at least not that I could see. No odd phone calls or hang-ups. No strangers showing up at the door, pretending to have the wrong address. I remember thinking that maybe my church friends had decided enough time and money had been spent trying to get to me. It had been a pipe dream.

CHAPTER ONE

The Beginning

❖

As I fought against folding under the weight of the threat of criminal investigation, I found myself thinking about my roots. I wondered how different my life might have been if my family had never moved to California.

I was heading into my junior year of high school when my stepfather relocated us from the small city of Norman, Oklahoma, to Los Angeles, where he could pursue his new job. My mother married Steve when I was in the fifth grade. This was her fourth marriage and his first. They met at a neighborhood bar where my mother worked nights as a cocktail waitress following her day job as a dental assistant and a student at Rose State.

Before that, it was just me, my mom and my

younger brother, Jeremy. We lived in a cramped apartment, all we could afford. Our living room was furnished with a rocking chair and a wobbly rolltop desk. The desk doubled as a stand for a small black-and-white television set topped with foil-wrapped rabbit ears. We ate our meals on the floor, sitting atop a spread-out blanket. My brother loved to complain: Why couldn't we have a table like normal people? Mom made light of it and scolded him to "get his knees off the table." Jeremy didn't laugh. But we did.

My mother was always chasing a dream. In so many ways, she and I were more like best friends than mother and daughter. Often, I acted the adult to her child. I didn't mind. I was born an old soul. Childhood games were of little interest to me. I had my own dreams to keep me occupied. In Norman, the highest a girl could aspire to was to marry a doctor, but I knew that living in someone else's shadow wasn't for me. From a very early age I was determined to do something great with my life, and because I came from modest means I knew I would have to work very hard to get there. Whether that meant becoming a surgeon to save people's hearts, or a lawyer to spare someone from a death sentence, my purpose would be about helping others.

I had a lot of responsibility growing up. My parents, high school sweethearts from the small town of Sparks, Nevada, split when I was three and Jeremy was two. We lived with our father as Mom started a new life with an abusive man I hated. At twenty-five, Dad was raising two toddlers and working long hours at the town's electric plant. We were often shuffled off to our grandparents' home, which I loved. Mom's second marriage ended after six months and we began seeing her more often after that. Soon Dad remarried, and he and his new wife had my half sister, Jessica. Jeremy and I went back to live with our mother. Not long after that, she reconnected with an old beau and decided we should move to Oklahoma to be near him. That marriage also failed. My mother seemed to always be searching for the perfect marriage just like my grandparents had for sixty-two years.

By the time I was in the third grade and Jeremy was in second, I was expected to take charge when Mom wasn't around, which was a lot of the time. Between taking college courses and working two jobs, she was away more than she was home, and it fell to me to fix dinner for Jeremy and me and make sure we got to bed on time. On the nights I was too frightened to go to sleep, I called my grandmother in Sparks and she read us bedtime stories.

I'm not sure how things would have turned out if it hadn't been for my grandparents. I longed for summer to arrive so we could stay with them, in a real house, with proper furniture, and dinner on the table every night. My father lived nearby, so

I got to visit with him and my baby sister when I was there.

Dad was a good man but strict with Jeremy and me. His rules became stifling and I chose to visit during the fun weekends to the lake or camping trips.

One summer, when I was visiting them, I mentioned to my grandmother that we couldn't afford to shop at Harold's, the department store back home where the girls who were well-off got their preppy plaid skirts and Izod shirts with crocodile insignias. My grandmother went out and bought plain pastel-colored golf-style shirts and sewed crocodiles she'd cut from Izod socks over the left breast pockets, assuring me that no one would be able to tell the difference. My grandmother was always trying to make up for the things that Mom missed because she was too wrapped up in her own life to notice the deficits in ours. I think she felt guilty that her daughter could be so neglectful of us. My mother didn't see that her neglect was taking a toll on my brother and me. She was trying to provide for two children with very little help. My mother and I were more alike than we were different. I didn't want her to know how scared and lonely I was as a child, and she didn't want me to know how scared she was raising two children on her own. We both put on a brave face for Jeremy and the outside world.

Eventually, Mom knew that Jeremy needed a

full-time parent. She decided to send him to Nevada to live with our dad, and I chose to remain with Mom because I didn't want to leave her alone. I needn't have worried. A short time later, she married Steve.

My life changed after that. Steve was a former Olympic swimmer, six years younger than Mom, and a successful land agent for an oil company. He moved us into a nice home in one of the newer developments in Norman. We had color TV and cable. For the first time I could remember, Mom and I didn't have to bring a calculator to the grocery store and we always had enough money for gas and my cheerleading uniform.

Steve was a willing father figure and he gave me a sense of steadiness and security I hadn't known before. If Mom couldn't make it to back-to-school night or to a weekend football game to watch me cheer, sometimes Steve sat in for her. His success meant Mom didn't need to work two jobs anymore, so she was home more often. Most nights, the three of us had dinner together, and someone was always there to help with my homework. I didn't feel like the poor, deprived kid anymore. I wasn't embarrassed to have friends over. I was an "A" student and popular with my peers. For the first time in my life, I could just be a kid.

Then, in my sophomore year of high school, life and all its uncertainty intervened. In 1986 the oil market crashed and more than a hundred thousand jobs in Oklahoma vanished, Steve's included. At first, I was too busy having fun with my friends to pay attention to what was happening in our household. What I did notice was the growing friction between my mother and Steve. They began arguing a lot. They usually took their differences to their bedroom and shut the door, but I could tell from the pitch of their muffled voices that my happy family was unraveling. My idyllic life was about to change.

As spring arrived, Steve was offered a good position purchasing land for a storage company. I was elated until I heard it was fifteen hundred miles away, in Los Angeles. Mom reluctantly agreed to go. The thought of leaving my life and my friends was devastating to me, but Steve thought the move was exactly what I needed.

"If you're looking for something to make you great," he said, "you have to get out of Oklahoma, because you won't find it here."

I'd never been to California. I pictured streets lined with palm trees, surfers riding aqua waves and movie star sightings everywhere. As intimidating as it was to think of starting over at fifteen, I was also excited to experience this whole new world. But the transition wouldn't be easy.

Los Angeles life seemed superficial and narcissistic compared with the traditional values we had left behind. When I think of Norman now, I recall a college town with football at the center of life, everyone flocking to the stadium for weekend games. Valencia, on the other hand, was a burgeoning Los Angeles suburb where the world turned on how you looked and how much money you had.

On my first day of school, I entered a new reality. The girls wore itty-bitty skirts with slouchy boots and tight tops designed to show off their cleavage. Handbags costing more than my first car dangled from their arms. I had on long khaki walking shorts, a buttoned-up oxford-style shirt and leather flats. The way they looked me up and down, slowly and with disdain, said everything. It was like a scene from the movie **Mean Girls**. When I got home that day, I cried to my mom that I might as well have been an alien from another planet. The kids drove Porsches and BMW convertibles to school! I was never going to fit in. I wanted to go back to Oklahoma.

"We're not going anywhere," she said.

Once we were settled in, Mom went to work as a consultant for a company called Sterling Management, where she gave seminars and sold management-training programs to health care professionals, predominantly doctors and dentists, who wanted to learn how to run the business side of their practices more efficiently. The position involved extensive travel, so Mom was gone a lot. Steve was usually on the road for his new company too, sometimes for two or three weeks at a time.

It quickly became obvious that our second chance wasn't working out the way I'd hoped. Mom spent more and more time at work, even when Steve wasn't away. She was taking self-improvement courses at night. Courses like "How to Communicate" and "Personal Values and Integrity." Steve complained about her attitude. She was becoming distant, and more independent in a way that didn't sit well with him.

I didn't like the changes I saw in my mother either. She adopted a strange, unemotional way of speaking that didn't sound like my mother at all. She even began using words and expressions I didn't understand.

For instance:

"Michelle, you and I need a comm cycle about this."

I roll my eyes impatiently. **A comm cycle?**

"What's that?"

Mom acts as if I should know this new lingo.

"It means, 'We need to talk.'"

I sigh in exasperation.

"Then why don't you just say that, Mom?"

Or:

"Michelle, we have to work on our 2D."

Here we go again: "What's a 2D?"

Mom raises her eyebrow. "The Second Dynamic. It means family," she says.
"Huh?"

And:

"That is so enturbulating."
"Enturbu-**what?**"
"Enturbulating, Michelle. Upsetting!"
"Oh, **that** enturbulating."

On and on it went. She was "hatting" (training) for a job. She wanted to improve her "beingness" (self). She "cognated" (realized) that I was upset. I couldn't keep track of the glossary of terms. There were too many words and they were too weird. Whatever strange new world my mother was living in, neither Steve nor I understood what was happening. Not until the day she came home with a pamphlet about a marriage course she wanted Steve to take at the Celebrity Centre in Hollywood. Mom told him she'd learned about the counseling through her company. She said if he didn't go with her, she'd divorce him.

Steve looked over the booklet. "This is Scientology!" he said, waving the pamphlet in the air.

I'd never heard of Scientology, but from his tone of voice, I knew it had to be bad.

He voiced his suspicions. "This is a cult!" he

said. "I'm not going there! Are you out of your mind? You're not sucking me into this!"

Was this the kind of thing she was learning at work? Steve asked. What was going on at that place anyway?

What was going on was that Sterling Management was run by Scientologists and it was the top recruiter for the church. My mother had no idea when she took the job, but not even six months later she was speaking the language and drinking the Kool-Aid. I hardly recognized her anymore. She said she finally had a purpose, and it was bigger than being a wife to Steve or a mother to me—she was joining the fight to save humanity! The church's mission, L. Ron Hubbard wrote in 1954, was to fashion "a civilization without insanity, without criminals and without war, where the able can prosper and honest beings can have rights and where Man is free to rise to greater heights."

"Who wouldn't be drawn to such ideals?" Mom asked with wide-eyed wonder after she read me this passage over dinner one night.

I didn't think my mother's transformation would last. This was just another phase, I thought. She had dabbled in other spiritual practices in a never-ending quest for enlightenment—Buddhism, Taoism, psychotherapy, yoga, you name it—but nothing lasted. It was the same with her marriages. She dove into relationships, tied the knot, got restless and bored, and moved on to the next man, hoping he would provide the missing piece to her quest for nirvana. **This, too, shall pass,** I told myself.

Steve didn't wait. He walked out. After that, Mom fell deeper and deeper into the church. Alone again, I quickly learned that, to survive in my new world, I would have to conform. My life became all about appearances and possessions. I quickly morphed into a person I hated. With no one at home to give me direction, I'd gone off course. Instead of the sure-footed girl I had aspired to be, I was suddenly lost and searching.

Rather than go home to an empty house every day, I spent more time with my friends. I was most comfortable with girls. I had plenty of opportunities to date boys, but the ones who liked me were usually the macho jock types, and I wasn't attracted to them. I was more intrigued by the butch girl in our class everyone was afraid of. She was interesting.

After months of quietly admiring this girl, I confessed my fascination to my best friend, Lacey, a sweet but wild soul who loved to party and would try just about anything. Not long after, Lacey and I were at her house drinking, which led to some kissing and a little fooling around, nothing very serious. I didn't think much of it. I figured most teenage girls experimented that way, and I knew Lacey had been with guys. I was sure I would be too. I was just a late bloomer.

———◆———

In June 1989, I graduated from high school with honors and an acceptance letter to attend the American University of Paris in the fall. Mom got me a summer job at Sterling so I could save up for my studies abroad. My title was "Hostess," and I helped the doctors and dentists taking management training at our Glendale headquarters with their travel and accommodations. I was only seventeen, but I was such a go-getter that in just a few weeks I was promoted to sales.

Sterling was a privately held company owned by Scientologists. It was built on, and licensed to sell, L. Ron Hubbard's blueprint for running a successful business, which he had developed more than a decade after founding the Church of Scientology in 1953. Hubbard's management training curriculum emphasized blanket marketing, high productivity and rigid ethical rules for employee conduct. It was one of three milestones in Hubbard's career that made a name (and a fortune) for him. The first, a self-help book published in 1950 entitled **Dianetics: The Modern Science of Mental Health**, was a runaway bestseller and transformed him from science fiction writer into pop psychology icon. Hubbard then morphed the book into a prescription for "a clear and scientific way to spiritual reality," which became the foundation for the church he founded three years later. And third, he came up with his blueprint for business success. This was the program we were selling, one based on Scientology principles, but with all references to the church deleted from our sales pitch and the course material.

I found I had a real knack for selling. My job was to follow up with medical professionals who had already spent thousands of dollars for the weeklong training program at our headquarters and convince them to buy the "Booster Program," or blocks of $250-an-hour personal consulting time, or perhaps the $1,500 set of Organization Executive Course (OEC) encyclopedias, which we called our "Green Volumes," seven books consisting of Hubbard's business "technology."

I had at my fingertips a three-ring binder called "The Hard Sell Pack," consisting of pages and pages of L. Ron Hubbard quotes to be used to counter obstacles I might face in the selling process. I was taught that the hard sell meant caring enough to get potential buyers to push past their "personal stops and barriers" and buy, because every sale was for the greater good. Accepting an excuse meant I didn't care deeply enough about the client or the future of humanity.

Most days at Sterling ran anywhere from twelve to fourteen hours. I rarely left the office before ten or eleven at night, and my supervisors were constantly applauding me for my job performance and my work ethic. At the time, of course, I had no idea that Sterling was a recruitment factory for the church and that I was one of its prime targets, or that dispensing praise was a key component of Scientology's methodology for luring new members. They build you up to hook you, then tear you down in order to take control of your life and convince you that you need the church in order to excel and achieve what the church calls "true spiritual enlightenment and freedom."

Every day that summer, I was pressured to postpone my plans for Paris and stay with the company, at least for a while. Instead of pursuing a college education, my supervisors asked, why not a career education at Sterling? All the education I needed was right there. I was young, they said. I could take their "real-life" courses, establish a career and study abroad later if I still wanted to. If I decided to stay, I would have a title out of reach of people twice my age and earn enough to be able to afford the Mustang convertible I'd dreamed of owning—white with matching leather interior. That car was a powerful incentive for a teenager.

Despite the daily flattery and cajoling, I was conflicted about what to do. If I'm being honest, the thought of flying alone to a foreign country and navigating a new city, language and culture was frightening. It would be easier to stay. At the same time, I wasn't completely convinced I could achieve my purpose in the cloistered world of Sterling.

To my sincere regret, after weeks of persuasion—

the Scientology "hard sell"—I began seeing things their way. "Okay," I said as the end of
summer loomed. "I'll stay." No one was happier
about my decision than my mother. I was doing
the right thing, she said. I was right where I
belonged.

It was the first of many big choices the church
would coerce me to make over the next twenty
years. These would be life-altering decisions about
my career, finances, marriage, children . . . even
who I should and shouldn't love.

———◈———

Later that fall, I was driving to work, panicked
about being late. The time had gotten away from
me that morning and I was a few minutes behind
schedule. I'd heard stories about what happened
to employees who missed roll call at the start of
"morning muster." They were labeled "enemies
of the group" and forced to submit to a series of
steps called "Conditions" in order to be accepted
back into it. Apparently it was a grueling and humiliating process, and I didn't want to go through
it. This may sound ridiculous to anyone with a
regular job, but for all I knew this was the way
corporate America worked. I didn't question the
rules; I just abided by them.

As I jumped on Interstate 5 for the drive to
work, my skin prickled with worry and my mind
raced with thoughts about the office. **I can't be**

late. I can't be late. If I'm late there will be hell to pay. I gunned the engine and shot over to the far left lane, ready to roll. But luck was not on my side. **Oh no! Please!** I thought as the logjam of rush-hour traffic slowed to a crawl in front of me. "C'mon! Move!" I cried. "I have to get to work. I have to be there for roll call!"

Looking over my shoulder, I saw an opening and quickly veered right into the next lane. I don't know what distracted me—whether I was looking down at my radio or glancing at my rearview mirror—but it wasn't until the last second that I looked up and saw the car in front of me stopped dead. As I slammed on my brakes, the back of the Mustang fishtailed wildly, lurching and spinning, first right, then left, then back again. I was swerving all over the highway. No matter what I did, I couldn't regain control.

All I could think about was saving my new car. **Mom is going to kill me if I crash it,** I thought. I couldn't remember whether to turn into the skid or away from it. Semis were bearing down on me—I heard air brakes spitting and the sickening screech of tires skidding on the roadway. All I could do was surrender, duck down as far as I could in the seat and brace for the impact. **Please don't let this hurt,** I prayed.

Shattering glass pelted my body like hailstones from a tornado cloud, and a fierce, hot wind swept over my face. Then it was quiet and I felt like I was floating in slow motion until suddenly everything stopped. I didn't know where I was. I could have jumped the guardrail, I might be badly injured, I might be dead. I stayed curled in my little ball, feeling numb and detached from my body.

A few minutes passed and I heard a voice.

"Honey, I'm a doctor. Help is on the way. Don't try to move."

The man's kindly manner gave me the courage to open my eyes. I was hurt all right, trapped down in my seat with my knees tangled under the steering wheel, but at least I was alive. I allowed myself a breath of relief. Then I looked up. The menacing undercarriage of a semitruck teetered over me, all its wires and springs and rusting pipes. I realized I was trapped in a cocoon of tangled metal.

Police cars, fire trucks and ambulances arrived, red lights flashing, sirens howling. For more than an hour, a team of rescuers, using the Jaws of Life, worked to extricate me from the wreckage. I would later hear the gory details of the crash, as told to my mom by the responders. The first semitruck ran over the rear of my car, propelling it under another tractor trailer ahead of me, where it got trapped. The only part of the car that wasn't crushed was the spot where I'd been sitting. Miraculously, I escaped without life-threatening injuries.

A few moments after I was admitted to the hospital with a cracked rib and badly bruised knees, my mother arrived. She came with a man I didn't know, a funky-looking little man with an angular face, a long nose and eyes that looked surprised. He wore an ill-fitting toupee, a disheveled crow-black mess I feared might slip down over his forehead at any minute. I remember thinking it odd that he wore white tennis shoes with his crumpled brown business suit.

I burst into tears when I saw my mother. I could see the fear in her eyes. I knew what she was thinking. What if the accident had been worse? What if I hadn't survived? What would she have done without me, her stability, her confidante, her best friend?

"Michelle!" she cried, rushing to my side. "What in the world happened? Thank goodness you're okay!"

I looked from my mother to her companion.

"This is Larry," she said. "He is a Scientology minister. He came because I was too upset to drive."

He sat down next to my bed and placed a reassuring hand on mine.

"Would you like to talk?" he asked.

I hesitated, not at all sure that I had anything to say to this stranger at my bedside. But Larry's voice was soft, on the effeminate side, which somehow made him seem safe.

"I can't believe I didn't die," I said, surprising myself with my words.

Larry smiled knowingly.

I had survived for a reason, he said. "I very much believe that accidents don't happen by chance," he said, pointing a long, thin index finger my way. "They happen because there is someone suppressing you or stopping you from being who you truly want to be or can be. And when you're feeling better, I'd like you to come and see me."

I couldn't explain why I took this stranger up on his offer, but he was kind to me and I was bursting to talk about my experience. I now understand this was a defining moment in my life.

I didn't grow up in a particular church. My parents dabbled in different faiths, but religion was never a mainstay in our lives. When I was three or four, Mom taught Sunday school at a local Methodist church. We attended services as a family on Christmas and Easter, and I enjoyed the holiday traditions. I was seven or so when they decided to explore alternative religions, some of which were quite bizarre. I remember going to a tiny metaphysical church, hidden in the woods, where people claimed to be healing each other with touch. At one of these out-of-the-way places, a woman asked me to apologize to a piece of furniture I bumped, "because everything in this world has feelings." Another time, I came home from school and a group of total strangers was chanting with my parents in their bedroom. These early experiences left me leery about religion. I'd always felt like a spiritual being, but I didn't know exactly what that meant or how to apply it.

My car accident was the first time I felt what I truly believed to be a higher power. I can only describe the experience as otherworldly. As my Mustang careened out of control toward what should have been my death, I was filled with the certainty that it wasn't my time.

The accident was a kind of spiritual awakening. Everyone said it was a miracle I didn't die. I was spared for a reason and I needed to figure out what it was. Larry's words about not allowing others to suppress me and taking control of my own destiny resonated with me. I longed to know who or what was holding me back from finding my purpose on this earth and I believed he could lead me in the right direction.

Two weeks later, I sat in a tiny, dusty office behind Larry's house in West Hollywood. The room was disordered and cluttered with furniture, papers strewn over the desk, and L. Ron Hubbard books stacked in lopsided piles on bookshelves. I knew little about Scientology except what I'd gleaned from my mother—that it was based on the concept that practitioners gained self-knowledge and spiritual fulfillment through graded courses and training fashioned after Hubbard's **Dianetics** self-help book.

Larry was a lapsed Jew from Brooklyn who'd

converted to Scientology while he was in college and, shortly afterward, moved to California after his parents disowned him. He told me that he was what the church called a "field auditor." His job was assessing the spiritual and emotional level of people who were new to Scientology or thinking about joining, and keeping them on track in their psychic journey until they were ready to enter the church. He explained that he did this by means of a process called "auditing," which was similar to psychological counseling, except that it required the aid of a Scientology device called an Electro-psychometer (or E-meter), which worked sort of like a lie detector. By reading the results of the E-meter, he said, trained auditors were able to help separate truth from fiction and help people retrieve buried memories from this and past lives—all for the higher purpose of reaching the next level of spiritual clarity and, ultimately, total spiritual enlightenment.

He reiterated his belief that negative events, such as illnesses and accidents, happened to us because toxic people or inner conflicts were holding us back from living our best lives—"the phenomenon of suppression," he called it. Once I was able to identify those psychic blocks through auditing, I could begin taking the necessary steps to become my best self. Only then would my true purpose be revealed.

What Larry wanted me to know was that even

though humans, by nature, tended to deceive themselves rather than face hard truths, there was no fooling the E-meter. If I lied or tried to suppress feelings or memories, the meter would catch it. That was the key to uncovering past traumas we didn't necessarily want to acknowledge, Larry said, all in an effort to save not just ourselves but the universe.

Each person saved brought us a step closer to the perfect civilization we strived for. Only Scientologists—as evolved, superior beings—could save the planet. I finally understood what my mother had meant when she talked about having a "higher purpose." It now made sense to me.

———◈———

During these weekly auditing sessions, Larry taught me the basics of the church curriculum and led me to embrace the belief system I would come to adopt as my new "faith." I had been right in thinking that Scientology was more a lifestyle than a traditional religion. The basic idea was that we were immortal beings—or "thetans," Hubbard's word for souls with bodies and minds—with emotional baggage from each of our past incarnations, which kept us from becoming our higher selves. Through a series of courses and the regular counseling sessions of "auditing," we could identify and address those issues and achieve a superior state of self-awareness and spiritual enlightenment. At the highest level of training, it was even possible to achieve superhuman powers and control over what L. Ron Hubbard called MEST: Matter, Energy, Space and Time.

I never asked Larry for proof. I was young and vulnerable and already under his spell. I truly believed when he said Scientology would lead me, as it had him, on a path of self-discovery and knowingness that would make anything possible.

What appealed to me most about these early sessions with Larry was that I could talk about my problems for as long as I liked. It was a lot like meeting with a psychologist, except a clock wasn't ticking. I could talk for as long as it took me to purge myself of whatever was bothering me, and, best of all, Larry didn't judge. He just jotted down notes.

A typical exchange would go something like this:

"Do you have a present-time problem, Michelle?"

"Yes. There is this girl, Candy, who has been mean to me since my first day at Hart High. I'm still hearing that she's spreading rumors about me. A friend told me she was telling everyone I hadn't been accepted to any good universities and that I was having sex with a thirty-year-old man. On the morning of my accident I was running out of my house in a rage, crying, 'Candy rules my life and I have no control!'"

"Give me an earlier time when it felt like you'd lost control," Larry said.

I gave him another example of something Candy did that made me feel helpless.

"Now think of an earlier time that you felt like you'd lost control."

At this point, I'm into it. I like that Larry is taking such an interest in my life and I want to see where this line of questioning takes me. By now, I have forgotten I am hooked up to the meter, even though I am clutching the metal cans that are supposedly measuring the truthfulness of my responses.

The succession of questions and answers continues until I "cognate," which, in Scientology, means I have dug down deep enough to get to the root of the problem.

"Oh my God!" I cry, breathlessly. "Candy makes me feel the same way I did when I was a kid and my stepmother was mean to me and I couldn't do anything about it! That's how Candy makes me feel! Wow!"

I feel unburdened because I appreciate that I am not a kid anymore and Candy is not my stepmother—which leads to the realization that I am a freethinking adult who can reclaim the power I gave away as a teenager. Success!

"Thank you very much, Michelle," Larry says. "Your needle is floating. You can put down the cans."

I dance out of his office, feeling euphoric. I can't

wait for the next session, the next adrenaline rush, the next life-changing epiphany.

That was the idea, of course. It's the Scientology trap. Indoctrination begins with these feel-good, build-you-up therapy sessions. At the same time, the metal cans of the E-meter are sending mild electrical currents through your body, which, studies have shown, stimulate endorphins for the same effect as highly addictive opiates. It's similar to being a heroin addict. Once the high wears off, you crave the next hit. But in the case of Scientologists, the craving is for another dose of auditing.

During one of our sessions, Larry instructed me to make a list of the toxic people in my life. With him as my guide, we labeled each person either "PTS" (Potential Trouble Source) or "SP" (Suppressive Person). SPs had to be eliminated from my life immediately with "disconnection" letters. The others were given a chance to redeem themselves by answering a few questions.

I wrote my first letter to Candy. I said our relationship had not been productive for either of us. I wished her well but was officially cutting ties with her. With the brush of a pen, Candy was banished from my life. Candy didn't respond to my letter. I heard she laughed when she read it. It didn't matter to me what she thought. I felt empowered and in control.

Once my disconnection letters were finished, I

tackled the names on the PTS list. This required more work. For each name, I was required to answer a series of questions. The questions were: "Is the person open to bettering him- or herself through Scientology?" "Does he or she make any comments about you practicing Scientology?" "Is he or she willing to be open and supportive of your choice?" One "no" answer meant that person was dropped to SP and rooted out of my life.

When I expressed regret over exorcising a friend, Larry reminded me that everything I was doing was for the greater good. Sentimentality was for the weak-willed. Scientologists were stalwart and focused on things of far greater importance than the petty struggles that emanated from useless human emotions.

How easy it was to be swept up in the grandness of our purpose!

At Larry's behest, I began attending night and weekend events at the church and met people close to my age. I lost touch with old friends and built new relationships with fellow Scientologists. Scientology quickly became the thread that ran through every aspect of my life. I worked with Scientologists at a Scientology-owned company. My social circle was made up of Scientologists. My free time was spent at Scientology functions. Before long, I was hooked.

Larry promised that, as soon as I was ready, he would turn me over to a church auditor for indoctrination on the Bridge to Total Freedom, which was a succession of steps to personal salvation. As a field auditor, Larry said, he was only eligible to take me to the level of "Clear," a pivotal point on the Bridge in which the auditor determines that your "reactive mind," or subconscious, is totally liberated from the damaging effects of the past, giving you complete control over your thoughts.

Once I'd reached Clear, my journey up the Bridge would consist of taking a series of expensive courses and auditing sessions that could only be performed in the church. When he determined I was ready, Larry said, he would turn me over to the Celebrity Centre International in Hollywood, the church's crown jewel, to pursue the rest of my journey. Mom had already agreed to open a new credit card to carry the cost of getting me started.

After spending nearly six months in counseling with Larry, clearing my mind of the human clutter that had stagnated my spiritual growth, I decided I had made enough progress to be granted the status of Clear. When I told Larry, he didn't agree or disagree; he simply sent me to the Celebrity Centre to undergo an extensive series of Security Checks, or "Sec Checks," to determine whether I was fit to move forward in my spiritual endeavors. Sec Checks are grueling interrogations by top-ranking church auditors. They pose questions designed to uncover any possible left-over "spiritual distress," running the gamut from whether you have ever had unkind thoughts about L. Ron Hubbard or the church, to lies you've told, to your sexual proclivities.

If I passed all the tests, I would be officially "cleared" to begin working my way up the Bridge to everlasting spiritual contentment. If I didn't, if a church auditor thought I was holding back any disturbing memories or past misdeeds, it would be back to the drawing board with Larry. But I wasn't worried about failure. I was confident that, at eighteen, I had progressed sufficiently in my personal and spiritual growth to ace the interrogations and be granted the status of Clear.

I couldn't wait to get started.

I was told that if I was dedicated, it would take me a few short months to attain the state of Clear. I was **not** told that "dedicated" meant twelve hours a day, seven days a week and tens if not hundreds of thousands of dollars—and that was if I was "perfect" and didn't get derailed by any "ethics" handlings.

It was impossible for someone my age to dedicate that kind of time or money to Scientology, but I loved the basic courses, which I could afford. I loved the idea of learning how to communicate better, spotting suppressive people in my life and learning how to have successful relationships. There were also marketing courses and sales courses that helped me in business. So I made progress, even if slowly.

Then there was another obstacle. Every so often, the chairman of the board would announce that some of the books and courses had been rewritten. At a big event, he would announce that some SP executive had screwed up the transcription of LRH handwritten policies into courses. Therefore, "key LRH data" had been left out, and everyone had to redo their courses with the "corrected" books. Some people had to start all the way down at the bottom of the Bridge and work their way up again. There was always some complaining, but the pressure from other Scientologists and staff was greater, so the noise would quickly die down and everyone would line up to start their new courses.

Between the demands of everyday life, limited financial means and the church constantly rolling out edited versions of coursework and auditing—well, months turned into years. But like any good cult member, I went with the flow. I had found my place.

CHAPTER TWO

Down to the Dungeon

❖

The Celebrity Centre is a kind of magical throwback to Hollywood's golden days. It is part five-star resort, part utilitarian conference center located on three pristine acres in downtown Hollywood. Built in the 1920s as a replica of a Normandy castle, it was originally called the Château Élysée and served as a long-term hotel for movie stars and other luminaries. In its heyday, it boasted a roster of guests that included Bette Davis, Clark Gable, Katharine Hepburn and Cary Grant. By the time the church bought the building in 1973, however, it had fallen into such a state of disrepair that it was targeted for demolition.

The church sank tens of millions of dollars into the structure to restore it to its former majestic state, a place fit for Scientology royalty such as Tom Cruise and John Travolta, who enter from a private parking lot through a private entrance to a private wing for celebrities. The private President's Office is up a series of narrow, winding stairs off an elaborate main lobby, which is open to the public. Auditing and course rooms take up the second and third floors, and the top floors are reserved for hotel guests.

Both the elaborate renovation and the name "Celebrity Centre" were a calculated effort by the church to bring in more congregants.

The Château Élysée was lavish and attracted the rich and famous to Scientology. The church used celebrity to help win acceptance as a mainstream religion and recruit members both here and abroad.

There was nothing churchlike about the Château Élysée. Every time I walked into the lobby, with its soaring gold-leaf ceilings and hand-painted murals, I felt as if I were checking into a plush European hotel—albeit one in which you have to pass an L. Ron Hubbard bookstore and a recruiting office to get to the fancy restaurant down the hall.

When Larry accompanied me there for the first time, in 1991, the renovation was still in progress and many of the programs were held in trailers and tents on the grounds. Larry walked me inside to the registrar's office, where Mom was waiting for us with her credit card. I signed up for a 12.5-hour block of time with an auditor and paid the $3,500 fee with my mother's card. My initial Sec Check auditing session took place in one of the trailers. The trailer was stark and brightly lit, furnished only with a desk and two chairs and a portrait of L. Ron Hubbard taped to the wall. My auditor was a woman not much older than me. Larry introduced us, and then left us alone.

I sat down across from the auditor and, at her instruction, took hold of the metal cans of the E-meter. My file—the one that Larry had kept of my weekly confessions over the last few months— was open on her desk. The auditor was stern and aloof, not at all what I was used to with Larry. She read robotically from the standard text most auditors use at the beginning of session:

"We are about to begin a security check. We are not moralists. We are able to change people. We are not here to condemn them. While we cannot guarantee you that matters revealed in this check will be held forever secret, we can promise you faithfully that no part of it nor any answer you make here will be given to the police or state. No Scientologist will ever bear witness against you in court by reason of answers to this security check. This security check is exclusively for Scientology purposes. The only ways you can fail this security check are to refuse to take the test, to fail to answer its questions truthfully or if you are here knowingly to injure Scientology."

I nodded.

The woman took a pen in her hand and, assisted by the confidential information in my file, began reading from a list of questions.

"We're going to address a certain area," the auditor said, pushing a sheet of paper in front of me. "I want you to read this policy."

I recognized the document as a "Tech Bulletin," red print on white paper. Tech Bulletins make up Scientology's scripture as written by L. Ron Hubbard. This one regarded homosexuality. Swallowing hard, I began reading. Hubbard wrote that sexual perversion, which included homosexuality, was contagious and threatened our society. On his "Tone Scale," a numerical measure of one's emotional state still used in Scientology today, he placed homosexuals and other "perverts" at level 1.1. People at that level are considered "evil, untrustworthy, a criminal."

My hands trembled.

"Have you ever had homosexual thoughts?" she asked.

I realized that the auditor must have been referring to my brief encounter with a classmate during my senior year, which I'd confessed to Larry during one of our sessions.

"Yes," I said. "I had thoughts about a high school friend."

"Okay. Thank you. Did you ever act on it?"

"No," I said, telling a white lie. "I did not."

The cans shook in my hands. The auditor looked from me to the E-meter. An idling or "floating" needle was a good thing; a jumping needle was a red flag for the auditor. I wondered what the needle was telling her.

"Okay. Thank you," she said, her expression as blank as the face of a porcelain doll. "Can you think of a time when you thought about a woman previous to that?"

"Well, there was another girl in high school," I said, referring to the masculine girl in my class. "I was fascinated by her."

"Okay. Thank you," the auditor said. "Did you act on it?"

"No, I didn't."

"Okay. Good. Thank you. And was there a time previous to that?"

I racked my brain, trying to think of anything that might be relevant to her line of questions.

"Well," I said, "I remember a time in the fifth grade. There was a girl, much taller than everyone and much better developed. I remember looking at the way her suspenders stretched around her breasts. I just wanted to hang around with her. I thought she was pretty cool."

"Did you ever act on it?"

"No, I didn't."

"Okay. Thank you. Give me an earlier time."

I had to come up with something. If I'd had even an inkling of a thought that I didn't recall, I feared the needle would betray me.

"Um, let me think," I said. "When I was nine my cousin and I played house and acted like husband and wife, but that would be it."

"Okay. Thank you. And why do you think this is significant?"

"I guess because I didn't want to play house with a boy," I stammered.

Before that interrogation, I'd just assumed that all girls experimented with each other. A part of me had always known enough not to broadcast it—not because I thought I was gay; it just wasn't something you talked about. Larry hadn't even blinked when we covered that territory. But judging from the reaction of the church auditor, my youthful indiscretions were much more serious than I had previously thought.

I felt so ashamed. The entire focus of my first Sec Check was the brief conversation I'd had with Larry about that very brief encounter with Lacey. The ethics officer looked at me with disdain, or at least that's what I read on her face.

"Okay," she said finally. "You have to go in for Handling."

My heart sank. I knew what "Handling" meant. I was certainly not getting out of there in a state of Clear. The auditor informed me that she would write up a "Knowledge Report" for my file. The next step after that would be a trip to the Ethics Department. Being sent to Ethics struck terror in even the most seasoned Scientologist, and I was an eighteen-year-old novice. **Oh shit,** I thought. **I'm in big trouble**.

———— ◈ ————

The Ethics Department was in the basement of the Celebrity Centre. It was dark and dank like a prison, and accessed by a single set of stairs, so you knew that whoever you passed on the way down or back up was in hot water. And they knew you were too. Scientology holds that anything that promotes or benefits the church is "ethical," and anything that is threatening to its core values is "unethical." L. Ron Hubbard defined "ethics" as "reason and the contemplation of optimum survival." "Dishonest conduct is non-survival," he wrote. "Anything is unreasonable or evil which brings about the destruction of individuals, groups, or inhibits the future of the race." It was obvious that my brief girl whimsy was considered a Scientology crime.

My legs could barely support me as I walked down the steps. The place was even worse than I'd imagined. I was instructed to sit on a bench in the hallway until an ethics officer was available to see me. People dressed in military-looking Scientology uniforms threw disapproving glances my way as they passed. No one smiled. No one said hello. It was simply, "Wait outside until we're ready for you." I waited and waited, trying to hide how frantic I felt.

Finally, a woman summoned me into the office. She was older than the auditor, but similarly stern and sour. She motioned for me to sit, and I lowered myself into the chair opposite her as she began to read through my file. She read each page with the intensity of someone who was proofreading copy, and it seemed to take forever. I didn't know where to look. At her? At my upside-down file? I'd better just look into my lap, I thought. It seemed like the safest thing to do. I felt as if I were back in school, in the principal's office, except that I'd never been sent to the principal's office—and this, I knew, was far more serious than anything an adolescent would have to repent for.

The woman turned the last page in the file, then folded her hands on top of it and looked at me.

"Are you aware of what these reports say?" she asked, her lips pursed, one eyebrow arched.

I thought my pounding heart was going to erupt in my throat.

"I think so," I replied sheepishly.

I could almost taste her revulsion.

"Okay," she said. She laid out a stack of paper in front of me: two Tech Bulletins this time, plus the Hubbard Chart of Human Evaluation, or Tone Scale, all of which declared that homosexuals needed to be wiped out of existence. **Oh my God!** I thought. I had no idea that what I'd done was that bad. **How will I ever work my way out of this mess? This is so embarrassing! I'm such a piece of crap!**

Larry never made me feel wrong or ashamed. Of course, I didn't know his job was to be kind and reel me in, and not to arbitrate my failures. That was the job of an ethics officer, and this one was clearly repulsed by me.

My ethics officer reached for her ethics book and turned to the chapter on "Ethics Conditions." "Conditions" define how spiritually and emotionally stable you are. There are twelve Conditions, arranged in order from the highest condition of "Power" to the lowest condition of "Confusion." "Preclears," or newbies to the church, like me, were classified as "Nonexistence," a kind of "let's get to know each other" condition that falls in the middle of the list.

The idea is that, over time, you work your way from Nonexistence to the top of the Conditions list, which you do through auditing sessions and coursework and by never doing anything "out ethics" to get yourself dropped down to the lower levels, which led to misery, worry and even premature death. Higher Conditions, on the other hand, promised happiness, security and overall well-being. It seemed like a clear choice to me.

"Read the list," ordered the ethics officer.

She sat stoically as I read the definition of each of the Conditions. When I finished, I looked

up at her. **What must she think of me?** I wondered. **She's an ethics officer. She's probably
never done anything wrong in her life. I'm still
on probation and here I am . . .** I just wanted to
please her.

"Where are you falling now on the Conditions?"
she asked.

"I think I'm in the Condition of Danger," I
said finally. The Condition of Danger was one
step above the entry level Nonexistence and,
defined loosely, meant I had done something
wrong and needed to get honest with myself and
others and stop my abnormal behavior by taking
assigned steps. Nice try. Wrong answer.

"Read further down the list," the ethics officer
said.

So I read, lower and lower, until I hit the very
bottom.

I looked at her, wishing I could read her
thoughts. "I guess, Confusion?" It was more of a
question than an answer.

To my surprise, for the first time during our
meeting, the ethics officer smiled, although only
slightly.

"Good," she said. "That's where we need to
start."

The ethics officer assigned me readings about
homosexuality from Hubbard's books, **Dianetics**
and the follow-up **Science of Survival**. I had a

lot of work to do to dig out of my lowly level 1.1, which was illustrated by a drawing of a gnome hiding a knife behind his back. Hubbard describes it as "the most dangerous and wicked level on the tone scale. . . . Here we have promiscuity, perversion, sadism and irregular practices."

The only way to move out of that category and up the Tone Scale to a better emotional Condition was by exposing and slaying my demons.

I was confused. "But I'm not gay," I said weakly. "I don't even know anyone who is gay."

The ethics officer sighed. "'Gay' is a 'psych' term that makes homosexuality less of a crime," she said. "Homosexuals get sick easily. They get AIDS. They cannot procreate. Many have committed crimes of sexual deviance. You don't know one because they hide their crimes. Is that the group that you want to be part of?"

"No!" I said, my eyes welling with tears.

"Which group do you choose?" she asked.

"The heterosexual group," I replied with newfound confidence.

"Good," she said. "You have been pretending to be part of a very bad group and in order for you to be accepted back into this group of ethical, successful, happy and healthy heterosexual Scientologists, you will have to do the work."

I knew what I had to do to be accepted by the church. The rulebook said that for me to move out of Lower Conditions I had to "strike a blow to the enemy." In my case, that meant forsaking homosexuals and finding a boyfriend.

I wasn't about to tell the ethics officer, but the idea of being with a boy left me feeling empty. I decided there must be something hormonally wrong with me and made an appointment to see a gynecologist. When I explained my lack of interest in the opposite sex, the doctor smiled reassuringly. "Oh, honey," she said. "You're so young. We can check your hormones, but you're only eighteen. Some people just mature later."

Just as she'd predicted, my hormone levels were normal. The doctor concluded that, because I'd started my menstrual cycle late, I would probably be in my twenties before I had sexual urges. My twenties? I couldn't wait that long. I needed a boyfriend now.

The subject of dating came up during my ethics sessions. Each time, I responded honestly that I couldn't find anyone I wanted to be with. The ethics officer complained that I was too picky. At the rate I was going, I would never find a mate.

I decided that lowering my standards and keeping an open mind was a small price to pay for a second chance with the church.

Not a year later, I met my future husband, Sean.

CHAPTER THREE

Sea Change

❖

I didn't have spare time to devote to a social life. I had a lot of responsibility for an eighteen-year-old. Lucky for me, the church placed ambition at the top of its list of desirable human traits. My average workday at Sterling was fourteen hours. It started first thing in the morning and ended when I made my sales quota for the day. I was selling packages of Hubbard management courses with thirty hours of private consulting time for $10,000 a pop. It took a lot of sales savvy and I was just a teenager with a high school education, but I was one of Sterling's top producers, and maintaining that status came with a lot of pressure.

At first I loved my job, especially when my sales were up and I was showered with accolades. But the work environment changed from harmonious to militaristic after **Time** magazine published a cover story about Scientology in which Sterling was revealed as a front for the church. The blockbuster story, with the headline "Scientology: The Thriving Cult of Greed and Power," was a scorching indictment of the church, calling it "a hugely profitable global racket that survives by intimidating members and critics in a Mafia-like manner." It quoted a spokeswoman for the Cult Awareness Network who said, "Scientology is quite likely the most ruthless, the most classically terroristic, the most litigious and the most lucrative cult the country has ever seen. No cult extracts more money from its members." As for Sterling, the **Time** story said it used "bait-and-switch" tactics, selling inferior products—"seminars and courses that typically cost $10,000"—when its "true aim is to hook customers for Scientology."

Understand, I didn't read the article until years later. Scientology had unwritten directives that were passed down through the ranks by word of mouth—usually by auditors and ethics officers. One was that we were "strongly advised" to avoid the news because the church was never given a fair shake. Translation: **Don't do it**. We were taught to believe that everything written by journalists was fraught with misrepresentations and lies. News sites were blocked on all church computers. We were told that whatever "news" we wanted could be provided by the church; all we needed to do was ask. Everyone I knew abided by the rule—or at least said they did.

Nevertheless, we heard rumblings and felt the shock waves that reverberated through Sterling's headquarters when the **Time** story ran. Sterling's management was so rattled they called an emergency staff meeting to refute the story. The story was garbage, they said. They had it with their lawyers for review. We were not to discuss the matter among ourselves. If we had questions, we were to book time with an ethics officer, who would provide us with any information we needed to know.

What Sterling couldn't hide was the fallout from the story. It was swift and severe. Sales plummeted and clients who'd already paid for courses called to demand their money back. In the months that followed, the pressure to sell—and the difficulty of making sales—intensified. We were expected to work more hours and were paid less, and sometimes not paid at all. Even Mom, who was in management, went weeks without a paycheck. She got so deep in the hole that she couldn't make her car payments and still pay for courses, so her car was repossessed. After six months of upheaval and relentless badgering from the president, she left Sterling to take a management position with the Los Angeles church. At least her courses would be discounted.

For me, things got tougher when I began putting in more time at the church to atone for my "crime," which meant less time honing my sales pitch at work. Sterling management didn't like me taking time away from the phones, even if it was for courses and auditing at the church. My bosses insisted I make up the missed time by staying late, sometimes until midnight, which was three or four hours later than my usual quitting time. The company had to sell to survive!

On those very late nights, one of the owners, a fast-talking alpha woman with flaming red hair and a nicotine gum habit, paced the halls maniacally while I left messages at doctors' and dentists' offices from Los Angeles to New York. She was supposed to be there to encourage us to sell, but she was hardly a mentor. The exercise was more about punishment than profit. Who was going to take my calls in the wee hours of the morning? When I was finally allowed to leave, I'd drive the forty-five miles home, sleep for three or four hours, then drive back to work for an early start. Sometimes I was so tired I closed the office blinds and put my head on the desk for a nap.

After a few of those grueling days, a woman who worked in the company's L. Ron Hubbard bookstore suggested that if I wanted to get out at a decent hour, I should do what she did and inflate my sales figures. We weren't being paid anyway, she said, so what was the harm in telling a white lie? I was desperate and sleep deprived enough to try it. The following night, when my supervisor came by to check on my progress, I told her I had good news. "Sale done!" I said. She looked pleased. "To whom?" she asked. I made up a name, wrote it on the sales board and left the office in time to get a decent night's sleep.

It didn't take long for the company to catch on to the ruse, of course. Faking a big deal was different than reporting a bogus book sale, like my coworker had. What did I know? I was still just a teenager, and the pressure to sell was so intense that I hadn't given much thought to consequences— not until the morning I was intercepted on my way into work and marched to the office of Sterling's very own and very unhappy ethics officer. My tearful confession was met with ridicule and scorn. The company ethics officer called me a criminal.

"But I didn't take any money!" I cried.

Just when I thought things couldn't get worse, she accused me of being a "CANPLANT," a mole for the Cult Awareness Network, one of the church's most fervent adversaries. (Members would rather be stuck in the eye with a pin than hear the church referred to as a cult.) I didn't even know what she was talking about. My punishment was a company Sec Check. Now I wasn't just "out ethics" with the church; I was "out ethics" with my employer. And just when I had thought I couldn't get any lower.

It surprised me, but my church mentors were supportive in my time of trouble with Sterling.

Mom kept them informed about what was happening, and every day, no matter how late I left work, people from the church were waiting to take me for coffee. Mom was caught in the middle of wanting to keep her job but also wanting to defend her daughter. Mom had not been paid either, and she knew that the grueling pressure was too much for me to bear. After a few weeks of watching me suffer, Mom suggested that I leave the company and come to work for the church. I could serve in the Sea Organization, or Sea Org, the order responsible for running the day-to-day operations of the church. Sea Org members lived together in crowded dormitories in communal compounds and worked for room and board, but despite the conditions it was considered a privilege to wear the uniform. Mom spoke to one of the top recruiters, who said they would be happy to have me.

I was ashamed that I'd faked a sale. After so many days of feeling worthless at Sterling, and the lack of sleep that accompanied my late-night hours, I decided to follow my mother's advice. Joining the Sea Org was the way to redeem myself. I would leave Sterling for what I believed was the most elite group on the planet. I was sure that once I was on the front lines of saving humanity, my Sterling indiscretion would be forgotten.

I signed the church's official "employment contract," in which I pledged to work for the Sea Organization for as many lifetimes as I had "for the next billion years." I was eager to get started. I was finally going to do something I'd always wanted to do: save lives!

My training for the Sea Org began with boot camp for new recruits. They called it Estates Project Force, or EPF. I reported to the church's "Big Blue" building, a former hospital on Sunset Boulevard that served as the local Sea Org barracks. Mom and Gavin, the recruiter, accompanied me. I was apprehensive because I wasn't sure what to expect, but super excited at the prospect of devoting my life to the church.

Enthusiasm quickly turned to apprehension, though, as I was ushered by my mother and Gavin through a series of dimly lit tunnels and down into the bowels of Big Blue. "Where are you taking me?" I asked, giggling nervously.

We finally reached the windowless basement. It reminded me of the Celebrity Centre dungeon, where the Ethics Department was. A fluorescent light cast a spooky glow over the reception area, where a large man with a permanent scowl met us. He introduced himself as "the Bosen." (German **Die Bösen** translates to English as "the wicked ones.")

The Bosen handed me a pair of tattered overalls that could have held two of me, and scuffed black combat-style boots. I swiveled around and looked at my mother in disbelief. "Do I really have to wear these?" Mom looked nervous. Gavin, who outranked the Bosen, intercepted the question. "I'm sure you can find a new pair of boots and better-fitting overalls, can't you, Bosen?" he asked.

The truth is, even with my mother there to support me, I was terrified. It was all so peculiar. The setting. The uniform. Especially the Bosen. I felt like I was trapped in a real-life scary movie. The urge to run was overwhelming, but where would I go?

A few minutes passed and the Bosen returned with newer gear. I pulled the overalls on over my clothes and handed Mom my white tennis shoes for safekeeping. As frightened as I was, and no matter how wrong everything felt, I did what I had been taught to do my whole life. I pasted on a smile and went along.

I relaxed a little when we went upstairs and I had a chance to meet some of my fellow recruits. All of them were around my age. We bunked together in dorm rooms on the upper floors of Big Blue. Female recruits stayed in one section, male recruits in another, with absolutely no sex allowed. (Premarital sex is forbidden for Sea Org members.) We were awakened at dawn by instructors who acted like robots and performed like drill sergeants. We addressed them as "Sir"—even the women. After morning classroom time to memorize church policy, we spent the next twelve hours performing our assigned tasks, from household chores to hard labor. We scrubbed floors and painted walls, pulled up bushes and planted saplings. The only purpose of some of our assignments was to humiliate and demean us—for instance, cleaning public toilets with my toothbrush.

I knew better than to question how picking up garbage or scrubbing urine stains off the insides of toilet bowls was teaching us how to save humanity. Complaining got you assigned to the lowliest of chores. Compliancy was rewarded. Once I learned the ropes, I sometimes got pulled off the dirty jobs to work at Bridge Publications, the publishing arm of the church. Those were better days, when I got to wear the navy Sea Org uniform and do office work. Still, I had grown to hate the long hours and the lack of freedom. I was working six and a half days a week—a hundred-plus hours—on three or four hours of sleep a night. I was told when to get up, when to eat, when to report for work and when to call it a day. My half day off was devoted to personal chores, like laundry and changing my bed linens. It was not the life I had imagined when I signed up.

After six weeks, I came down with the flu. I couldn't shake it. When Mom realized how sick I was, she pulled strings and got me a pass home to recuperate. That brief taste of my former life was enough to convince me that I wasn't going back to Big Blue. I told my mom that I would still be a member of the church, but I wasn't ready to commit my life to the Sea Org. Maybe when I was a little older. I could tell she was disappointed, but she appealed to higher-ups and I was allowed to put my billion-year commitment on hold. I was lucky Mom had sway, but I really think the Bosen knew I wasn't Sea Org material and was happy to get rid of me.

I didn't work for the rest of that summer. For the first time in my life, I could be carefree. I re-connected with old high school friends who had tired of my constant nattering about Dianetics and repeated attempts to recruit them. They wel-comed me back into the circle, as long as I didn't talk about Scientology. I was still devoted to the church, but I felt like I needed time away from all their rules and restrictions, not to mention the complex and loaded language they used. Half the time I still didn't know what the words meant: He committed an "overt"—a sin or crime. She was "downstat"—not producing enough. It was "entheta"—negative.

My friends urged me to be a teenager. They told me that I'd never allowed myself to behave like a regular kid and have some fun. They were right, and this was my chance to make up for lost time.

On most days, I slept in, spent afternoons at the beach and came home whenever I felt like it, which didn't please my mother. She was con-stantly complaining about me hanging out with my "Wog" friends (a pejorative church term for non-Scientologists). It drove her crazy when I didn't make my bed, or came home late, or when she found cigarette ashes in her car. According to her, these were bad habits I was picking up from the Wog world. I didn't care what my mother thought. I loved my newfound freedom.

One weekend, my friends and I packed up my car and drove eighty miles south to Newport Beach. We'd rented a place on the beach, which, as it turned out, was next to a house full of boys around our age. One of them approached me as I was sunning myself on the first day. He was small, thin and clean-cut—a good-looking guy in a feminine kind of way who came across as painfully shy even though he had made the move to talk to me first. He said his name was Sean. He was four years older than I was, attending school and working at a sporting goods store while pursuing an acting career. Small world—he lived in Valencia too. We talked for a long time that day and the next.

I wasn't attracted to Sean—not in that heart-thumping way my girlfriends described when they liked a boy—but he was nice and nonthreatening. While everyone else spent their time playing beer pong and drinking way too much, I was happy to have someone else who wasn't into clubbing and the party scene. Sean seemed perfectly content to sit with me on the swings and talk about our families. I developed a sense of security with him. By the end of the weekend, I felt as if we'd become good friends.

Sean called a few days later and invited me to come for lunch with his family. They lived in a large Tudor-style house that looked like a mansion to me. His parents were welcoming and made me feel right at home. He had the kind of family I had always dreamed of, with parents who were happily married and made their children the center of their universe. Meanwhile, my mother was more dedicated to the church than she was to me. She was always there. With no one at home and no job to go to, I began spending a lot of time at Sean's. He quickly fell in love with me and I loved his parents. I told myself that, in time, I would grow to love Sean too. His family became my family.

That fall, I got up one day and found a note from my mother on my bed. "If you don't get your life in order, you can move out," it read. Accompanying the note was a flyer from an insurance marketing company that was hiring—a company affiliated with the church, of course. At that point, I didn't know what I wanted to do with my life, but being a carefree teenager was getting old and I was bored. I'd worked since I was fourteen and I missed being productive and challenged and making my own money. I decided she was right: I needed to get my life back on track and find a job.

I applied to the company that Mom had recommended and was hired on the spot. The company required that I stay on top of my "overts" (sins) and "withholds" (secrets). At around the same time, my mother got me back into session with Larry, my former Scientology counselor, to get me away from my Wog friends and on course with the church. Back into the church for auditing and coursework I went.

In auditing, the theme of my sexuality sometimes still popped up. Every new auditor who read my file asked me about it. How many times did I have to repeat that I understood any sexual act other than intercourse between a man and a woman for the purpose of procreating was considered deviant social behavior? I wanted to pursue a "normal life" and have a successful career, a happy marriage and children. And now I had a boyfriend! Problem solved.

I was back on track in the church and dedicated to being the best I could be at everything in my life: the best Scientologist, the best salesperson in my company, the best girlfriend to Sean. Time passed quickly. I was on my way to attaining the level of Clear, and I'd come to crave my auditing sessions again. Every time I unburdened myself, I came away feeling high. Mesmerized, really. I felt like I could conquer the world. Sometimes I spent entire weekends at the church, being audited and taking courses. The more I did, the more I wanted. And it was working! My career took off and a larger insurance company recruited me as a sales manager for more money. I was happy enough with Sean and shut off my occasional, fleeting thoughts about women. Sean and I got engaged. At the urging of my mother, I got him to join the church.

———◆———

In June 1994, exactly two years after we'd met in Newport Beach, Sean and I were married in a traditional Scientology ceremony with bridesmaids and groomsmen and vows written by L. Ron Hubbard. Photographs from the wedding show a beautiful young couple, faces flushed with the joy of the moment and the promise of the future. That picture was only partly true. There was a side of Sean I'd begun to see that gave me pause—times when, out of the blue, he erupted in anger and was verbally abusive. One of the worst occasions was the night before our wedding.

I was sharing a room at the Mandalay Beach Resort in Ventura with my mother, my half sister, Jessica, who'd flown in from Colorado, and my friend Shannon. My mother was in the Sea Org by then and living on a "berthing" floor at the LA church. She'd received special permission for a two-day leave to attend the wedding. The four of us enjoyed a relaxing day, getting in facials and beach time before the big day. After dinner, we gathered in my suite, drinking wine and chattering happily, when Sean called from our house. As soon as I answered the phone, I knew something was wrong. Sean began shouting at me. "This fucking dog! This is your fault!"

"What are you talking about?" I asked. "Calm down, Sean."

Over the phone I heard a commotion and Sean yelling at our new American Eskimo puppy, a little white fur ball named Chloe. Then I heard a thud, like something hitting the wall, and yelping.

"Sean, stop it!" I cried. "You have to calm down. Sit down. Talk to me. What is happening?"

"I just came in the house from having drinks with the guys," he said. "It's late. There is no way that I will have enough sleep for tomorrow. I'm going to spend my fucking night cleaning up this mess!"

At that point, he sounded like a mental patient. He was breathing hard and making no sense.

"Tell me what happened," I said, trying to stay calm, but frantic about what was happening to my sweet new puppy.

"Well, knowing you, you must have left a pen somewhere that Chloe could get it and she chewed it up," Sean said, spitting his words into the phone. "We have black ink all over our white carpet and she walked in it and it's everywhere. I will be up all night cleaning this up. We just need to cancel the wedding!"

I should have agreed with Sean and canceled the wedding, but I didn't. I chose to ignore major red flags—namely, my lack of interest in him sexually and his increasingly volatile temper. My Scientology training had taught me that any situation could be "handled." Besides, all of my family had come to town and they were expecting the fairy-tale wedding I'd been planning for months. So instead of running, I took a deep breath and said, "Sean, this is not worth it. Leave the mess. Chloe is probably scared to death. She is a puppy. Just go to bed and get some sleep. I'll take care of it when we get home from our honeymoon."

Sean was quiet for a moment. I thought I had convinced him to go to bed. Naive me.

"You know, that's exactly why you are the mess you are," he said, his words dripping with contempt. "You never handle anything. No, Michelle, you just enjoy your time at the hotel. I'll see if I decide to show up tomorrow or not." He slammed down the phone.

My mother, my sister and my friend, witnesses to this row, all stayed quiet when I hung up the phone. They knew not to give their opinions or advice. I was too headstrong to listen and too staunch a Scientologist to be deterred from my mission by a petty argument. As we so often said in Scientology, "There are no such things as problems, just situations and solutions." I repeated the mantra over and over that night.

Sean showed up the next day. Neither of us mentioned the phone call. We got married and acted as if nothing had happened, until after the last of our two hundred guests left the reception and we went to our hotel room. That's when Sean picked up his rant from the night before, as if no time at all had passed. "Fucking dog! Why did we get the fucking dog, anyway? Why did you leave a pen around? What the hell is wrong with you?" We went to bed angry, without consummating our marriage.

The next morning I put a big smile on my face for my friends and family. This good little Scientologist couldn't let anyone know how bad I was feeling on the inside. I especially did not want my mom to know. She was headed back to her cloistered quarters and didn't know when she'd be free to see me again, and anyway, I knew what she would say—what every Scientologist would say: "There are no such things as problems, just situations and solutions." Finding solutions always meant casting a critical eye on your own actions.

What are you withholding from Sean, Michelle?

What have you done to cause this?

What have you done to him?

I knew my answer. I didn't want to be married and I didn't want to be married to him, but I was stuck.

———◆———

I started another new job when we returned from our honeymoon in Hawaii. I had been thinking for a while that the company I'd been working for was limiting and stringent. I was confident I could make more money someplace else. A week before the wedding, I landed a position with a bigger, more prosperous insurance company. The commute was shorter, the money was better and I was my own boss. For the first time in my career, my employer had no ties to Scientology. I was working for and with Wogs. Of course, I couldn't have taken the job without the church's blessing, which Larry gave gladly, pointing out that Wogs were potential recruits and an opportunity for me to bring in "raw meat."

I dove headfirst into my new job. Sean worked part-time doing fieldwork for his father's geology company. He groused about it constantly. I encouraged him to go back to school to train for something he loved. I was the main breadwinner, and I could cover him for a while until he determined what he wanted to do.

Sean decided he'd like to pursue acting once again. We paid for acting classes at the Beverly Hills Playhouse, but he went once and lost interest. When acting didn't pan out, he decided to pursue work as a personal trainer like his best friend, John. If it meant he'd like a job enough to stick with it, I was all for it.

He spent his days training with John at the gym and I put in long hours at my company. Our busy schedules meant less time for church activities, auditing and coursework, and we started to stray.

Sean introduced me to his new group of friends from the gym. They were the typical Valencia "beautiful people," most of them self-indulgent twenty- and thirtysomethings with perfectly toned bodies and permanent tans. I could see why he was attracted to them, with their good looks and their lavish lifestyles.

In the beginning, we spent most evenings partying with them at posh clubs, but the routine got old quickly for me. Sean often ended up staying out later than I did and getting a ride home. The arrangement worked for a couple of months before he became resentful and started picking fights. Why couldn't I stay out late like everyone else? Why was my job so important that I had to tuck in early every night? Why did my fucking career always come before him? I told Sean the partying had become too frequent for my taste. I wasn't a big drinker and the late nights made it hard for me to be my best when I was working. I wanted to say that I wasn't fortunate enough to have parents who employed me, and bought my cars, and paid my car insurance, and gave me a company credit card, but I didn't want to stir up trouble. I just wanted to get along.

Sean was becoming increasingly aggressive and confrontational with me. His moods often ranged from sullen to belligerent and I was never sure what to expect from him. Our arguments were mostly about money and sex. When he started a fight, I usually walked into another room, or grabbed a blanket and went to sleep on the couch. That he couldn't get me to respond infuriated him even more. He called me vile names: **Fucking liar! Suppressive. Bitch. Cunt.** He threw things at me—pillows, keys, suitcases, whatever was within reach. I told myself that everyone had problems. I knew how to handle ours. Every time his anger flared, my Scientology training kicked in. **Let it go. Don't react. Emotions are for Wogs. Be in control.** But his withering attacks left me humiliated and afraid, and wondering what could happen next.

Then it did. On a Friday night I arrived home from work and found Sean dressed and ready to go out on the town. He said he'd made plans for us to meet John and his new girlfriend, Lisa.

I'd had a long day. All I wanted was to put on my pajamas and collapse. "You go out," I said, tossing my briefcase and purse on the couch. "I'm exhausted."

I had barely gotten the words out when Sean erupted. "That would suit you just fine, wouldn't it?" he shouted, clenching his fists at his sides. "For me to go out and you to stay here. Why can't you be normal like everyone else?"

I was genuinely puzzled by his reaction. "Why are you yelling at me?" I asked.

Sean got up in my face. "You give me every excuse about why you can't go out and that leads to excuses about why you don't want to have sex!" he said, seething. "Well, guess what. We are going out and then we are having sex like every normal couple should!"

"Really?" I said, raising an eyebrow. "I'm sorry if I'm working hard and bringing in the majority of the income, but I'm not going to be told when I am going to have sex with you!"

Sean had fire in his eyes. I sensed we were headed in a direction I didn't want to go and I quickly shifted gears. I told Sean he was right. We needed to go out and have fun with our friends.

I quickly changed clothes, and we met John and Lisa at a Mexican restaurant nearby. Sean began nitpicking everything I said. This was something new. He'd never been critical of me in front of his friends before. Yielding to his wishes obviously hadn't been enough. He was holding a grudge.

I managed to stay cool and smile my way through his insults and criticisms. Toward the end of the meal, he finally got to what was bugging him. "So Michelle thinks she's **all that** now with her big job," he said. "She almost didn't come out."

I saw John and Lisa glance at each other uncomfortably. "Dude, leave your wife alone," John said. "We can't stay out late anyway. I have an early-morning client and Lisa has had a long week too. We were planning on calling it an early night."

Sean didn't respond. We all drank down what was left of our margaritas, split the check and said our good-byes.

The drive home was tense. I tried making small talk to bring Sean out of his funk, but my efforts were futile.

"It was good to see John and Lisa tonight," I said. "She seems happy in her new job."

"Yep."

"So what are your plans tomorrow? Should we ask your parents to dinner?"

"I don't know."

We arrived home and I took Chloe out for a short walk. When I returned, I found Sean lying naked on the bed, clearly aroused.

I took a deep breath. "Sean, can we plan this for another night?" I asked. "I'm really tired and I don't feel like we're in a good place right now."

Sean grabbed my arm and yanked me down on the bed. When he tried to kiss me, I turned away. "I don't know what you are doing, but this is not working for me tonight," I said, my heart starting to race. "You're acting strangely and I don't like it. It certainly isn't a turn-on."

When he let go of my arm, I breathed a quiet sigh of relief. I told myself he'd had too much to drink and needed to sleep it off. Everything would be back to normal in the morning.

I walked into the bathroom to get ready for bed, certain that by the time I was finished Sean would be dead to the world. But when I came out, he was stroking himself.

Grabbing my pillow and a blanket, I turned to leave the room.

"Where are you going?" he asked.

"Have at it," I said. "I'll sleep in the living room."

I made up the couch, turned out the light and curled up with my back to the bedroom. No sooner had I closed my eyes than Sean padded past me into the kitchen. I heard the freezer open and ice tinkle into a glass, then the sound of the faucet running. I was relieved he was drinking water. Hopefully it would help sober him up and he'd go to sleep.

Thinking the worst was over, I began settling in again when—**whoosh!** Freezing water rained over me. Gasping, I opened my eyes and saw him standing over me. "That's what you get for being such a bitch!" he said. "Did that wake you up? Are you ready to have sex now?"

I was looking into the face of evil and I was petrified. I didn't move for fear of what he would do next. I had never felt so demeaned or so vulnerable. Sean was trying to provoke me, but I knew not to fight back. Not at that moment. I closed my eyes and lay there, motionless, until I heard him stomp back to the bedroom.

As soon as it felt safe to move, I got up and tiptoed to the kitchen. It was dark, and I slipped as I felt around for my car keys. I didn't know where

I was going to go, but I had to get out of the house. With ice water still dripping off me, I finally found my keys and rushed toward the garage door. As I did, I saw Sean coming toward me.

"What are you doing?" he asked, his voice as cold as the water he'd thrown on me.

I started to cry. "I can't believe that you threw ice water on me! I'm going for a drive. I think we both need to cool off."

I took another step toward the garage and he leapt for me. I tried to run, but the floor beneath me was slick and I couldn't gain traction fast enough to get away. Sean was too quick and too strong an adversary. He grabbed me around my waist and tried to wrestle the keys away from me.

"Give me the fucking keys!" he shouted. "You aren't going anywhere."

I was hysterical by then. He twisted my arm behind my back and the keys fell to the floor. He let go of me for a split second, trying to grab the keys, and I ran for the front door. But it was no use. He was on me before I could get out of the kitchen.

Swooping me up from behind, he threw me over his shoulder. This time, he slipped and we went crashing to the floor, him on top of me. When I hit the tile, a wrenching pain shot through my hip.

"You broke my hip!" I screamed. "Oh my God! You broke my hip!"

Sean looked as if he'd been Tasered. His mouth was agape and he didn't move.

"I'm so sorry," he said. "I didn't mean to drop you. There was water on the floor and I was trying to stop you from going out in the dark. I wasn't trying to hurt you. I am so sorry."

I writhed in pain, shaking and sobbing. Sean helped me to my feet and guided me to the bedroom. He brought me ice to put on my hip and I eventually fell asleep.

I walked with a limp for days afterward. When his parents asked me what happened, I said I'd slipped on wet tile. Sean said nothing.

As miserable as I felt, leaving the marriage wasn't an option. What was it that L. Ron Hubbard said about people who walked out on their spouses? "People leave because of their own overts and withholds. That is the factual fact and the hardbound rule. A man with a clean heart can't be hurt."

I told myself that I needed to get back to the church. A clean heart would be the armor that protected me from Sean's cruelty. I promised myself to get back into session, and get Sean back into session too. Then I pasted on a permanent smile and pretended that all was right with my world. No such things as problems, just situations and solutions.

Sean and I never talked about that night. Everything went back to normal. After a few weeks of relative calm, I told myself that getting back to the church could wait after all. I was too busy with work to do much of anything else.

It was during our truce that I was shopping for groceries after a long day and heard someone call my name. I turned to see Lacey standing there, the girl I'd shared a kiss and a few touches with when we were in high school. It was good to see her after so long. We talked briefly, then exchanged phone numbers and promised to get together.

I was excited at the prospect of seeing Lacey again. I had no intention of resuming our sex play—at least that's what I told myself. I'd spent too much time getting "cleansed" in the church to make that mistake again. But I missed our friendship and the easy conversations we'd had.

Not long afterward, Lacey called, asking if I wanted to meet for a drink. I said I'd have to check with Sean and get back to her.

To do right by my marriage and be honest with Sean, I told him about Lacey and our history together. I assured him I had no romantic feelings for her. I just wanted to catch up with an old friend. I prepared myself for Sean's reaction, certain he would be furious and forbid me from rekindling the friendship. Instead, he encouraged me to go.

I met Lacey on a Friday after work and we spent hours talking over cocktails. It had been a long time since I'd spent an evening without talking about work or Scientology and it was a refreshing change.

A week later, Lacey called to invite both Sean and me to a party. I was surprised when he agreed to go. It turned out to be a pleasant evening of drinking wine and playing board games with new friends. Sean seemed to enjoy it as much as I did.

Lacey and I continued seeing each other. One evening, she asked if I'd ever thought about having a threesome. I was shocked because all of our conversations until then had been strictly platonic. I told her honestly that Sean had suggested it, but I'd never taken him seriously. Then I quickly changed the subject.

The next time the three of us were together, driving back from a dinner date, she broached the idea with Sean. "I understand you want Michelle to have a threesome," she said. "I'm guessing with another woman?" I stayed quiet while the two of them bantered back and forth.

After we dropped Lacey at home, Sean brought it up again. "Well, that was interesting!" he said, grinning. I laughed it off. We had all had too much to drink, I said. I was sure most people our age thought about such things when they were tipsy, but they didn't necessarily act on it. "It was just talk," I said.

Sean initiated sex when we got home, but rather than make an excuse, I responded by closing my eyes and fantasizing about Lacey.

She called again and asked us to come to dinner at her place. We took a good bottle of wine and our favorite board game, but I was pretty sure I knew her real purpose for inviting us.

After a few glasses of wine, Lacey made her

move. She sat down next to me on the couch and began rubbing my leg. "Here's how I think things should go," she said, looking at Sean. "Michelle and I have to get comfortable with each other before you are included. Why don't you give us a moment upstairs?"

Sean looked like a kid who had just been given the keys to a toy store. "Take whatever time you need!" he said.

Lacey took my hand and led me toward the stairs. I turned to Sean, uncertain how I felt about what was happening, and he smiled his approval. My body trembled with excitement and anticipation, but my conscience reminded me of the consequences of my actions if the church found out.

As conflicted as I was, when Lacey and I reached the bedroom, my body took over. We fell onto the bed in a passionate embrace. A moment later, I heard Sean on the stairs. Reality set in. I was a wife and a Scientologist and what I was doing was wrong. Very wrong.

I looked up at Sean, now standing in the doorway. "I can't do this," I said.

I was appalled that I had considered committing adultery.

I was scared that the church would find out and I would get into trouble.

I was nervous about being with a woman, but I was aching to feel her touch. My body was telling me that this was more right than anything I had ever felt, my mind was telling me that it was wrong because I was married and a Scientologist, and my soul was screaming, **RUN!!! Just get out of here!**

Sean looked at me pleadingly. "It's fine—there's no rush. I can just watch."

"I'm sorry. I can't."

We all went back downstairs. "I think we should go," I said. My remorse was immediate. How could I have been so dumb? After all the work I'd done in auditing!? On the drive home, I told Sean how worried I was the church would find out. No one had to know, he said, conspiratorially. It could be our little secret.

And so . . . it happened again. A few more times, actually. I told myself it wasn't a betrayal of my marriage because Sean was a willing participant. I knew what I was doing was risky. If the church did find out, I'd be severely punished for having had sex with a woman again. But how would they find out? Lacey wasn't associated with the church. And Sean promised not to tell.

CHAPTER FOUR

Indiscretions

◆

Larry began calling, asking when I planned on getting back to the church. Soon, I said. As the weeks passed, the trysts with Lacey became fewer and farther between. Any pleasure I'd felt at the beginning was eclipsed by the guilt over flouting church doctrine and, perhaps even more so, fear of being found out and punished.

In the summer of 1995, shortly after our one-year anniversary, I learned that Sean had cheated on me with one of our friends from the gym. It happened one night while I was sleeping. My brother, with whom I'd kept in close contact after he'd gone to live in Nevada with our father, had recently moved to California and was staying with us until he found his own place. He told me he'd walked in on Sean and the woman and got a weird vibe. I chose to ignore it.

Weeks later, I came home from work and found Sean packing an overnight bag.

"Where are you going?" I asked.

He was frantic, angry. "I have to get away and think a bit."

"I don't understand. What do you have to think about?"

Without answering, he picked up his bag and walked out the door.

I was dumbfounded. Where had this come from? I wondered. What was he talking about?

Sean called me that night and said he was staying at a cabin in Big Bear for the weekend.

"What's going on?" I asked.

"I'm just very confused about what I want," he replied. "I just need to think."

Talk about confused. On one hand, I was grateful to have time to myself, to go to bed early, rather than on his schedule, and not have to fight off his unwanted sexual advances. On the other hand, I was bewildered by his need to get away from me.

He returned on Monday. I had just finished dressing for work and was packing up my briefcase when he dropped to his knees next to me with tears in his eyes.

"What's wrong, Sean?" I asked, genuinely concerned.

"I cheated on you," he said, bowing his head.

I never saw it coming. "What? . . . What do you mean?"

Sean explained that he'd cheated with our friend from the gym. She had driven him home. He'd invited her in. One thing led to another. He was drunk at the time, but otherwise confused about why he'd done what he did, he said.

My brother's intuition—that "weird vibe" he'd told me about—had been valid. I was furious. To my way of thinking, this was totally different than what had happened between Lacey and me. Sean had pushed for me to be with Lacey, and he was there **with** us.

I know it seems like I shouldn't have cared that he'd been with someone else, but for some crazy reason, I did. I believed in marriage and I looked at our experience with Lacey as the equivalent of watching porn together. But Sean had gone behind my back. He had cheated on me at the same time we were supposed to be working on our marriage.

The anger I felt wasn't out of any grand jealousy or fear of losing Sean, because I felt neither. I cared for him, of course, but it was hardly the passionate kind of love I'd read about. I supposed I loved him, but as Scientologists we were taught not to focus on the word "love" per se. Hubbard dismissed it as having "too many meanings." Romantic love was for the weak, for people who operated out of their "reactive minds" and allowed their emotions to control them. As Scientologists, we were always striving to eliminate the reactive mind and develop our "analytical mind," which gave us full control to make decisions that promoted survival. The anger I felt was less about romantic jealousy than it was about his betrayal of our partnership.

I did the only thing I knew to do. I contacted Larry for advice. Larry instructed me to write up a Knowledge Report for the Ethics Department, which I did: "Sean told me he kissed her; he touched her; he told her his heart was breaking, but she gave him more attention than I gave him. He didn't know what to do. I left the house when he told me this." I concluded the report the way we did in the church: "This is True. Michelle Seward."

Larry submitted the report to the Ethics Department and the church called to schedule a meeting with Sean and me. A few days later, we arrived at the Celebrity Centre to talk things over with the Chaplain, the highest-ranking officer there. He read us church policies on the sanctity of marriage and related quotes by L. Ron Hubbard. To sum up, the Chaplain said, when couples betray each other and trust is breached, the only way to repair it is with communication, and that could be handled with auditing. The Chaplain prescribed the church's marriage counseling, the "2D Co-audit," which the church touts as "an exact procedure for alleviating marital problems." He sent us to the registrar to buy a 12.5-hour block of auditing time for $5,000 and schedule our first appointment. Our auditor was a young girl, no more than twenty.

Our first session together was relatively benign. I was hooked up to the E-meter first. I knew the drill. As much as I wanted to complain about Sean—about his poor work ethic, his bad temper, his fling with the woman from the gym—the purpose of auditing was not to blame, but to acknowledge our own misdeeds and mistakes.

"What have you withheld from Sean, Michelle?" the auditor asked.

Here we go. What have I done? Can't we just concentrate on Sean? He's the reason we're here.

"Well, one time I went shopping and hid the shopping bags in the trunk of the car," I said obediently.

"Thank you. What else?" she asked, scribbling notes for my file.

"I had credit card charges I didn't tell him about."

"Okay. Thank you. What else?"

"That's about it."

"Okay. Thank you," she said, motioning for me to switch seats with Sean.

He took the chair opposite the auditor and grabbed the cans.

Looking down at the meter, the auditor asked, "Sean, what have you withheld from Michelle?"

Finally!

"Um . . . um . . . Well, I think I may have complained about her to one of our friends," he said quietly.

"Thank you. What else?"

"I may have yelled at her once."

Yelled at me once? **And what about the time you threw ice water on me? The time you pushed me?** I wasn't allowed to respond to Sean, so I just rolled my eyes.

The auditor looked at me with indifference. I looked at her face and wondered, **What could you possibly know about marriage?**

On it went for more than an hour. At least it was a start, I thought.

With each session after that, Sean opened up a little more, but he would never volunteer the more egregious things he'd done. He guessed he'd raised his voice at me. He might have called me a name one time. How about picking me up and dropping me on the floor? Blocking the front door so I couldn't run away when he was berating me? But I couldn't prompt Sean. My role was to confess to my own failures and let the auditor worry about getting him honest.

During the third or fourth session, with the auditor pressuring Sean to come up with anything else he might be suppressing or avoiding, he started shaking his head from side to side, as if trying to shake loose some deeply buried thought. **Tell**

her about forcing me to have sex, I thought. After several minutes of silence, he finally spoke. Yes, he said, he'd had a brief encounter with a woman from the gym and that was wrong. "And, well," he said, pursing his lips, "I guess I haven't talked about another thing I've done." **Now we're getting somewhere,** I thought. **Let the auditor see who you really are!** Sean paused. The auditor signaled for him to continue. "Well," he said, haltingly, "I really haven't confessed that Michelle cheated on me." I stifled a gasp. **What? . . . Are you really going to go there?** "I guess I'm kind of responsible because I knew Michelle was going to have relations with a woman and I allowed it to happen."

Tears of anger and frustration stung my eyes. I was stunned by Sean's deviousness. He was ostensibly taking responsibility for withholding information from the auditor, but in a way to make me look bad. I looked at Sean and sensed the glee concealed behind his rueful expression. It was the first time I realized just how calculating he was.

Just as he had planned, the auditor abruptly switched her attention to me again.

"Thank you very much, Sean," she said.

At the instruction of the auditor, I switched seats with my husband and grabbed the E-meter cans.

"What have you done to Sean?" she asked.

I knew the drill. Attempting to justify my actions or place the blame on Sean would only get me more trouble. My role was to accept responsibility for what I had done and take my punishment.

"I was with my friend Lacey," I said.

The auditor wanted details. My face was red with humiliation and I tried to avoid specifics, but she insisted I give her a step-by-step recounting of what Lacey and I did together. When she was satisfied that I'd told her everything, she called for a break.

"Let me get this written up," she said, "and I'll see you next session." With that, she headed out, leaving Sean and me to sit there, staring at each other.

Sean taunted me all the way home, laughing as he recalled how embarrassed I'd been when I'd revealed what Lacey and I had done. He clearly felt in control. He said he didn't even know if he wanted our marriage to work anymore, that I had a lot of making up to do if there was a chance of us staying together.

I returned to the auditor's office for our next appointment, expecting that Sean and I would go back in session together, but I was sent alone to the case supervisor and grilled about what else I was withholding from the auditor. My file had details of my history with Lacey. Had I been with her more times than I'd admitted? Had I been with other women? Had I ever spoken in derogatory terms about LRH or Scientology? No, no and no, I said.

Two days later, I was released back to the Ethics

Department and dropped down into Lower Conditions again. Sean was assigned readings and sent home.

For the next two weeks I spent endless hours with a male ethics officer in order to determine "who I really was." The sessions often lasted from early morning to late at night, with only short bathroom breaks, and they wiped me out. I was bombarded with readings from L. Ron Hubbard and questions about my innermost thoughts and beliefs.

"Do you fantasize about women when you masturbate?"

"What exactly is your fantasy?"

"Tell me how you touch yourself when you think about women."

He told me I had a choice. Did I really want to be part of a damned culture, one prone to promiscuity, AIDS and a lifetime of sickness and misery? Or was I really a High Ethics, highly productive, morally sound heterosexual who was just pretending to be attracted to women? I chose the latter.

Once I made my pronouncement to the ethics officer, my penance came in four parts. First, I had to promise Sean that I would be a good, faithful heterosexual wife.

Next, I was to make a list of policies for myself to prevent me from committing the same transgression again. Third, I would avoid all association with homosexuals.

The final step was seeking forgiveness from the

"group" I was seeking to rejoin: heterosexual Scientologists. My assignment was to write up a "liability" report, a painfully intimate and vividly detailed accounting of what I'd done, followed by an explanation of what I did to atone for my actions. Once the ethics officer approved it, I was ordered to walk the halls of the Celebrity Centre asking random members—most of whom would be complete strangers—to read and sign my confession. They were allowed to ask questions before they agreed to sign.

I needed twenty-five signatures in order to be allowed to get out of Lower Conditions and rejoin the church. Imagine my complete and utter shame, standing before my Scientology peers while they pored over the details of my sexual encounters, and then asking each for forgiveness and the opportunity to dig out of the hole I'd dug for myself. If that didn't deter me from my evil ways, nothing would, and that was the idea.

I braced myself as I left the Ethics Department, my confession in hand. My first encounter happened as I walked out the door into the hallway, with a man I'd never seen. "Excuse me," I said, handing him my confession with all its raw particulars. "I am in liability. I would love to ask you if I could rejoin the group." The man took my statement and read it over quickly. I think he took pity on me, because he signed and walked off without a word.

Another man glanced at my declaration, then asked, "When was your last donation to the church?"

"I just wrote a check for $5,000 this morning," I answered. He signed too.

I came upon a middle-aged woman with a kind face.

"I am in liability," I said. She took my confession and read it carefully.

"What is your blow to the enemy?" she asked. I was armed and ready for that one.

"I know homosexuality is wrong and I will never be around that person or any homosexual again," I said. Satisfied with my answer, she scrawled her signature on my confession, smiled condescendingly and walked on.

With each request I felt smaller and smaller. Most of the people I approached were kind enough. They'd scan my declaration of guilt and sign off with an expression that seemed to say: **Hey, I've been there. I know what you're going through.**

But there's a jerk in every bunch and this bunch was no exception. I came across a familiar face, a man I recognized from the Celebrity Centre, and explained my situation.

"Aren't you married, Michelle?" he asked smugly.

"Yes, I am," I responded sheepishly.

He glared at me. "How did this happen exactly?"

"It's kind of ridiculous," I stammered. He asked for details, which I was required to give him.

"Well, you won't do that again, will you?" he asked, aghast. "My God! That's disgusting!"

I assured him I wouldn't, and it was. "I know what I did was wrong," I said. "Yes, it was disgusting, and I'm over it. I don't know what I was thinking, but I've made a blow to the enemy."

The man stared at me for a moment, signed my confession, turned on his heel and marched away.

I felt like throwing up. I was so mortified by the experience that, after ten or fifteen requests, I ran to the bathroom, locked myself in a stall and sobbed. I was a terrible, repulsive person who'd committed treason against the church and I deserved everything I got. It didn't matter that Sean had cheated on me and then gotten away scot-free. I accepted the fact that you don't second-guess the church. If the church said I was wrong, I had to make it right. I decided to start by making an appointment with my doctor to check my estrogen levels again. Maybe something had changed and that was contributing to my sexual dysfunction?

That evening, I went home and asked for Sean's forgiveness. I had been broken down during auditing and gotten "honest and straight," I said. I finally understood that any homosexual tendencies I thought I had were made up in my reactive mind. I had no choice but to believe I was over it, and committed to a future as Mrs. Sean Seward. Part of my penance was that I had to work harder at being a good wife and commit to sex at least two or three times a week.

Sean was satisfied with that and we vowed to put the past behind us and give our marriage another chance. He promised to try harder to find a job and contribute more to the household. I complied with my commitment to regular sex, but I usually had to drink two or three cocktails beforehand to make it tolerable. The act itself was physically painful for me, but when I told Sean he brushed it off. "Your body is made for this," he said. "It can't hurt that bad." Sometimes, afterward, I felt like throwing up. Often my mind wandered and I'd find myself thinking about how repulsed I was by the look of his manhood and how much I hated the way he smelled. **Why?** I asked myself. **Why am I this way?**

I suggested to Sean that we see a sex therapist. He refused, saying it was me who had a problem. I tortured myself with guilt over not wanting him. I wondered if I would feel differently if he pulled his weight at home. I told Sean he wanted more than I had to give; surely there was someone who could love him better than I could. When I tried to talk things out, he shut me down. He went weeks without speaking to me. And when his frustration boiled over into anger, he had his way with me.

Crying and pleading got me nowhere, so I just succumbed. Eventually, I figured out a way to avoid sex without blatantly rejecting him. If I booked client meetings in the evening and got home late enough, he was usually already asleep. **Not my fault!** If he groused about the lack of sex, I told him there had been many times that I'd been ready but he was already asleep. I asked if he wanted me to curtail my schedule, knowing the answer. If I cut back on work, he would have to step up and contribute more or we wouldn't be able to afford our lifestyle. That would usually stop his complaining, at least for a little while.

After a few short weeks, our fresh start withered on the vine. I never showed the outside world my unhappiness. As Scientologists, we were taught to present a positive image to the public because we were, first and foremost, representatives of the church. Our problems were to be "handled" in the church with an auditor or ethics officer. Wallowing was for Wogs.

My work was my coping mechanism. When the opportunity arose for me to advance my insurance territory to the northern part of the state, Sean and I decided to sell our home in Los Angeles and move three hundred miles north to the San Francisco suburb of Danville. The move would be good for us, I told myself. A new place would mean a new beginning. We agreed that once we were settled into our new life, we could think about starting a family.

CHAPTER FIVE

Clear

◈

People often asked when Sean and I planned on having kids. My standard answer was "two years." Two years turned into six. We were in the new house for a year when we decided to start trying. Getting pregnant was more of a scientific project for me than an act of love. I kept track of my ovulation cycle and informed Sean when it was time for sex. I knew the moment I conceived, in February 2000. I was elated not just to be expecting but because it meant nine months of prescribed celibacy; the church's view was that sex in the presence of a developing thetan (being) was both inappropriate and dangerous. According to L. Ron Hubbard, intercourse caused the fetus pain that lingered after birth in the "reactive mind," which he claimed was responsible for most mental, emotional and psychosomatic ailments. Whenever Sean pushed for sex, I pulled out Hubbard and reminded him that the well-being of our child was at stake.

Church policy called for a silent, or at least quiet, delivery: "labor done in a calm and loving environment with no spoken words by anyone attending." According to Hubbard, his own research showed that commotion surrounding a normal birth often caused psychic scars that presented as aberrations later in a child's life. "Chatty doctors and nurses, shouts to 'PUSH, PUSH' and loud or laughing remarks to 'encourage' are the types of things that are meant to be avoided."

Sean and I agreed that a silent birth was the way to go. Finally, we had something in common, something we could look forward to together: our first child.

I interviewed a few doctors before I found one who agreed to do things my way. The pregnancy was relatively easy and I went into labor in early October, right on schedule. Sean called my mother to let her know the baby was on the way. Five years earlier, my forty-five-year-old mother had given up her job, her apartment, her car and all of her belongings and signed a billion-year contract with the Sea Org, thus trading her independence for a life of servitude to the church. In exchange, she was promised a bunk bed, three meals a day and a fifty-dollar weekly stipend for the rest of her life.

I was proud of Mom. She had accomplished what I couldn't. She had given herself over to the church. She was always on the move, helping to fix this church or open that church. At the moment she was helping to oversee the reorganization of churches in Canada, which were mismanaged and in a state of disarray. The assignment was supposed to last a few months, but she'd been in Toronto for nearly four years, and I rarely saw her.

I admired my mother's altruistic spirit and her commitment to the church's mission, but even as a grown woman, I found myself wishing I were her priority. Unfortunately for me, she was first and foremost a Sea Org foot soldier and needed permission to do anything outside of the church, including visiting her children. So I was shocked that she convinced the leaders that I needed her, and she managed to make it to California in time to be in the delivery room with me.

My labor was long and arduous, but I refused anything for the pain. The church had convinced me that medication was of no value; its only purpose was to enrich the greedy pharmaceutical industry. The medical team was briefed about my preference for a silent birth. Of course, I didn't speak during labor, but used hand signals to communicate with Sean and Mom. After twenty-five hours of contractions my blood pressure skyrocketed. The baby was in danger. I had two options: an epidural to help relax me or a C-section. I chose the epidural and slept for the next five hours. When I awakened, the doctor whispered and a nurse tapped me on the shoulder when it was time to push. Finally I gave birth to a boy we named Sage. Scientologists have a special way of welcoming their babies into the world, a way even newborns understood: "You tell a little baby, 'It's okay. We're going to keep you.' And you always get a sigh! They're so happy. It's such a relief to them." When my baby looked up into my eyes for the first time, I assured him that he was a keeper. I had never felt such love for anyone.

When we brought the baby home, I slept on the living room couch with Sage in the bassinet beside me. I had the perfect excuse for not staying with Sean in our second-floor bedroom. My delivery had been painful and I couldn't easily walk up the flight of stairs. Mom slept on an air mattress nearby and helped with the baby, but Sean made himself scarce, which was fine with me. On most days, he disappeared with his computer until bedtime. I knew my mother sensed the tension in the house. But she didn't ask about it. I didn't offer anything, except to say that I was lonely being so far away from Los Angeles and everything I knew there. I hadn't had time to make friends because I was always working, and the closest church was forty-five minutes away, so I hadn't been active since we'd moved. I worked twelve-hour days and most evenings. Who had time for weekend auditing marathons?

I assured my mother that I was still a believer. Scientology was who we were, after all. I applied it every day in my personal life and in my business, just as she did. I blamed the friction between Sean and me on everyday stressors. I knew that going into any detail would have forced her to write me up in a Knowledge Report to the church. As a Scientologist, she was obligated to report others for "nattering," or "negative chatter," even if the offender was her daughter.

Mom blamed whatever differences Sean and I had on what she called our lavish lifestyle. We were living in a big house, driving luxury cars and making a lot of money—hardly extravagant by Hollywood standards, but to a woman making fifty dollars a week and living in a dorm room in an old converted hospital, it must have looked like a life of extreme excess. She accused me of "going PTS [Potential Trouble Source] to the middle class." In other words, I was feeling the consequences of living the shallow existence of a Wog, which she defined as "money, materialism and keeping up with the Joneses." This is what caused my loneliness and unhappiness, and the solution was to get back to Los Angeles and the church, my mother said. I needed to be with the people who shared my values and ideals. If I wouldn't do it for myself, I had to do it for the sake of the baby, "who will have to be raised in Scientology," she said.

My mother's words resonated with me. She believed that Scientology solved everything and I agreed. Before she left, she had almost convinced me to move back to Southern California, but Sean and I owned a house. I'd built a significant client list in San Francisco. Now we had a new baby. Could we just pick up and leave?

When she returned to Toronto, my mother called Larry to enlist his help in getting me to return. She told him about the conversations we'd had while she was visiting and her thoughts about why I was resistant to coming home.

Sean was the problem, she said. He was stingy and didn't want to move back because he didn't want me putting as much money into the church as I did when I was active at the Celebrity Centre. She'd heard Sean say things to make me feel guilty about uprooting the family again. She had done all she could do to convince me to come back. Now she needed someone in higher authority to intervene.

Larry promised to get his wife on the case. I'd lost touch with Larry and Julianne after moving away from LA. But before that, Julianne had become my advisor once Larry became too busy with other church responsibilities to continue counseling me. A chain-smoker with a raspy voice, she was strong-willed and bossy, and had always been able to talk me into almost anything. As a field staff member (FSM), she, like Larry, was responsible for keeping members coming to church and moving along on the Bridge. For every course, or book, or block of auditing time she sold, she earned a 10 or 15 percent commission.

Julianne began calling me every day, sometimes more than once, telling me all the reasons I needed to come home. She knew from Mom that I was now earning somewhere in the six figures. My potential to be even more successful was staggering, Julianne said, if only I'd get back on the Bridge.

"Come back, Michelle, and we'll get Sean moving again too," she implored me. "You know it's the right thing to do."

Talking to Julianne, I realized how much I missed daily involvement in the church. I used to spend at least some time there every day. The auditing and courses had been such a large part of my life, and I missed the social events and the support of my Scientology friends. I'd grown tired of being the breadwinner while Sean contributed nothing to our household. His temper tantrums were getting worse and he was increasingly angry and abusive. I had no one to turn to in Northern California. If we returned home, I could ask the church to intervene. Sean could work for his parents again. I could still make regular trips back up north to stay in touch with my clients. I knew Sean's mother would help with the baby when

I traveled. Going back home made sense. A call from the Chaplain of the Celebrity Centre sealed the deal. "Michelle," he said, "we really think you need to get back here."

It wasn't every day a parishioner received a personal call from a church leader, and I was duly impressed. But even more than the call from the Chaplain, I sensed that the tension in my marriage was building to a climax again. The baby was growing and I was running out of excuses for refusing Sean sex. It was only a matter of time before his frustration exploded in violence again, and I didn't want to be far away and isolated when it did.

I finally convinced Sean that going home was the right move. We would be close to his family again and his mother could help with the baby when I was working. We packed up our house in Danville and returned to Los Angeles in the spring of 2001. It felt good to be back home and close to Sean's family again. My mom was thrilled we were back in Scientology territory. The news of our return traveled quickly. Within a week, the Chaplain called again. "Welcome back, Michelle," he said, his voice warm and welcoming. "I understand you're anxious to get back on the Bridge. When will we see you?"

I returned to the church that week, signed up for a block of auditing time and resumed my walk up the Bridge to Total Freedom. Everyone was so welcoming and so happy to have me back. Like them, I had been trained to believe that anyone outside the church was to be pitied. Wogs weren't necessarily bad people; they just weren't "enlightened" the way we were. Because of their inferior standing, they could only play peripheral roles in our lives. I was cordial to my Wog acquaintances. I could share a meal with them. They could work for me. But they were never going to be business partners or best friends because they weren't on my spiritual level. It felt good to be back with "my people," the spiritually enlightened masters of the universe.

Before Sage, Scientology was more about taking courses and attending events. It was also about having someone to run to when Sean's abuse got to be too much to take. It was a safety net of sorts. Auditing was very expensive, and the significant levels on the Bridge were gained through auditing, not through courses. Even though I was making good money—around $200,000 a year—there was rarely enough left over to plop down $10,000 for a couple of auditing intensives.

After giving birth to Sage, though, I felt a much bigger sense of responsibility. What kind of mother was I if I wasn't moving up the Bridge to my spiritual freedom and my son's spiritual freedom? It was my duty to raise Sage as a Scientologist; I needed to be "all in" for him. I couldn't have Sage growing up with an angry father and be witness to the abuse, so I had to do something about it. I believed that intense auditing and courses would fix Sean and make me a better person too.

Scientologists believe that "outflow creates inflow," so if you have to borrow the money to get started, then you borrow it! We sold the house in Northern Cal and moved back to Valencia, and kept some money out so that Sean and I could be in session—because that was the "greater good"!

———◈———

I began spending most of my free time at the church, and in no time I was "all in" again. My spiritual practice came before everything else. Once you start auditing and coursework intensively, you crave it every minute. I spent part of every day at the Celebrity Centre and scheduled my work and parental duties around coursework and auditing. The more I immersed myself, the more I wanted to be there.

By my baby's first birthday, I had worked my way up the Bridge to the coveted state of "Clear," the launchpad to ultimate spiritual enlightenment and superhuman powers. The Clear designation meant I was permanently freed from my "reactive mind," the part of the brain that stores memories of past traumas and provokes destructive emotions and behaviors, which prevent us from achieving happiness and success. The route to Clear had involved a dozen courses and hundreds of auditing hours, at a cost in excess of $100,000, but I felt it had been worth every dollar and every moment of suffering and angst to rid myself of the barriers that come with human emotion. I had been broken down and built up. My confidence was at an all-time high. I felt like I could fly. Nothing and no one could bring me down.

That September, my certification was announced in grand fashion on the stairs of the Celebrity Centre. As I stood at the top of a staircase, my host, the leader of Hubbard Guidance Center (HGC), where most of the auditing took place, called for everyone to gather in the reception area. It was dinnertime, the busiest time at the Celebrity Centre, and people scurried toward the area from all directions. Sean and Mom were in the audience.

"Attention, everyone!" my host said. "Attention! We have an announcement!" My heart pounded with excitement. "Ladies and gentlemen! Michelle Seward has attained the state of Clear!"

The room exploded in cheers and applause. People shouted, "Speech! Speech!" I felt like a queen looking down at her subjects. My host stepped back and motioned for me to take her place at the podium. All eyes were on me as I began to speak. I was euphoric. "I want to thank the HGC, my auditor, the RTC"—or Religious Technology Center, the church's ecclesiastical authority—"and, always, L. Ron Hubbard for creating the technology to clear this planet!" I said. "There are times in your life when you feel like you are walking through the mud and you're trying to hold on so you don't go under. Well, when you are Clear, you float above the mud and help pull everyone else out!"

At that point, Michelle the saleswoman kicked in. I wanted to share the elation I felt with anyone who would listen. I had achieved a level of clarity that I wanted everyone to experience. For the first time in my life, I felt truly content. I had unburdened myself of my human weaknesses and I was ready to conquer the world. Nothing and no one could stop me from achieving whatever it was I desired.

Speaking specifically to the preclears in the room, I said, "You need to do anything you can to buy your next intensive! Your life will never be the same again! It's worth everything!" The crowd roared.

My host presented me with a large mahogany-framed certificate and a bouquet of flowers. People ran up to hug and congratulate me. My face ached from smiling. After everyone dispersed, I sat on the stairs, staring at my certificate. In beautiful cursive, it read: "The Church of Scientology, Qualifications Division, Department of Validity, does hereby certify that Michelle Seward has attained THE STATE OF CLEAR." It was a moment I could only describe as magical.

CHAPTER SIX

Moving On Up

By going Clear, I had abilities the average person couldn't even imagine—at least that was what I believed. I was taught that without my "reactive mind" and the negative thoughts contained within it, I could control everything from my career success to my health. I sincerely believed L. Ron Hubbard had blessed us, the chosen ones, with his universal wisdom. I had come far in my epochal journey to enlightenment and I couldn't fathom stopping now. My goal was to reach the uppermost plateaus of the Bridge: the Operating Thetan, or OT, levels. Going Clear was the gateway to OT. Nirvana was within reach.

The eight OT levels are an exploration of one's own spiritual immortality through the study of

Hubbard's most advanced research, leading to what the church describes as spiritual benefits that "surpass description." As I understood it, an OT gained a supernatural level of awareness of his own immortality and reincarnations. His psychic powers made him capable of curing illness and psychological disorders in himself and others by sheer force of will.

The highest OT levels promised to reveal "the secrets of a disaster which resulted in the decay of life as we know it in this sector of the galaxy, and, even more importantly, how to fix it." Hubbard said he had made the discovery during a trip to North Africa in 1967. "Somehow or other I brought it off, and obtained the material and was able to live through it," he wrote. "I am very sure that I was the first one that ever did live through any attempt to attain that material."

This extraordinary knowledge forms the core of the church's methodology for saving souls and repairing the universe, but most Scientologists can't afford to access it, and those who do are sworn to secrecy. So mind-bending are the revelations, Hubbard said, that years of costly auditing and church coursework are needed to prepare for them. Anyone who is exposed to the information prematurely will fall sick and die.

Before pursuing my OT levels, I set my sights on an optional auditing procedure called the New Life Rundown, or L-11. The course was taught by only the highest-level auditors at the church's worldwide spiritual headquarters, the Flag Land Base in Clearwater, Florida. It promised to increase one's "havingness," defined by the church as "owning, possessing, being capable of commanding, taking charge of objects, energies and spaces."

"Money is a trap," a high-level auditor told me. "The more you outflow, the more you inflow. If you hold on to it, you will stick your flows and you'll never make more. The more that you help others with the gifts you have been given, the better you will do."

In the spring of 2003, I wrote a check to the church for $50,000 for the course and arranged for Sean and the baby to stay with me at Flag's Fort Harrison Hotel for the two weeks of the course. I couldn't tell Sean what I'd paid, but it nearly drained our bank account. Sean always complained about the amount of money I spent on auditing and courses. He was content to do just enough to stay off the church's radar. I, on the other hand, was committed to the idea that there was nothing more worth spending my money on than my spiritual being. By the time he saw the canceled check for Flag, it would be too late to do anything about it. If he reacted badly, I would get the church to handle him.

On our first day in Clearwater, I filled out the necessary paperwork and took the Oxford Capacity Analysis test, "a scientific barometer of whether a person is getting better." The test consisted of two hundred "yes, no or maybe" questions ranging from practical to silly and was designed to detect a person's weaknesses, or what your "ruin" was: **Do you often make tactless blunders? Are you aware of any habitual physical mannerisms such as pulling your hair, nose, ears or such like? Is your voice monotonous, rather than varied in pitch? Would you "buy on credit" with the hope that you can keep up the payments?** And so on.

It took about an hour to complete the questionnaire. Then I was escorted to meet my high-priced auditor. Class 12 auditors are the crème de la crème, highly experienced, clairvoyant and capable of auditing without a meter. They become your greatest spiritual guide.

The auditor assigned to me was a woman who appeared to be in her late seventies. She was different from the other female auditors I'd had. She was stylish, with designer-label clothes, hair cut in a trendy short bob and tasteful makeup. The Ls, as the New Life Rundowns are known, are also super secretive. You're not allowed to talk about what takes place in session with anyone. I had heard only that the very first question was so profound that many people were thunderstruck (or, as we said in the church, "blown out of their minds") when they heard it. Supposedly it was very short, and answering it gave you the ability to have anything your heart desired. The idea was both daunting and exciting.

My über-auditor knew all about me. She'd already outlined some of the trouble spots we had to cover. Based on the review of my file by an anonymous case supervisor, she said she had a good idea of what we needed to accomplish in our time together. The course could take months to complete, but we were going to work at an escalated pace, with auditing sessions twice a day.

Then came that legendary first question: "When was the first time your power was held back?" the auditor asked.

As a Scientologist, I believed we all had past lives that went back billions of years. Now images of past lives flickered before my eyes. Back and back and back I went over the course of our twice-daily sessions together. My head hurt from thinking so hard. Each night, I fell into bed from mental exhaustion. Little by little, we began to piece the images together to form a finished picture. With the help of prompts from my auditor, I was finally able to conclude that I'd been a warrior in a galactic confederacy and had become drunk with my own power. I'd eventually been stripped of my authority and had not felt powerful in any of my lives since. Through uncovering and acknowledging this seminal event, the auditor said, my power was restored. I was free to be me. The sky was the limit. Nothing and no one could stop me now. There wasn't anything I couldn't do!

I felt euphoric when I finished, the way you might after hurling yourself off a rock ledge into the ocean, or walking a tightrope, or reaching the peak of a challenging mountain. Auditing has that effect on people, which is why it is so addictive. You're always looking for that next high.

I was so grateful for my new insight that I committed another $40,000 to the church, on top of the $50,000 I had paid for the course. It was money I could hardly afford, but it got me on the "big donor" list.

"Big donors" were awarded celebrity status. They got the best hotel rooms at Flag and the best tables at fund-raisers. As a big donor, I would no longer be picked up by a church van with ten other people when I traveled to another location; I would get my own private limousine. If I didn't like a certain auditor, I could request a new one. If I was late to a course, I wouldn't be reported. Money brought immediate deference and respect.

Sean and I came home broke, but I was confident that my contribution would pay off quickly. The course had given me the extra fire I needed to take my career to the next level, and the added donation set me on a trajectory toward acceptance into an elite group of successful businesspeople—most of them men—in the church.

I was on my way to becoming one of Scientology's movers and shakers.

———◆———

From an early age, I knew my purpose in life was to fight for something worthwhile. I remember lying next to my grandmother during naptime at her house in Nevada and her telling me, "Michelle, you will do something great in this world." I was seven or eight at the time, but I **knew** that Grandma was right. I was destined to do something useful and in a big way.

I thought I'd discovered what that was when, the summer after I returned from taking the course in Florida, Mom mentioned that a human rights conference was being held at the Celebrity Centre. I'd always been interested in human rights issues, especially children's rights, so I decided to go. It was a major conference, cosponsored by the church and a nonprofit foundation for human rights that had been founded by a Scientologist, Mary Shuttleworth. More than a thousand people were attending, including government officials and foreign dignitaries. I showed up late and took one of the only available seats, up at the front of the room, next to one of the heads of the California Democratic Party.

For the next couple of hours, I listened intently as the panel onstage spoke of human rights violations around the world, such as discrimination and racism, poverty, violence against women and the abuse of children. The stories about children really spoke to me. They were haunting and heart-breaking and I found myself eager to do anything I could to help. As the conference was ending, I stood to speak. "You have a captive audience here," I said. "Can we sign up to do something? Do you need money? You have a roomful of Scientologists. What do you want us to do, because we're ready to do anything you need!"

Once the applause died down, a pair of church executives approached me privately. Both welcomed me warmly. Leisa Goodman introduced herself as the human rights director for the church. Standing beside her was Heber Jentzsch, the president of Scientology International. Leisa, a tall, pretty woman who spoke with the accent of her native New Zealand, said they liked what I'd said. She wondered if I'd be willing to meet with her the following week to talk about ways I might become involved. I was awestruck. Over the years, Mom had introduced me to some of the higher-ups in the church, but these two were top executives and they had sought me out!

"A meeting?" I stammered. "Yes, sure—of course!"

A few days later, I was in the lobby of the Office of Special Affairs on Hollywood Boulevard waiting to be escorted upstairs to the executive offices. It is top secret and only people with the highest-level security clearance work there. Every door had a card access pad, and security guards or staffers escorted all visitors. I walked to the front desk and asked for my mom, who was by then back from Toronto and working in the OSA building.

She arrived to escort me upstairs, and I could see how proud she was that I'd been invited there. We stepped off the elevator into what I can only describe as something out of a spy novel. The windowless reception area was expansive, with walls of mahogany. It was dim and eerily quiet. A receptionist sat behind a high U-shaped desk. Behind her were three doors with card readers. Offices for the bigwigs, I assumed.

"Good morning," she said quietly.

Mom responded, "I have my daughter here for a meeting with Leisa Goodman." The receptionist nodded politely and picked up a phone.

"Sir . . . Yes, sir . . . Michelle Seward is here . . . Yes, sir . . . Thank you very much, sir." My face must have given away how intimidated I felt, because Mom touched my hand and smiled reassuringly.

A moment passed and Leisa appeared from behind one of the thick wooden office doors. She was dressed in a fashionable suit and heels, her hair perfectly coiffed, her makeup flawless. She smiled warmly, but I could see that she was checking out my clothes.

"You look lovely," she pronounced.

She barely acknowledged my mom, who was a lower rank than she was. I thought it odd.

I hugged Mom good-bye and followed Leisa

into a large conference room. The room was vast, with a cherrywood table at the center, leather chairs, bookshelves stuffed with L. Ron Hubbard books, and framed portraits of the late founder lining the walls.

Leisa introduced me to Mary Shuttleworth. They explained that the foundation needed a U.S. president.

"We have checked your background and you are exactly the person we've been looking for. You're young, you communicate well, you're successful and you're a mother. These are all things we think are important to the foundation."

Mary nodded her approval. I was flattered, but I couldn't imagine I had the time for such an important role when I had my burgeoning career and an active toddler at home.

Sensing my uncertainty, Leisa dropped a three-ring binder on the table in front of me. The cover was stamped "Confidential." "Go ahead, take a look," she said. The book was filled with photos and stories of human rights tragedies she said the church had uncovered. I felt sick as I turned page after page of stories and pictures of victims of genocide and massacres around the world. I broke down when I got to the section about starving slave children in Africa. I was in tears as I closed the binder. "I can't look anymore," I said.

Only much later did I learn that Leisa had asked my mother probing questions about me and that

Mom had given her everything she needed to reel me in. She fed Leisa information about my job, how I was the breadwinner in my family and I made all the financial decisions, and most notably the size of the donations we made to the church. She shared that I had a love for children and a passion for Africa—that I'd even talked to Sean about adopting an African child. The binder had been tailor-made for me based on the input from my mother. And it worked.

"What do you want me to do?" I asked.

Three months later, in August 2004, in my new role as the volunteer U.S. president of our church-sanctioned group, I was speaking to an audience of delegates and advocacy leaders at the United Nations Human Rights Summit in New York City. I was so green I could barely say my foundation's name without stumbling over my words, but somehow I made it through my speech without embarrassing myself. I had found my niche. I threw myself into my new volunteer position, learning about human rights violations around the world, raising money for the foundation, educating schoolchildren and business executives about human rights abuses in South Central LA. My function was to promote the United Nations Universal Declaration of Human Rights and specifically to advocate for children, a role that I relished.

Most of our events were arranged and supervised by Leisa Goodman. She had a say in everything we did. I thought it odd that she was calling the shots when the foundation was supposedly separate from the church, but I knew the church was always looking for ways to enhance its public image by attaching itself to good causes, and this was one. They called it "safe-pointing," a term for counterattacking critics by promoting a positive public image.

As L. Ron Hubbard wrote in one of his policy memorandums: "Continuous good works and effective release of material about one's good works is vital especially in a Black Propaganda war. . . . One can't just dedicate his life to eradicating the enemy, even when that is tempting. On the other hand, within the dictates of safety, one cannot hide continuously. One must, through his good works and actions, at least be visible. So a continual truthful and artful torrent of public relations pieces must occur." What better way to get good publicity than working with an organization that promoted human rights?

I was surprised to discover that the mission of my new foundation involved more administrative than hands-on work. As a volunteer, I didn't have the authority to change it, so I questioned why we weren't getting our hands dirty more. Educating the public and printing brochures was certainly worthwhile, but the people who needed our help were starving **now**. While we were hosting banquets in Hollywood, children overseas were suffering from malnutrition and hunger. I took my concerns to Leisa Goodman.

"You showed me a binder of children starving and dying," I said. "Are we providing them food?" She stared at me blankly, and I got angry. "We're just talking; we're not actually giving these children what they need."

Leisa listened attentively. My concerns were well-taken, she said, but we were unique in our mission. Other organizations provided food and shelter. Our focus was educating needy children about their basic human rights. We were teaching them to save themselves as well as the generations that followed. I decided that what she said made sense. Teaching children about their rights was in some ways just as important to their survival as food and shelter.

And we were getting good PR.

At the same time that I was making a name for myself for our human rights initiatives, my career continued to flourish. I was the top manager and producer for a nationwide insurance company and bringing home more money than I could spend. I wrote a check for $100,000 to the church and promised there would be more—much more—where that came from.

❖

My mother spent most of 2004 in New York City with the Sea Org team in charge of preparing the church there for its grand reopening in the fall. Many millions of dollars were being spent on the renovations to the building on West Forty-Sixth Street near Times Square. I tried seeing Mom that August while I was at the United Nations, but she said she was too busy.

"Not even for a dinner out?" I asked.

"Sorry, Michelle," she said. "You know how it is."

I knew about the rigors of Sea Org life. It certainly wasn't the glamorous job that the crisp blue uniform implied. Although it was considered a privilege to serve in the church's "fraternal religious order," it was a punitive culture. The rules were strict and the punishments harsh. You never knew which of your comrades were watching and judging you until you were written up and called in to Ethics to defend yourself. It was a tough life, hailed by the church as "composed of the singularly most dedicated Scientologists—individuals who have committed their lives to the volunteer service of their religion."

That was my mom. She worked eighteen to twenty hours a day at the New York church, six days a week. She got Sunday afternoons off for personal chores, like hand washing her clothes and her bed linens. She slept on a bunk bed with rusty springs and a stained mattress in dormitory rooms that had bedbugs and cockroaches, showered in cramped communal showers (in and out in three minutes) and ate crummy food. She didn't seem to mind the oppressive rules, or the physical and mental stresses of the daily grind of Sea Org life, or that most of her colleagues were in their twenties. It wasn't for everyone, she admitted, but she had known what she was doing when she signed her billion-year contract, and she wouldn't change it for anything in the world.

Mom had always had trouble committing to anything, including her husbands and her children. But she was unwavering in her commitment to the church. I couldn't have been prouder of her dedication and sacrifice. I think it was her way of making up for things. Every time I saw her, she was smiling. She never complained about the poor living conditions, or the slop they were fed, or the lack of sleep, or the hard labor they were often assigned. Of course, if she did, she knew either I'd have to write her up or she'd be coerced to confess it in auditing; either way, there would be hell to pay. Badmouthing the church was a punishable crime. Speaking ill of our leader was even worse. If you said things "out PR," you were in a lot of trouble.

Which was why my mother didn't tell me at that time, and I found out only years later, that David Miscavige had gone on a two-and-a-half-hour tirade during an inspection of the New York church. Red-faced and stomping his foot, he screamed that the project was late and over budget. Things were poorly run and sloppy. Mom and the others were stupid and incompetent. Nothing was right.

"You have twenty-three people here on mission and I could get this done with three!" he shouted at the workers. "You don't belong in the Sea Org. You're a bunch of worthless slobs and you're fucking up. NOW WHAT ARE YOU GOING TO DO ABOUT IT?"

I'm sure it didn't occur to Mom to complain. Her devout belief in the church and in Miscavige as a divine figure higher than God drove her to blindly accept the principles and practices of Scientology and, above all, obey our leader. She didn't ask questions. She did what she was told, and she told me only good things that happened while she was in New York. She bought a new bedspread for her bunk with the money I gave her, she told me, and Tom Cruise, who was in the city filming, had brought his kids through the church.

"We were told not to gawk, just to nod and say hello and continue working. So many bodyguards surrounded him! He's not very tall, but he's taller than Mr. Miscavige."

I pretended not to hear that last part. I knew Mom didn't mean anything malicious by it and I didn't want to report her and get her in trouble for something that had been said innocently.

There were times I wished I were as reverential as my mother. She'd given up so many human pleasures to serve in the Sea Org. Cars, clothes, vacations, her own toilet, a cell phone, the freedom to say and do whatever she wanted whenever she wanted. I, on the other hand, was pampered and indulged because I was able to afford the celebrity status. I took any occasion to give Mom some of the creature comforts she was missing, things like chocolates, and Starbucks gift cards, and winter coats, and rain boots, and tickets home for Christmas when she could get permission for the time off. I wanted the grand reopening of the New York church to be one of those opportunities to treat her. She had worked so hard for so long on the project and I thought she deserved some reward in return.

The ribbon cutting was set for September 26, and I flew in the day before with Anne Archer and her husband, Terry Jastrow, who were in my circle of big-donor friends. I'd booked a thousand-dollar-a-night suite at the St. Regis Hotel, hoping that Mom could stay with me for at least one night. I'd planned to take her to an elegant dinner, but she declined. She was too busy, she said, tying up loose ends for the opening. She invited me over for a quick tour. When I arrived, I was brought to a special lounge and treated like royalty while I waited for Mom. She looked tense when she walked in, but, as always, she managed a smile and hug. I couldn't imagine the stress she must have been feeling just twelve hours before the main event. After a quick tour, she said she had to get back to work, and I returned to my hotel.

The church sent a car for Anne, Terry and me the following afternoon. I loved my status as an important person in the church. I was escorted and catered to wherever I went. Anything I wanted, from a bottle of water or a glass of wine to a tour of the city or a ride to the airport—just ask, our attendants said. When the ceremony was about to begin, I was led to the front row of seats facing the stage. The stage was outdoors and the sky was a radiant blue. The church must have called in favors to get that done, I thought. While I was being fussed over and smoothing my suit in anticipation of meeting our leader, Mom was scurrying around behind the scenes, tending to last-minute details. She was checking out the uniforms of newbies to make sure they were crisp and correct. She was leading rehearsals so participants knew how to answer questions from the public. She was making sure staff members were in their assigned positions.

As I watched my mother, I remembered a story she had told me recently. She said she was at the church in Los Angles when she heard I was in the building. She'd gone to the lobby and asked where she might find me, to which the receptionist responded with disdain, "And you are?" Mom was wearing her Sea Org uniform, which usually commanded respect, and she was a bit taken aback by the young woman's condescending attitude. "I'm in the marketing unit," she said. "I'm Michelle's mom." That got the young woman's attention, Mom said. "Oh! You're Michelle's mom?" she cried. "That's awesome!" It was the first time she realized that our roles had changed, she said. Before, it was always someone asking me if I was her daughter.

Ten thousand people crowded onto West Forty-Sixth Street for the grand reopening of the church. The busy city block was cordoned off and secured by the NYPD, causing massive traffic tie-ups in Times Square. As trumpets blared, streamers and confetti rained down on the sea of people. Everyone from Tom Cruise and John Travolta to United Nations dignitaries and U.S. senators were in attendance. The roster of speakers included the vice president of the Times Square Alliance, an undersecretary of the United Nations and U.S. congressman Charles Rangel. At the last minute, David Miscavige swooped in in his blacked-out Mercedes. Flanked by bodyguards, he made his way to the front row, where I was sitting. The crowd roared.

Miscavige is a tiny man, probably five feet one, with a powerful presence. It's almost as if he compensates for his diminutive height with his booming voice. He personified confidence. I'd heard that someone once asked him how he'd ended up running the church. He'd looked them straight in the eye and said it was all about ethics. His were stellar, he said. That's exactly how he came across. As if he did everything right all the time. He hugged Anne warmly and shook my hand heartily. He bounded up onstage and began speaking.

"As we look out across the world, we can speak of international conflict, of economic instability, and yes, of terrorism. . . . Let us speak in terms of solutions, solutions that can solve every one of them."

I turned to look at the crowd and glimpsed my mother standing at the back. Her face was filled with awe. Miscavige had that effect on people. He oozed charisma. Listening to him speak, I resolved to get to know him better. I wanted to please him. To let him know he could count on me. It was time for me to step up and do more for the church. To give more of my time. To donate more of my money. Looking back at our leader, I was overtaken with a feeling of euphoria. I was going to help him save the world. The crowd was chanting and I joined in. **Hip-hip-hoorah! Hip-hip-hoorah!**

CHAPTER SEVEN

Meeting Dror

❖

I was making money hand over fist in insurance commissions. As a top manager at my company, I had more than thirty insurance agents working for me and I was earning in the top 10 percent of agents nationwide. My company rewarded me with free trips and bonuses. Sean and I moved to a million-dollar home in a gated community.

At the same time, my charity work was paying off. I was working with officials at the United Nations to teach human rights to children and had partnered with the America's Schools Program to get the first human rights curriculum into a school district—Clark County, Nevada, one of the largest in the country. I told everyone that I owed all my success to the church. Because I was up on my courses and auditing (defined by the church as "on lines" and "upstat"), I was "pulling in" all good things (think "karma").

I decided to keep the momentum going by opening my own business. With financial backing from a large insurance broker, I started my own firm. I recruited some of the top people in the field. The business took off immediately. Within months, I was selling huge insurance policies to the rich and famous. With my first multimillion-dollar sale paying a $2 million commission, I wrote my largest check ever to the church.

The church took full advantage of my good fortune by showing me off at galas and celebrity events. I was Scientology's poster girl. Look at Michelle! She's young and happily married with a beautiful child and a winning business! Scientology can do that for you too!

It was at one of these dog and pony shows that I was introduced to Dror Soref, a fellow Scientologist. The black-tie gala at the Celebrity Centre in Hollywood was a star-studded evening: John Travolta and his wife, Kelly Preston; Leah Remini; Anne Archer; television actors like Sofia Milos, Danny Masterson and Erika Christensen; and the musician Beck among the thousand guests. It was hardly your typical church dinner; it felt more like being at the Oscars.

I was seated next to Dror at a table purchased by a mutual acquaintance. Dror was introduced to me as an award-winning filmmaker. He was probably twenty years older than me and spoke with a slight stutter. With uncombed, spiky hair and rumpled clothing, he reminded me of my first auditor, Larry. He seemed nice enough, but he quickly monopolized my time, asking me questions about the insurance business and my human rights work. I really wanted to mingle, but I didn't know how to extricate myself without seeming rude. Finally, about halfway through the evening, I managed to get away and do some table-hopping. At the end of the evening, Dror caught me on the way out.

"I'd love to get your information," he said. "I would love to support your human rights foundation."

I pulled a business card from my purse and handed it to him.

"Thank you—that's very kind!" I said. "I'll let you know when we have our next event."

Dror called several times the following day while I was tied up in client meetings. When my assistant announced his fifth call, I picked up. He asked for a meeting to discuss how he could support my charity work. I said I would get back to him to set up a lunch, but time got away from me and I didn't follow through.

A month later, I was invited to a summer party at the sprawling Hollywood Hills home of a wealthy Scientology couple. He was a business magnate and she was an aspiring actress. Sean didn't want to go, so I was by myself. The first people I spotted when I got there were Dror and his wife. I was new to the church's celebrity inner circle and relieved to see someone I recognized. Dror jumped to his feet when he saw me and greeted me warmly, almost in a fatherly way.

"What a coincidence!" I said. "Here we are together again!"

Dror said he'd called me many times. Had I received his messages? I told him I'd been swamped with work and apologized for not getting back to him.

He introduced me to his wife, Virginia, and the three of us ended up talking for most of the party. I especially liked Virginia. She was around my age and very "LA," a former actress with a bohemian-chic fashion sense and a nose for where to go to "be seen." She and I bonded quickly. We found we had a lot in common, like our Southern upbringing—mine in Oklahoma, hers in Texas. We shared stories about where each of us was on the Bridge, and the challenges of balancing career, family and kids. It turned out that Virginia was interested in adopting a child, as I was. Saying good-bye, Virginia and I promised to see each other again soon. Dror asked if we could schedule a business meeting.

"I'd love to get together with you, Michelle," he said. "I hear your business is very, very successful." I thought perhaps he wanted my advice on life insurance or annuities.

"Sure!" I said, thinking I had a potential new client. "Call the office anytime."

Two weeks later, Dror was sitting across the table from me at the Marmalade Cafe, where he spent the better part of the meeting telling me all about himself. **What a fascinating man,** I thought as I listened to his story.

Dror was born and raised in Israel. He attended the University of Haifa and earned degrees in economics, sociology and anthropology. When he was a student, he started a repertory theater before being drafted to serve in the Golani Brigade, an elite unit in the Israeli Defense Forces. He founded a new political party in Israel and, at the age of twenty-three, was nominated to run for the Knesset, the Israeli legislature. When he decided to pursue a film career in the late seventies, he emigrated from Israel to the U.S. to study at the cinema school at the University of Southern California.

Around that time, he was introduced to Scientology. L. Ron Hubbard was still alive then; Dror had the opportunity to get to know him and said he was one of the most charismatic men he'd ever met. Over time, Dror rose to serve under Hubbard in the Office of the Guardian, the intelligence-gathering arm of the church (later renamed the Office of Special Affairs). **Oh my God,** I thought. This man had worked beside LRH! How many people could say that?

We never got to talk business that day. We

simply ran out of time. But I ended the meeting thinking that this was someone I liked and wanted to see again.

———◈———

Over the next few months, my friendship with Virginia developed at warp speed. She was always around, inviting me to lunch or dinner with her and Dror, or to do some shopping, or offering to do whatever I needed for my human rights events. I usually brought Sage on our dates while Sean stayed at home alone, playing war games on his computer. Virginia was so attentive that sometimes it seemed as if she were courting me, and I enjoyed the attention. Virginia was an original. She smoked and cussed and you didn't want to incite her Cuban temper, but at the same time, if she was on your side, you could do no wrong. I didn't have many friends who were that encouraging and supportive, and I soaked it up.

There was only one slight drawback, in my mind, which was that Dror was around more often than I would have liked. I enjoyed the girl time, but he and Virginia came as a set. Wherever she was, he was usually not too far away. And whenever he was with us, he dominated the conversation with talk about filmmaking. I tried to be polite and seem engaged, but I'd never been a big movie fan and the business side of moviemaking didn't interest me. My business was insurance, not Hollywood, but Dror aimed to change that.

After months of friendly lunches and dinners, Dror asked if I would be willing to meet with some people he was considering doing business with. He said he had a film deal in the works and a plan to start his own production company. He admired my good judgment and business acumen. Mostly out of my loyalty to Virginia, I agreed to help, even though, I pointed out, I didn't know anything about the movie industry, nor did I have any interest in it.

One day, over lunch, Dror invited me to "consult" on the film project he had under way. It was a thriller called **Not Forgotten**, for which Simon Baker, famous for the hit TV series **The Mentalist**, had been cast in the lead role. It was a surefire hit—backed by a bond with international distributors on board, which he explained was a filmmaker's dream. Distribution deals were tough to get, he said. They guaranteed the film would have a wide release in theaters in the U.S. and abroad, which was what lenders looked for before agreeing to finance a project. With my business savvy, he said, I would be a real asset in helping him raise funds. I thanked him for his confidence but said I lacked both the time and expertise in the film industry.

A short time later, Dror invited me to a meeting with a wealthy and well-respected businessman who was also a top donor in the church. I was impressed. "Is he going to be involved in the film project?" I asked. Dror said it looked like it. "Let me know when and where and I'll be there," I said.

The meeting took place at the man's Spanish-style estate in the La Cañada hills. It was a turning point for me. The man appeared to have great respect for Dror and total confidence in the movie. If he was behind it, I thought, maybe I needed to take a closer look to see what was in it for me.

When I expressed an interest, Dror seized on it. He said the way he'd figured it out, with the help of some financial experts, the deal would pay double-digit returns a couple of years after the film's release. He had already signed on A-list actors and an executive producer who owned over 1,200 theaters in the U.S., and distribution was certain.

The timing was right. It was late summer of 2007 and the robust economy of the previous decade was showing signs of strain. Lax lending practices had led to debt obligations in the hands of people who were unable to pay them. The housing bubble was starting to deflate and investors whose pockets were deep with mortgage-backed securities were worried. Investors who'd made a killing in mutual funds, including many of my own clients, were nervously watching their portfolios decline and asking about alternative investments. I thought Dror's deal was something to consider.

I decided that I would introduce the film opportunity to some of my high-end clients and family, like my father, as a great "extra thing" they might want to take a look at as a possible investment to prop up their declining annuities. Between guaranteed distribution, top actors and a script by the writer who worked with Scientologist Paul Haggis on the movie **Crash**, the deal, which Dror sold as "no risk," seemed like no-brainer.

I did a huge amount of due diligence. I spoke to attorneys, friends and even my VP, and everyone thought it looked good. I also trusted Dror because that's what we did as Scientologists. To question the integrity of a fellow Scientologist was an affront to the church. "Mutual trust is the firmest building block in human relationships," L. Ron Hubbard said. "Without it, the whole structure comes down."

Putting my faith in Dror would turn out to be a colossal mistake and one for which I would pay an awful price. At the same time, our friendship helped me to make one of the best decisions of my life. He and Virginia encouraged me to follow through with my dream of adopting a baby girl.

CHAPTER EIGHT

Savannah

❖

One of the greatest moments of my life was when I looked into the face of my new baby girl for the first time. It was Monday, October 2, 2006. I was sitting in the rocking chair in the hospital room when a nurse picked the baby up from her bassinet and placed her in my arms. I'd never held such a tiny baby. She was wrapped in a blanket with a knit cap on her head, but I could tell how very small she was. Sage was nearly double her size at birth. I got the feeling she was confused. **Who am I? Where am I? What's this all about?** Cradling her in my right arm, I placed my left hand on her head. At that moment I felt as though we were the only two people in the room. Sean and the nurses seemed to have faded out of the picture.

"Do you feel this beautiful little head?" I asked her. "That beautiful little nose? Those beautiful little lips?" Scientology taught me to get in touch with the body in order to get in touch with the soul. But this was more than a religious ritual. This was a mother's instinct.

I continued caressing the baby's soft brown skin. **Your beautiful arms. Your beautiful hands. Your beautiful fingers. Your beautiful feet.** When I finally reached her toes, she peeled one eye open. "Hi, little Savannah," I said. "That's your name! Savannah! I'm going to be your mommy." The hours-old child looked into my eyes. "I promise to always take care of you," I said. "We will be so happy together." Suddenly, stunningly, her mouth turned up in a half grin. It was as if she understood all that I had told her, as if I had touched her soul. A nurse's voice broke the silence in the room. "Oh my goodness!" she said. "I have never seen a newborn smile like that!" Both of us started to cry.

Through my tears, I noticed my attorney walking toward me. It was time to give the baby back, he said. Time to meet the birth mom. I could barely stand the thought of letting her go. Looking at her sweet little mushed-up newborn face, all I could think was that she had been given up once and now I had to hand her back to the nurse and walk away. **What is she thinking? Is she afraid?** My tears turned to sobs. **Is my beautiful little**

**girl going to think I'm abandoning her when
I just promised that I would always be there
for her?**

"It's only until tomorrow," my attorney said, trying to comfort me.

I pulled my baby close. "Savannah," I whispered, "I will be back. I promise I will be back
tomorrow to take you home."

<hr />

I had learned about the baby's birth only a few
hours earlier. I was at the Burbank airport, having just returned from a business trip to Dallas,
and waiting at the luggage carousel when my cell
phone rang. I saw that it was Durand Cook, an
adoption attorney I'd once met over the phone.
The actress Catherine Bell had heard the scuttle-
butt in the church that Sean and I were looking
to adopt, so she approached me one afternoon at
the Celebrity Centre to say her stepfather was an
adoption attorney in Beverly Hills and she thought
he might be able to help me. Sean liked the idea
that Durand was somehow attached to Catherine
Bell and all of a sudden he was more interested
in the idea of adoption. Catherine was a naturally
beautiful woman, and Sean spoke of her looks
to me quite often. Looking back now, I realize
that he was trying to impress her. Catherine had
oohed and **aah**ed about the idea of adoption. As
we were driving home, I asked Sean where this

new state of mind regarding adopting had come from.

"I've been giving it some thought, and although I would rather have our own, I think we should help a child that needs a home."

That this came out of Sean Seward's mouth was surprising to me, but if he was going to give me an inch, I would take a mile—yet I knew I needed to be calm and not get too excited, or he would back down. "Okay, so would you like me to reach out to Durand and set up a meeting for us?" I held my breath.

Sean paused, the way he always did. He liked to make me wait when he knew that I was on the edge of my seat for an answer.

"Why don't you meet with Durand and then you can let me know how it goes?"

I started to get a little worried that he was slipping away from the idea.

"But he will want to meet us both, and I'm sure there are classes and things we have to do to be prepared." My voice was getting higher as I felt myself starting to plead.

I could see the veins popping out in his temples from clenching his teeth and I knew I needed to get him back on track.

"I have an idea. Why don't I talk to Catherine? I'll get her to explain to her stepdad who we are and that I will handle everything for now. How's that?" I begged.

A long silence was broken by Sean saying, "Okay."

Durand and I had a phone conversation that same week. I could tell that Catherine had spoken highly of me, and Durand never asked to meet with Sean and me together. He did warn, as I'd anticipated, that adopting a baby could be a long, expensive process. When I received the application package Durand had put in the mail, I was so excited I immediately ran upstairs to Sean, where he was playing a computer game. Even though I knew interrupting him was a no-no, I plopped down on the floor and started reading the application questions to him.

"What's your mother's maiden name again?"

No response.

"Sean, please take a minute to talk to me. This is very important—I need to fill out the paperwork for our application to adopt a baby."

As his fingers were frantically moving to kill something in his game, his character died. "FUCK!" he screamed. "I've just let my whole team down because you interrupted me!

"I don't give a shit about your application!" Sean screamed as he frantically logged back on to his game. "You want information, then you call my mom! I've told you before. You want to adopt, then you handle it. I don't have time for this!"

"Sean, please don't get mad. This is about a baby and not about some fake game!" I knew the minute the words came out of my mouth there would be hell to pay. I literally ran from the room and shut the door, hoping that the pull of his game was more important than dealing with me. I knew I had to get out of the house with Sage and fill out the application on my own.

After looking over the paperwork and the "happy family" pictures I'd enclosed, Durand called me again a few weeks later.

"I noticed on your application that you said you would take an African-American child," he said. "Why?"

I explained that, for many years, I'd thought about adopting a black child. For some reason I'd always imagined myself with an African daughter. My best friends growing up were black, as was my best friend in the church, and I loved reading about Africa and its rich mixture of cultures. I loathed racial discrimination and I wanted my children to grow up amid diversity, I said. Durand sighed.

He explained that he had a client, a woman with African heritage who'd had a one-night stand during a trip to Las Vegas and gotten pregnant. She wanted to give the baby up for adoption at birth. Unfortunately, he said, a family in Canada had already started the process of adopting the child. He wished he'd seen my application earlier. "I'll call you if anything else comes up," he said.

Then, on that October day, Durand called again, his voice urgent.

"Michelle, where are you?" he asked.

"I'm at the airport," I said. "Why? What's going on?"

Durand explained that a baby girl had been born recently and she was available for adoption.

He needed a decision right away. "Are you interested?" he asked.

I didn't hesitate. "Of course!" I said.

"Michelle!" he said. "She's an African-American baby girl."

I was overcome with emotion.

"Oh my God, Durand!" I cried. "This is my child! It's her!"

I asked when the baby was born.

"Thirty minutes ago," he said.

"Where do I need to fly to see her?" I asked.

"She's right here at St. Francis hospital in Lynwood," he said. I knew of the area, but I'd only driven through on my way up and down the California coast.

"I need you and Sean to get here right away," the lawyer said.

"I'm coming," I replied.

Despite the cracks in my marriage, I kept telling myself that bringing a child into even an unhappy marriage was better than a baby languishing in foster care.

I hadn't expected things to move so quickly,

but I was beside myself with joy. My exhilaration was tempered only slightly by the trepidation I felt about telling Sean. He was indecisive by nature and we couldn't afford to waste time while he tried to make up his mind. The baby was available now and I felt she was meant to be mine. I couldn't let the opportunity slip through my fingers.

Sean and I didn't have a normal couple's way of communicating. Partially because I didn't want to be yelled at and he didn't want to be bothered during his daily computer games, everything was done by text. In hindsight, I feel embarrassed that I texted him rather than calling him about something so important, but this was how our relationship functioned at that time and I didn't want to do anything to harm our chance of adopting this baby. At least by texting I could gauge his reaction before we actually talked. "Baby girl just born," I wrote. "She's ours! Meet me at St. Francis in Lynwood."

I grabbed my bags, rushed to my car and quickly got on the road. I was giddy with excitement and I wanted to share my news with someone who would revel in it with me. I called my sister, and for the hour-long drive we batted around possible names for the baby. Elia. India. Savannah? Yes, that was it. Her name would be Savannah. Closing in on the hospital, I ended the call with my sister and called Sean's cell.

"Where are you?" I asked. "Are you almost at the hospital?"

I met him in the parking lot. I could tell he was in a sour mood.

I was over the moon and I tried to get him excited too. At least he had come! I was certain that once he met the baby he would fall in love with her and any anger he'd felt would evaporate. My heart pounded with anticipation and exhilaration as we walked into the hospital lobby. Durand was waiting for us there with the sweetest, most welcoming smile. I'd never met him in person, but I felt as if we were longtime friends, bonded by the beautiful child I was about to meet.

Durand and I embraced. He led Sean and me into a small conference room. He handed us the birth mother's medical records. He said that when she first realized she was pregnant, she inquired about having an abortion, but she was too far along, nearly four months. After that, she'd made every prenatal medical appointment. She had no history of drug or alcohol abuse. She admitted she'd had a single glass of wine before she knew she was carrying a child, but that was all. All she remembered about her one-night stand in Las Vegas was that he was tall, handsome and black. She didn't even know his name. She hadn't seen the baby and didn't want to. She just wanted to get this over with and resume her normal life.

"This is the baby you told me about," I said.

"The one who was being adopted by the Canadian couple?"

"Yes," he said. "That fell through."

The fact that there was no history of addiction and no sign of fetal alcohol syndrome was a huge relief to me. I didn't want a special-needs child. Scientology held that someone with afflictions was being punished for "poor ethics." I'd seen my fellow Scientologists shake their heads condescendingly when they saw a special-needs child. "Must've 'pulled it in,'" they'd say, meaning it was the child's fault for attracting the misfortune, probably a transgression in a previous lifetime that had never been "handled."

When I was finished asking questions, Durand pulled out the adoption papers for Sean and me to sign. Sean hadn't said a word the whole time. I asked for a moment alone with him. We were about to make a life-changing decision and I wanted to make sure he was on board.

"Look at me, Sean," I said, when Durand left the room. "This is the time to say it if you are not ready to do this. You have to tell me now. You can't tell me after we've seen the baby and met the birth mother. There's a lot at stake here. A lot of people's lives are involved, including an innocent child. Once we sign the papers, there's no turning back."

Sean remained quiet. His eyes were vacant.

"Well?" I asked. "Sean, please say something. What are you thinking?"

"I'm fine," he said absently.

I foolishly took his response as a sign that he was coming around. Once he saw our child, everything would be fine.

But Sean didn't even try to connect with the baby. The whole time I held her, he stood off in a corner with his arms folded across his chest. When I asked if he wanted to hold her, he shook his head and said, in a frosty voice, "No, that's okay." I understood that I'd put Sean in a difficult position by agreeing to the adoption without first consulting him, but I hoped he would give it a chance. I needed to know now that he was at least willing to try.

Before I got the chance to question Sean further, Durand said it was time to meet the birth mother. The three of us headed upstairs. My head was spinning as we approached the room. I wondered what she would think of us. What would she look like? How would she act? Would she like me? Would she be leery because we were white?

When we walked into the room, she was propped up in the bed, dressed in a hospital gown and head cap. Durand had said the birth was by cesarean.

"These are the people who want to adopt the baby," Durand said.

She didn't say anything at first. She just looked

at us with a blank stare. Once again, Sean stood at the back of the room while I took the seat next to her bed. Self-consciously, I dropped my handbag beside me. I studied the woman's face.

"Hi, I'm Michelle," I said gently.

An awkward silence followed. The birth mother and I had nothing in common except for the baby she was giving away, whom I wanted so desperately. When she did look at me, I tried not to read her thoughts. It was too frightening.

I noticed she was holding a pamphlet in her hand and rubbing it with her finger.

"Oh," I said. "You are holding the Lord's Prayer. I love that prayer. It reminds me so much of my father. The Lord's Prayer was his favorite."

She seemed unmoved. "I'm not very religious," she said. "The nuns just walked in here and handed it to me."

I don't know what came over me, but I took hold of her hand then. I was surprised she didn't pull it back.

"You have given us the greatest gift," I said. "I do not judge you for making the decision you made. I am grateful to you. I promise you this little girl will be loved more than you can imagine."

For the first time she smiled, ever so slightly.

"What will you name her?" she asked.

"We have named her Savannah," I said.

She laid her head back on her pillow and looked

up at the ceiling. "I love that name," she said. Finally, a connection.

"Do you have any other questions?" I asked.

"No," she said, turning her head away.

"What if she wants to contact you when she's eighteen?" I asked.

She paused, looked back at me. "Well, I guess if she has to," she said.

With that, our meeting was over.

"Thank you," I said.

She didn't respond. As Durand led us out of the room, I looked at Sean, who was distinctly pale.

"Sean," I said, "you don't look so good."

"I'm just trying to take it all in," he said.

Of course, I thought. How could I blame him? This was a lot for Sean to digest. I'd sprung it on him so abruptly. We had agreed to adopt, but it may have seemed only theoretical to him. Now there was a real baby in the picture. What if he backed out? I'd seen him break promises before. It never mattered whether it hurt someone else, as long as everything went his way. What if this was one of those times? What if we went home and he said he didn't want another child? I knew how that went. He'd fight until he wore me down, the way he always had. But this was too important. I was not going to leave the hospital committing to the baby only to have him ruin everything later.

I tried talking to him one last time. "Sean," I said. "Sean, please. Tell me you're sure about this. I know this came out of the blue, but you have to be honest about what you're thinking. We are talking about a child's life here. We cannot mess around. There is no backing out once we leave this hospital. There is no stopping it at that point." He didn't blink.

"I'm fine," he said finally.

"Okay," I said. I tried to empathize with his hesitation, but I actually never doubted that he would love our little girl. He just had to get used to the idea. I knew I could get the church to help if he had trouble adjusting.

Durand walked us back downstairs. He said the baby would be ready to go home at ten the following morning. Birth mothers normally had thirty days to change their mind, he said, but ours had signed a waiver saying she didn't need the time. Her mind was made up. The baby was free for us to adopt her. I hugged Durand good-bye and promised we'd be there at ten sharp the next day.

I could hardly contain my excitement as Sean and I walked to our cars. I couldn't wait to get home to tell Sage, I said. Our six-year-old son had wanted a sibling for so long. He was going to adore his baby sister! After dinner we could all go shopping for baby things! We'd need to get a crib and formula and bottles and diapers . . .

"Oh my God, Sean!" I cried. "Can you believe it? We have a daughter!"

Sean pulled the keys from his pants pocket and opened his car door. He didn't seem to be hearing a thing I was saying.

"I didn't think she was going to be that dark," he said.

I felt like someone had knocked the wind out of me. "What does **that** mean?" I asked. I couldn't believe what I was hearing.

"No, nothing," he said. "The mother. I just didn't expect her to look like that."

———◆———

I barely slept that night. All I could think about was bringing my baby home. There had hardly been time to wrap my head around it. Only twenty-four hours earlier, I'd been standing in an airport, listening to an attorney I'd never met tell me about a newborn. Now she was coming home with me and I was overwhelmed with joy and anticipation. Ten o'clock couldn't come fast enough.

The night before had been just Sage and me. As expected, he was beside himself at the thought of having a baby sister. His birthday was a week away and this was the best birthday present ever! he said.

"I love her and I haven't even met her yet, Mommy!" my sensitive son squealed.

I'd called my family and friends to share our good news and gathered up Sage to go baby shopping. The two of us ran around the department store until closing and checked out with two big cartloads of baby things. Sean was sleeping when we got home, which was what I'd hoped for. The less time we spent in each other's company, the more unlikely it was that he would question the adoption.

It was ten thirty p.m. by the time I got Sage into bed. I slipped gingerly into mine so as not to awaken Sean. After hours of tossing and turning, I rose at five. After getting Sage off to school, I spent the morning organizing the baby's room. I began getting ready to go to the hospital. I was toweling off in the bathroom when Sean came in and sat on the edge of the tub. We had less than an hour and he still hadn't showered or shaved.

"I'm not going," he said.

"What do you mean, you're not going?" I asked.

"I can't do it," he said.

"What do you mean, you can't do it?"

"I'm not adopting her."

At that moment, I gained another kind of clear: I finally understood that my marriage was never going to work.

I was so sure that Sean would come around, that he would realize this little girl was meant for us and we could offer her the loving home she deserved. But ours was not a loving home. For years, I had done a stellar job of pretending to the outside world that we were a model family. Sean was the perfect stay-at-home dad, taking care of our adorable little boy, while I worked to provide us with a comfortable living. The problem was, the marriage didn't live up to the image. I couldn't remember the last time either of us had been happy together. There was constant simmering tension. I couldn't stand to be around him most of the time, much less give him sex, and he resented me for being the elusive wife he couldn't quite conquer. The only people who knew the truth were our auditors and the Chaplain. Give us your money and we will save you, they'd promised, but all they ever did was tell Sean to get a job and me to start acting like a real wife.

I was done kidding myself. The marriage was over. It probably should have never been.

There would be no more pretending. There would be no more emergency meetings with the Chaplain. There would be no more putting up with his pushing and shoving and calling me names. There would be no more soliciting auditors or the Chaplain for advice about how to get him to work. There would be no more asking how to save our marriage. I was going to divorce him and raise this child. He had forced me to choose and I chose her.

"I'm going to pick up our daughter," I said. I could feel his eyes burning into my back. My eyes welled with tears.

I quickly finished dressing, loaded the car seat in the car and drove to the hospital alone. Any anger or sadness I felt when I left my house melted away after I walked into the nursery and saw Savannah in her bassinet. The nurses welcomed me warmly, then crowded around as I scooped up the baby and cradled her against my chest. I was a bundle of nerves, but nothing ever felt so right as holding my daughter. I rubbed Savannah's swirly black curls. "Girl! You're going to have to learn how to do her hair!" one of the nurses cried. Everyone laughed, but I could hardly wait.

I said my good-byes to the nurses with hugs and words of gratitude. On the way to the car, I had a paralyzing thought. I remembered that the car seat was still in its box. Sean would normally have handled installing the car seat, and the idea of doing it myself filled me with trepidation. **What if I can't do it?** I thought. The nurse is going to think I'm completely unqualified to take this child home.

The nurse held Savannah while I pulled the car seat out of the box. Nervously, I read the instructions, and within a few minutes the car seat was secure. I took the baby from the nurse and strapped her in. She looked like a peanut in that big seat. I thought about what this was supposed to look like, the new mother sitting in the backseat with the baby while the other parent drove. But there wasn't anyone in the backseat. It was just Savannah and me, and I was petrified. What if something happened while I was driving? I wondered. What if she stopped breathing?

I steered the car with my left hand and held my right hand on her chest. To calm myself, I talked to her all the way home to Valencia: "Savannah, this is you and me. It is going to be you and me and you are going to be fine. The beauty that you are will shine so brightly that every person who meets you will love you. I don't want you to worry. Everything is going to be okay."

My house was full of friends when we arrived. Dror and Virginia brought food and drinks for the occasion. Mary Mauser, my new FSM and spiritual advisor, scurried around, making sure everything was perfect. My friend Alana came in juggling a stack of baby gifts. Everyone took turns holding Savannah. The baby seemed to revel in the attention. It was such a happy occasion, except that Sean was sulking. I listened as people congratulated Sean, telling him how beautiful the baby was and what a great day it was and what a wonderful thing he had done. He barely acknowledged them. After an hour or so, when it was time to put the baby down for a nap, I walked upstairs and Sean followed.

"You have seven days to find her a home," he said, as if talking about a stray dog.

"Excuse me?"

"I'll let you keep her for a week," he said.

You'll let me keep her? I thought.

The strangest feeling of calm came over me. I knew Savannah wasn't going anywhere. Sean could protest all he wanted. I wasn't afraid of him anymore.

"You heard what I said, didn't you? Didn't you? You have a week, Michelle."

"Okay, Sean," I said, turning to walk back downstairs.

❖

Sean didn't follow through on his seven-day ultimatum and Savannah was still living with us, but I was planning for a future without him. I began taking control of my life in anticipation of being a single mother. I could no longer rely on his family to babysit while I made evening sales calls or took weekend business trips. My solution was to take the kids everywhere with me. They went to meetings and church functions and my human rights talks and conferences. We were the Three Musketeers and I loved it.

Waiting for the adoption to be final, Sean and I entered the most dangerous phase in our marriage. He didn't care if the kids were around when he shoved me into a wall or screamed that I was an "out-ethics cunt." I fantasized about the day I never had to share the house with him, but I wasn't about to let him know I was leaving him and risk delaying or even forfeiting the adoption. Until he signed the adoption papers, I had to hold on.

CHAPTER NINE
Endings and Beginnings

◈

Savannah was three months old when we got the news that the adoption was final. Sean had come to love her but it was too late for us. We barely spoke anymore and when we did it always turned into an argument. I didn't care what he told the ethics officer—about what a bad wife I was, so cold and unfeeling—because I was on the way out of the dysfunctional mess we called a marriage. I wasn't prepared to spend one more miserable day of ugly accusations and name-calling and physical abuse than I had to. In fact, I had signed us up for a marriage course at Flag in Florida to assist with the split. Once we got to Clearwater, I would beg and plead with the auditors and the Chaplain to let the marriage be over. I was certain when they saw how unhappy I was, and how hopeless another crack at reconciliation would be, they would agree to assist us with a divorce.

Sean had agreed to the trip, but I'm sure he had a different scenario in his mind about how it would play out. Why wouldn't he? He didn't believe we would end up getting divorced. Every time we turned to the church with our marital troubles, the same thing happened: I was blamed for our problems because I was not performing my wifely duties; he made promises about finding a job and curbing his temper; and the church pressured me to give the marriage another try. I was sure he expected the same routine again.

Not this time. I was finished negotiating. They could keep me in session for weeks or months and browbeat and bully me until I couldn't take any more. They could threaten to take me down on the Tone Scale and label me a Suppressive Person. They could lock me in a room without food, water or a working toilet. But I was done.

I didn't think it could get any worse between Sean and me. But a few weeks before we were due to leave for Flag, it did.

That monstrous night—one I could never have imagined—began with a neighborhood birthday party. Our next-door neighbor, Mr. Johnson, was celebrating his eightieth birthday and his wife wanted to mark it in style at a fine local hotel. The Johnsons were two of the few neighbors I knew, because they were retired and I often saw them coming and going. Residents of our neighborhood had the big jobs they needed to afford the multimillion-dollar homes in this gated community in the Santa Clarita Valley. I might see other people on the weekend and get a wave or a quick hello. The Johnsons owned one of the biggest estates on the block—a home measuring six thousand square feet—and even then they had downsized from a much larger home in Brentwood after Mr. Johnson retired.

Mr. Johnson had made his millions in the disability insurance business, and even in retirement the couple maintained an extravagant lifestyle. Mr. Johnson had a wandering eye, and Mrs. Johnson pretended not to notice when he flirted with me. Both were jealous of anyone who had more than they did, and Sean and I were in our thirties and owned the only house in the neighborhood worth more than theirs. This made us competitors of a sort—at least in the Johnsons' eyes. Mr. Johnson had often made innuendos about how we were making our money, but I always just smiled. I let his comments slide because I assumed he didn't mean any harm, and I never wanted to get on the Johnsons' bad side because I'd heard the resulting freeze could take forever to thaw.

Whether to accept the invitation to Mr. Johnson's birthday extravaganza wasn't even a question. The Johnsons ruled the neighborhood. I told Sean we were going, like it or not. He didn't like it, he said. I told him to make sure to get his tux out of storage. The party was black-tie. That didn't go over well at all, but I didn't care. "We have to go, Sean," I said.

"So you're going to force me to dress up and you're going to pretend?" he asked.

"That is exactly what we're going to do," I said. "So you can put on your tux or I'll go alone."

We were among the last people to arrive at the hotel. The banquet room was grand, with over-sized crystal chandeliers, thick gold velveteen drapes, bone china on white linen tablecloths and white roses on every table. It looked like a wedding was about to take place. Sean and I took our as-signed seats. I knew the neighbors on the opposite side of the table, but the two women next to me were pretty much strangers. I'd gotten glimpses of them because they lived in the house across the street from ours, but I had never actually met either of them. They were a handsome couple, I thought. One wore makeup and was dressed in a feminine black suit and ruffled white blouse; the other had short, slicked-back hair and wore an ex-pensive man-tailored tux. She introduced herself as Charley Harper. The other woman was her wife, Maria, she said. I was intrigued by the couple and wanted to engage them in conversation. Surely the church wouldn't object to a little neighborly chatter.

Maria didn't say much. She just sat there, sipping champagne while everyone else drank margaritas. I thought she seemed annoyed. But Charley was just so open and warm that we hit it right off. She asked about our kids and said she saw Savannah playing outside when she was walking her dog. Her accent was unmistakably Southern.

"Where are you from?" I asked. Charley said she was born and raised in Mississippi. "I'm from Oklahoma!" I cried. Two girls who said, "Y'all." We bonded instantly.

Sean didn't seem interested in joining the conversation. Like Maria, he sat there without saying a word. For the rest of the evening, Charley and I chatted about everything from the difficulty of finding places in California that served good fried chicken to how West Coast folks knew nothing about fried okra and didn't know what they were missing. We talked about the unique beauty and culture of the South and how LA could really benefit from a lesson in good old Southern manners. She was so confident. She offered no excuses for who she was or what you saw. She was comfortable in her own skin. I envied her that. Listening to her talk, I imagined sitting on a porch with her somewhere in the South, drinking sweet tea and hearing all about her life. For just a moment I forgot what my life was like outside of that beautiful room.

Charley seemed particularly interested in Savannah.

"Your little girl is so cute," she said. "I think it's so great that you have an African-American child. My niece adopted three girls and one is African-American."

I knew I could safely open up to this woman. She was so warm and nonjudgmental.

"You know what I hate?" I asked. "I hate it when people look at us and say, 'Oh my God! She's so lucky!' I always say, 'No. I am the lucky one.'" She nodded and smiled.

Four hours went by at lightning speed. When I realized the party was wrapping up, I glanced at my watch and was stunned to see it was almost midnight. Sean and Maria were just sitting there, looking bored. With everything going on around us—including a spirited performance by ballroom dancers—Charley and I had been in our own little world. I'd forgotten Sean was even there.

As Charley and I hugged good-bye, I couldn't help but think about how she would be classified by the church. L. Ron Hubbard wrote, "The sudden and abrupt deletion of all individuals occupying the lower bands of the Tone Scale from the social order would result in an almost instant rise in the cultural tone and would interrupt the dwindling spiral into which any society may have entered."

As a lesbian, Charley would be branded a lowly level 1.1 on the Tone Scale—unless she was "handled" in Ethics, the way I had been. My exposure to homosexuals had been pretty much nonexistent, but if she was an indication of what most of them were like, then maybe the church should reevaluate its judgment. **There is nothing covert or hostile about this woman,** I thought to myself as we were preparing to part ways. **She is warm and kind and she seems to be living a very normal, happy life.**

I could tell that Sean was furious once we returned home. He didn't say a word. Even during the worst of times we always made small talk if we weren't fighting. I walked upstairs, checked on the kids and went to our room to get ready for bed. Sean was already there. As I stood in front of the bathroom sink, washing my face before I turned in, I could feel him staring at me. He was eerily quiet. **Don't provoke him,** I told myself. **Finish up and go to bed.**

"Who do you think you are, ignoring me and talking to a lesbian all night?" Sean finally asked.

The glacial tone of his voice frightened me. He was livid. Apparently the neighbors who had been sitting across the table from us were teasing Sean that he'd better watch out because it looked like he had some competition from the lesbian. Did I understand how embarrassing that had been for him? He was shouting. **Don't respond,** I told myself. **Hold on. Only a few weeks to go before he's out of here.** The cold granite of the countertop pressed against my stomach as I prayed he would leave the bathroom. But that wasn't going to happen. I would have to be punished for humiliating him.

I was bent over the sink when Sean grabbed me from behind. He held me so tightly around my chest that I couldn't breathe. I tried to turn to get away, but I could not move with the weight of his body pressed against mine. The more I resisted, the more he seemed to like it. I pleaded for him to stop and calm down so we could talk it out.

"Please, Sean!" I whispered. "The kids are in the other room."

Sean didn't say a word. He just pushed me harder against the bathroom counter.

"Not tonight. Please not tonight!" I cried.

I knew what he was doing. His intention was to remind me that he was the man and I was his wife and shouldn't ever forget it. I heard the zipper on his pants unzip. I couldn't fight anymore. When he finished, I fell to the floor and shook uncontrollably.

"You have no idea how done we are," I said. "You have no idea."

From that moment on, Sean and I lived separate lives. I ordered him to sleep in the guest room. He didn't argue. We stopped talking, eating meals together or even sharing brief moments together with our children. To keep my sanity, I began counting down the days until we could leave for Clearwater.

Freedom was so close I could almost taste it.

———◈———

Several weeks flew by. I'd committed to helping Dror get his film funded, and he was ready to start filming. He called constantly. If he wasn't telling me about a budget or scene change, which I didn't understand anyway, he was pushing for me to come to the set to meet the actors. I was too busy with my own business, I said. I had a big deal pending. I was headed to Flag as soon as the matter closed. I'd see him when I returned to California.

The week before our scheduled flight to Florida in April, I came down with symptoms of flu. I was nauseous and so fatigued that I couldn't lift myself out of bed. On Sunday night, after sleeping for a solid twenty-four hours, I hobbled downstairs to check on the kids. Sean was in the kitchen, boiling hot dogs for dinner. I took one whiff of the hot dogs cooking and fled to the bathroom. I threw up until I was gagging on air. **I know this feeling,** I thought. The sensitivity to smells, the bone-tiredness . . .

Once I felt steady enough to stand, I stumbled out to the kitchen and told Sean I was running to the store. I got to the drugstore just before closing and purchased a pregnancy test, then sped home and ran into the house without closing the garage door. Into the bathroom I went. My hands trembled as I did the test. The instructions said it would take two minutes for the results to appear. I placed the stick on the side of the sink and waited, checking every couple of seconds. After a few minutes that felt like a few days, a big blue "X" appeared in the window. The reading was positive. I was going to have another child.

A sense of strength washed over me, dousing my moment of panic. **Okay,** I thought. **I am having a baby, but I will not change my plans. I will go through with my divorce. There is no going back. My mind is made up. If I can't do it for myself—because the timing seems wrong or the idea of raising three children alone is too daunting—then I will do it for my children. They deserve better than the life they are living with Sean and me. They deserve to just be happy and carefree and loved.**

Throwing the test in the wastebasket, I walked upstairs to the bathroom, where Sean was giving Sage and Savannah a bath.

"Guess what, guys," I said. "Mommy is having a baby!"

Savannah was a toddler, still too young to understand, but Sage yelped with delight. Sean looked smug and knowing. I knew what he was thinking. His place in my life had just been secured. Surely I wasn't going to leave him when I was having his baby. I hoped he could read my expression because it said that I was determined to do this without him. As tired and sick as I felt at that moment, I would not allow my confidence to be shaken. He could think whatever he was thinking. I would not be deterred. No matter what the church said or did.

◈

I was nodding off to sleep on the flight to Florida when I had a vision. Part of my old self was dying. My eyes were closed but I was watching it happen. Far from feeling fearful, I was in bliss, content. All my life I'd had a sense of foreboding and fear. For as long as I could remember, I was always worried about something. Can Mom make the bills? Can we afford to buy groceries? Will I pass this test? Will I get that job? Now, as my head bobbed and the voices of my chatty children turned to echoes in the distance, I felt free. For the first time in my life, I wasn't afraid. No matter what, I had me, and I could overcome anything.

As my mind drifted from one pleasant thought to the next, the pilot's baritone voice awakened me. We were starting our final approach into Tampa International Airport.

"Sorry, folks, but it looks like the weather is un-seasonably cold and rainy," he said.

I looked down at Savy, who was asleep in my lap. Sage was coloring in the seat next to my personal assistant, Monica, who was accompanying us on the trip. I looked over at Sean, who stared straight ahead.

We landed in driving rain, but my mood was

still bright from my dream sleep. I was headed to a new and better life for my children and me.

Because I was one of the top donors, we received VIP service when we arrived in Florida. A representative from the President's Office was at the airport to greet us. We piled into a limo for the thirty-minute drive to Clearwater.

Flag's Fort Harrison Hotel was under renovation, so we were lodged in a large suite that resembled a New York City penthouse apartment in one of the newer buildings. Monica settled into her room, and I checked into the suite with Sean and the kids. I was dismayed to find only one bedroom. Sean sneered, but I wasn't having it. I called downstairs to tell the concierge we would need another room, for Sean. Of course, he said. But it was very late. They would make the arrangements for tomorrow. By then it was midnight. **Okay,** I thought, **so what's one more night?** I was six weeks along and so tired all I cared about was falling into bed and crashing. I didn't care who was beside me.

I tucked myself tightly under the covers and turned out the light. A moment later I felt Sean slide in beside me. I cringed in the darkness. A few seconds passed and he tossed his arm over me. Sitting straight up in bed, I pushed him with the full force of my body weight. **How dare he?** I thought. I was seething.

"Don't you come near me!" I hissed, unable to conceal my loathing for him.

Sean launched into a tirade. I was worthless, a Suppressive Person, a horrible wife, a liar. This was the usual rant. I didn't know what to do, so I took it. **Don't fight back,** I told myself. For four hours he ranted until he finally wore himself out. It was four thirty a.m. when I turned in. At sunrise, I crept out of the room. I called Mary Mauser back home to tell her what had happened.

Mary had been my spiritual advisor since my previous advisor and I had had a falling-out a couple of years earlier. I liked Mary. I found her to be a breath of fresh air because her predecessor's gruff, controlling style could be overwhelming. Mary was a lot more like me in many ways, only older. She was petite and blond and successful in her career in computer software technology. She lived in a nice home in Santa Clarita and seemed to know everyone. I thought she was steady and strong, which made me feel secure in her counsel. The only thing that bothered me was that she gossiped a lot. She was always telling me unflattering stories about the people she worked with, and I couldn't help but wonder what she told others about me. Every time she spoke ill of someone, I let it go, just as I'd been trained by the church to do with all negative thoughts.

In exchange for her service as my spiritual

guide, Mary received a commission on the courses I bought and my donations to the church. She was making a good buck on me, but she seemed to really care about her church work. Mary was aware of my marital struggles. There had been many times when I'd called upon her to get Sean calmed down, and she'd always managed to do it. That alone was worth the money.

I told Mary about how we'd arrived in Florida and experienced a terrible night. I'd had two or three hours of sleep at most and I was exhausted. Mary was sympathetic. She promised to contact Flag's Ethics Department to let them know what I'd told her. It was the proper chain of command. Sean knew he was in trouble when he was routed to Ethics that day. As soon as he left, Charmaine Roger, one of the church's chief fund-raisers at Flag, swooped into my suite.

Charmaine and her husband, Bruce, were a power couple in the church. Their primary role at Flag was fund-raising. They were based in Florida but often traveled to the Celebrity Centre to solicit donations from stars and wealthy businesspeople. I was always on Charmaine's target list. I was fond of both, but I especially admired Charmaine. She was a tiny woman but a fireball. Mary had told her what had happened and she was furious. When I said I was pregnant, she picked up the phone and arranged to have Sean's belongings moved to another room. Within minutes, the housekeeping staff was packing up his things. I was comforted to know Charmaine was in my corner, but my peace of mind was short-lived.

After Charmaine left, I was freshening up in the bathroom while Monica played with the kids when I heard banging on the door. Sean had come back to the suite from Ethics and noticed his things were gone.

"Where are my clothes?" he screamed. "You are not going to separate me from my children!" I was shocked.

"You just get back from Ethics and this is how you act?" I asked, trying to control the fear in my voice. He raged louder. I was trapped in the bathroom as he stood blocking the doorway. I felt desperate to protect my body because of my pregnancy; I tried to keep myself calm and as far away from Sean as I could be in the bathroom. The louder he yelled, the more concerned I became about Sage and Savannah hearing him. I wanted to shut the bedroom door and do everything I could to get Sean calm and out of this room. When I pushed past him, he grabbed my arms and started to push me back. I knew that I needed Monica's help and I screamed, "Sean, let go of me!"

Monica ran in from the other room. "Let her go, Sean!" she cried. "What is wrong with you? She is pregnant! Are you crazy?" Her tone of voice seemed to stun him. He released his grip and ran from the room.

I called downstairs for help. "This is an emergency," I said, barely able to catch my breath. "I need to see an ethics officer immediately."

While Monica stayed behind with the kids, I rushed down to the Ethics Department. The ethics officers were behind locked office doors with keypads. "Just a moment, please," the receptionist said, disappearing behind one of the doors. I was terrified that Sean was about to come barging in. Only a moment or so passed when an ethics officer introduced herself.

"Come back with me," she said, motioning toward one of the doors. She ushered me into her office and asked what had happened. I told her everything.

"Okay," she said when I'd finished. "Now go back to your room and we will get on this immediately."

It was the early evening by the time I got back to my suite. The kids were reading with Monica. I had been told in Ethics that Sean was being ordered to stay away. I needn't worry. Security would be watching.

I was back for only a few minutes when Charmaine appeared with a butler carrying a tray of cookies, fruit and tea. The kids filled their plates with goodies and Monica took them to another room so Charmaine and I could talk privately. I poured my heart out to her. There was only one solution, she said: I had to divorce him. It wasn't what I expected to hear and I was flush with gratitude. Charmaine had influence, and she was on my side.

Charmaine switched the conversation to fund-raising. For the next two hours, she talked about the benefits of giving generously. Considering my future plans, she said, I would need the church more than ever. Increasing my membership from Silver to Gold was essential. The upgrade would cost $250,000. I thought her timing was off. I was going through one of the worst periods of my life and she was there to sell me an upgrade. The church was always looking for more. Whatever I gave was never enough for very long. Whenever I found myself thinking about it, I tried to remind myself that altruism came at a price. It took a lot of money to serve our larger purpose: the fight to save mankind. And better the church got my money than Sean, I thought. I wrote the check that night.

The following day, Sean and I were called into session together. **The sooner, the better,** I thought. **Let's just get this over and move on with our lives.** I was thinking we'd have a couple of days in session and then the powers that be would concede there was nothing left to salvage. I would then be free to go home and proceed with the divorce.

The auditor began by asking Sean to sit next to her while she hooked me up to the E-meter.

"Hold the cans," she said. I did what I was told

and waited. "What have you done to Sean?" she asked. **What? What have I done to Sean?** "What have you withheld from him?"

My head was filled with thoughts I wasn't supposed to be thinking: **This guy's an abuser. I want a divorce. Why are you asking me these stupid questions? Can we please just get this done?** I tried to clear my head, to stop the negative thoughts, knowing that the needle wouldn't float if I continued to think them. Then there would be more questions. **Stop!** I told myself. **Clear your head. This is all good. The auditor is good. The process is good. The church is good.**

Hours passed, with only a short snack break. It was late evening. I just wanted sleep. I reminded the auditor that I was pregnant. I was feeling nauseous. She accompanied me to the cafeteria for sparkling water to settle my stomach. "I need a bathroom break," I said when we returned to the room. With Sean and the auditor on the other side of the bathroom door, I retched over the toilet. After a few minutes, I heard a knock on the door.

"Okay, are you done?" the auditor asked. "Would you like to come back to session now?" **Do I have any choice?** I wondered. I felt like I was in the **Twilight Zone**.

The following morning it was Sean's turn on the cans.

"What have you done to Michelle?" asked the auditor.

"Nothing major," he said. For the next hour, he recited what amounted to nonsense. "I didn't tell her I was on the computer. I left dishes in the sink. I didn't give Sage a bath one night." My face twitched. I wasn't allowed to interject, but I wanted to scream. **C'mon, Sean! Let's get honest. I don't want to be here forever. Tell the lady the truth . . .** "I screamed at her all night. I forced her to have sex." If only I could get him mad. Maybe then he would break down, if he was angry enough. **I know! He hates when I roll my eyes at him.** When Sean gave another innocuous answer, I made sure the auditor wasn't looking, then rolled my eyes. He went berserk.

"Look!" he cried. "She's rolling her eyes at me!"

I shrugged as if I didn't know what on earth he was talking about. Another safe answer, another roll of the eyes.

"See!" he shouted, pointing at me. "She's doing it again!"

The auditor looked at me. I shook my head, as if to say, **Cuckoo!**

Another ten-hour day, another few thousand dollars, and I knew we were getting nowhere. How many times did I have to say it? I didn't want marriage counseling. I wanted a divorce.

"See you back here tomorrow," the auditor said at the end of each day.

Why? I wondered. Why did we have to come back? I was spending a fortune on auditing hours and I wasn't even interested in fixing things with Sean. I wanted out of the marriage. Even Charmaine agreed a divorce was the logical answer for us.

Something didn't feel right. I had expected to be at Flag for a week and spend a couple of days in session. But we were stuck, going over the same stuff. We weren't having sex. Why? Because I couldn't stand the thought of him touching me. Why? Because he was cruel and abusive. What had I done to him? Withheld sex. What was I hiding that I would deny my husband sex? Really? We're still talking about a sexual urge I had for a girl fifteen years ago? **Cha-ching . . . Cha-ching.**

After two weeks of ten-hour days of being grilled about the same topics, listening to Sean hem and haw and contribute nothing meaningful, and, later, when we were unwatched, come banging and screaming at my door at night, I was at my wit's end. I was writing $5,000 checks every couple of days for something I didn't need. I was running my business by phone and trusting my staff with my biggest accounts. No one seemed to care.

I complained. I wrote reports. I was noisy about wanting to go home. I had a business to run!

In the fourth week, I was called one afternoon into session. Alone. I was overjoyed. I expected to hear that Sean was not participating with honest intentions, so there wasn't any sense in continuing with marriage counseling. I would receive the church's blessing. I would be free to return home and start divorce proceedings. **Glory be!**

But that was not what happened.

I was told to sit and was handed a form with red writing. I knew that meant trouble. Red writing conveys instantly that something needs to be repaired. The form noted that I was "pulling withholds," which meant I was hiding something. My needle wasn't floating. Was there something I wanted to say? the auditor asked.

I couldn't believe it. "I am newly pregnant," I said. "This is probably why my needle isn't floating. I am uncomfortable and nauseous and tired. That has to account for something!"

"Thank you very much," the auditor said. "But we're concerned there may be withholds that have been missed and we are going to send you for a withholding check." In other words, be prepared for a merciless inquisition by Ethics.

I wanted to scream. "Why are you not pulling in the abuser?" I cried. "Why is it always me?"

I had been in Clearwater for nearly a month and I was no closer to my goal of a divorce settlement than I had been when I first got there. I was trapped.

The auditor hooked me up to the cans and started down a list of questions on the form, making notes along the way.

"Have you thought badly about L. Ron Hubbard?"

"No," I answered.

"The church? Mr. Miscavige? If so, what kind of thoughts did you have?"

"I didn't," I replied.

"Have you withheld from the auditor?" she asked.

I stared at her blankly.

"Have you given an untruth? A half-truth?"

I was exasperated. "I have told everything I can possibly tell," I said.

"Thank you very much," she said. "What have you withheld from the auditor?"

"Really?"

"Thank you very much. What have you withheld from the auditor?"

My chest heaved and I collapsed in tears. "I have told everything!" I cried.

"Thank you very much. Okay, now what have you withheld from the auditor?"

I wondered if they were trying to drive me crazy. I couldn't think of a thing I hadn't told the auditor. What was there to tell that I hadn't already revealed during the other four marriage counseling sessions that Sean and I had attended over the years?

"What have you withheld from the auditor?" she asked again.

While Sean was doing who knows what, I was being held hostage by a high-placed Scientology auditor who probed my every feeling and thought, all to determine whether my marriage could be saved. I already knew it could not. She poked and prodded my fragile psyche for hours, allegedly to help me discover why I couldn't make my marriage work. I wanted to get the hell away from them, from Sean, and return home.

"What have you withheld from the auditor?"

I hadn't eaten since morning and I was beginning to feel faint. Now I'm thinking, **This is so horrible. I am pregnant and I have an abuser sitting outside while** I'm **the one on trial.**

I snapped.

"Okay!" I said. "I'll tell you what I didn't say. This whole thing is ridiculous. I think it's all bullshit."

"Thank you very much," she said. "Was there an earlier time you felt this way?"

I thought my head would explode. Obviously, my fucking needle still wasn't floating.

"I've been through hell because you guys can't get this right!" I shouted. "I'm here because I want to end this marriage, not because I want to fix it! I'm done! I want out of here!"

"Thank you very much. I understand," she said. "Now let me repeat the question. Was there an earlier time that you withheld something from the auditor?"

"You need to let me out of here!" I sobbed. "My needle isn't floating because I'm pregnant and hungry and tired. That's against LRH policy that dictates we have to be properly rested and fed before these inquisitions!"

She kept pushing and I panicked. We were going down a rabbit hole and I wondered if I would ever get out. What was going to happen to me? What was she trying to accomplish? We were going in circles.

I was becoming hysterical. If I hadn't been pregnant, I would have forced my way out of there, but I knew part of her auditor training was to physically stop me. What if I was thrown to the ground and the life of my unborn child was jeopardized?

Another hour passed. It was late, very late. I had to get control of myself. **Take a breath,** I told myself. **Calm down and say whatever you have to to get out of this room.** "I'm sorry," I said, slowing my breathing. "I'm very hungry now and I need to eat. I am extremely unhappy. I am being interrogated and you are doing nothing to address the years of abuse that I have endured with Sean. Unless you do something about it, I will not donate another dime and I will not return to Flag!"

The auditor was stone-faced. "Thank you very much, Michelle," she said. "I understand. I will make sure that this is written up for the case supervisor."

She had apparently had enough. Or was it the mention of money that did it? She advised me that the needle had floated and the session was over.

I dragged myself out of the room and headed

down to the lobby to get a snack. Bruce Roger, Charmaine's husband, was waiting when I stepped off the elevator. The thought crossed my mind that he was there to solicit yet another donation, but if he was, he apparently thought better of it when he saw the condition I was in. Bruce looked shaken when he saw me. "Oh my God, Michelle," he said, holding his hands to his face. "You look terrible! What happened?" I told him how long I'd been in session and that I was pregnant and sick. He took me to the restaurant off the lobby and fetched me some chicken soup. He looked at me like I was a broken child.

"May I be honest?" Bruce asked.

"Of course," I said.

"We are all hoping you can get out of this marriage. You are always so uptone [upbeat] and we get so excited when you come here. But every time you're with Sean it's like a black cloud following you. I shouldn't be saying any of this, but I have to tell you, you deserve so much better."

I was grateful for his kind words. I felt as if, at that table, we were just two people, one helping the other during a difficult time.

I felt comfortable talking to Bruce. I wasn't worried that he'd write me up or report me for talking about my personal business.

"Bruce, I'm done!" I said. "I'm done with this marriage and I'm done with auditing and I'm done with being dragged through the mud for overts that Sean has committed. This trip has been so disappointing. I came to end an abusive marriage and I thought I would get help. I've complained about his abuse for so long and nothing is ever done. What is it going to take? For one of my children to be hurt?"

For good measure, I threw in, "If you want another dime from me, get someone to listen and help me get a divorce now." Was I testing Bruce? The church? Myself? Probably all three.

Bruce changed the subject to my kids. "We love seeing them running around here," he said. "Tell me about them."

Talking about my children was exactly what I needed to calm down.

"They are everything to me," I said. "Savannah is sweet, strong, funny and determined. I wish I had her spunk. She has taught me there is no difference between a child you bear and one who comes into your life after birth. Sage has been a big brother to her in every way. My son is a gift. He's smart and thoughtful. I just worry that he holds too much inside. I'm so sad they have had to experience the turmoil of our marriage at such a young age."

Bruce listened quietly until I was finished. I felt as though he really cared.

"Let me ask you something," he said. "What kind of person do you picture yourself with?"

Wide-eyed, I glanced down at my tiny bump. "Bruce! Really?"

"I mean it," he said. "I'm talking about after you have the baby. Who do you see yourself with next time around?" It was almost as though he were giving me permission to escape from my personal hell for a moment.

I thought about what he'd asked, trying to get past my original thought, which was that I was trying to get out of a relationship and couldn't see myself with anyone at that point.

"That's the furthest thing from my mind. But, you know, it's an interesting question." I thought for a moment. "Well," I said finally, "whoever I'm with next needs to be older than me and definitely well established because I need someone who doesn't depend on me." Bruce nodded and smiled. "I want someone I can learn from and I want to feel that I can lean on that person for advice and direction." Bruce urged me on.

"What industry would he be in?" he asked.

I laughed. "What popped into my head was the music industry, but I have no idea why," I replied. "I don't know anyone in the music industry! But not a singer—someone who is behind the scenes. An executive, maybe. A person who travels a lot so they don't have to be by my side twenty-four/ seven. And they would have to be kind and sweet and love children. Maybe have a child of their own so they understand the love for a child. And I want to be madly in love."

Only much later did I realize that I never said the word "he."

I felt calmer after talking with Bruce. When I got back to my suite, Sage and Savannah were sound asleep. Monica retired to her room, and I crawled into bed and fell fast asleep.

The following morning I was advised that I was to meet with the Chaplain to proceed with divorce negotiations. **Money talks,** I thought. I'd been trapped there for four hellacious weeks, paying for auditing that was useless, and all it took was a threat about withholding future donations to finally get what I'd come for. Bruce had obviously reported back to Charmaine, and—just like that!—the edict was given to facilitate the divorce. It was my first clear glimpse behind the veil of deception that shrouded the church, and I didn't like what I saw. A coincidence? I convinced myself it was, and fought the feeling that I was being played.

———— ⊕ ————

At the end of May, two weeks into our divorce mediation with the Chaplain, I received word that my beloved grandfather was on his deathbed. My grandparents had helped raise me and I was devastated at the thought of losing him. I already felt guilty that I hadn't been to see him in a few months. The divorce negotiations with the Chaplain were ongoing, but my priority was seeing my grandfather before he passed.

"I have to fly to Nevada," I told the Chaplain. "My grandfather is dying and I must be by his side the way he was always by my side."

"We're not finished yet," he said.

Yes, we are, I thought.

"I have to go," I said. "Monica will take the kids home to California. Please keep Sean here until after I'm gone. Otherwise, he'll try to delay me and I won't make it to my grandfather."

I spoke with a new certainty and the Chaplain knew there was no stopping me.

He made me sign a pledge that I would return as soon as my grandfather was gone. I scribbled my signature, agreed to write another big check to the church to secure my release, and told Sean not to be in our house when I returned to California. I'd been at Flag for six grueling weeks and left feeling adrift. One minute, the church was my savior. The next, I was a pawn in a game. I struggled to see clearly in my pursuit of the truth.

Two steps forward. One back.

Mom was already there when I arrived in Reno. My grandfather died two days later. I had made it in time and I was grateful. I stayed for the funeral and then it was time to go home. I found an excuse for not returning to Florida. I learned I was carrying twins and I was too sick to travel.

Sean moved in with his parents, and I had a

huge amount of work to catch up on. My life was chaotic, but for the first time since I was very young I wasn't afraid or worried about anything. Our home was peaceful, the kids were happy, I had twins on the way and our financial future was secure.

At my five-month checkup, my doctor informed me that I would have to start taking it easy. Most twins were delivered prematurely, he said, and I was already having mild contractions. A month later he put me on bed rest. Talk about chaos! I had to hire a team of nannies to watch my children day and night. It was all I could do to get to the bathroom, much less tend to my business. My executive team picked up the slack and Monica became the liaison between my employees and me. I tried to stay in the game by doing conference calls from my bed. Dror took up a lot of my time. **Not Forgotten** was in production and going to be phenomenal, he said, but he needed additional funding. He had an international distribution deal in place, which meant a major payoff for our clients. I had already recruited investors and pitched in with my own money in exchange for an executive producer credit, but he needed more up front. It would all be worth it when the film eventually paid dividends, he said. I promised to do my best to help.

My home confinement didn't keep the church away. The top "regs" (fund-raisers) had me on their target list and they'd show up at all hours. I didn't know it at the time, but they were getting daily reports from my mother about every aspect of my life, everything from how much money I had coming in to the status of my marriage and my pregnancy. Mary Mauser, who acted as my confidante, was also sharing everything I told her, giving the fund-raisers information to help them get me to donate more. The fund-raisers would come to my home, plant themselves in a chair by my bed and stay until I made a donation.

One night, three of them showed up and pitched me about donating to the expansion project at Flag's Clearwater headquarters. The plan was to resume construction of the new Flag building, which had begun a few years earlier. The seven-story building would house the church's highly classified "Super Power" program and state-of-the-art equipment to empower spiritual beings to clear the planet of all its perils. Saving the planet—wasn't that what we as Scientologists aspired to? I knew they weren't leaving until I paid up. Finally, at two a.m., bone-tired and heavy with my growing twins, I wrote a large check to get them out of my house.

I gave birth to the twins on September 27, 2008, five weeks earlier than their due date. Jadon and London were both healthy, and we went home the following day.

The first week was hell. I didn't sleep. I couldn't eat. I was distressed and depressed. Virginia, Dror's wife, came to my rescue. She rounded up another friend, Alana, and they spent a day helping to take care of the babies and cooking a week's worth of meals, which allowed me time to take a bath and an afternoon nap. Virginia came back every day after that. **What a kind and loving friend,** I thought. She picked me up and encouraged me when I needed it the most.

I finally settled into a routine. I was raising four children as a single mother. The idea was intimidating, but I was so happy to be free from Sean. Whatever I had to do to keep up with the crazy production that was my life—my children, business and divorce negotiations—I was willing.

I worked from home for the next couple of months. My kids needed me, so I conducted whatever business I could from my bedroom. My time was limited and I began refusing visits from church members. The break gave me even more clarity about Scientology. Since Florida, I had really begun to question what the church stood for. **Where is the substance?** I wondered. **They have all this money but none of it is spent on bettering the world. They don't build hospitals or orphanages or support animal rights. All they do is build their own beautiful buildings and tout their wealth and their celebrities.**

For my entire adult life, I had lived under the church's rule, by the words of L. Ron Hubbard, thinking his thoughts, suppressing my own, never questioning church doctrine or how the church spent my money or why it treated people so cruelly. Were my beliefs and values really my own? Or had the church planted them in my mind, then watered and fed them during all those weekly sessions with auditors and ethics officers? Was I brainwashed? Had I been intentionally trapped in a warped bubble so I couldn't think for myself?

I wasn't sure anymore.

One morning in February, I was nursing when the phone rang. The twins were turning five months old, and I was beginning to get back on my feet. The caller was Lindsey Sutton, a Scientology friend who worked in the entertainment business. Lindsey was with the musician Chaka Khan, who had performed at church functions. "I'm sitting here with Chaka and her manager, Tammy, and we want to talk to you about something, Michelle," Lindsey said. "We heard you put a lot of money behind Dror's film, and we want to talk to you about our project."

Chaka was looking for investors for an album being developed by a promising new artist who also happened to be a Scientologist, Lindsey explained. I thanked them for thinking of me but said I didn't know a thing about the music business—maybe I could recommend some people who might be interested.

Lindsey urged me to at least agree to meet with the producer of the album, a really talented woman, she said. I demurred. "I'm sorry, guys," I said. "I'm already drowning in commitments and I can't take on one more thing right now. Let me try to come up with some names of people who might be more open to this kind of project."

A week later, they called again. I agreed to meet Lindsey for coffee.

"You're not going to believe this," Lindsey said. "But the woman lives in your neighborhood."

"What woman?" I asked.

"The music producer. She lives in Valencia, near you."

"Where in Valencia?" I asked, more out of politeness than any real desire to know.

"A place called the Woodlands," Lindsey said.

"The Woodlands? That's where I live. I don't think any famous music producers live in the neighborhood. What street?"

Lindsey named my street.

"Oh my gosh! That's my street! Tell me her name again?"

"It's Charley Harper," Lindsey said.

How did I know that name? It sounded so familiar. **Charley Harper . . . Charley Harper . . .**

Lindsey said Charley was a big deal, a famous songwriter and record producer. All of a sudden it hit me. Charley Harper was the neighbor I spent the evening talking to at the neighborhood birthday party exactly one year earlier—that handsome lesbian from Mississippi who lived across the street. As much as we'd monopolized each other's time that night, neither of us talked about what we did for a living.

"Oh my gosh!" I said. "Charley Harper! Wow! Please tell her it's me—Michelle! The woman she talked to a year ago at the birthday party."

It wasn't ten minutes later when the phone rang again.

"Girl, where have you been?" the voice with the sweet Southern drawl asked.

"Charley! How are you?! It's been a long time," I said.

"I thought you had fallen off the face of the earth," she said. "But then I saw two storks in your front yard and I heard you had twins. You and your husband must be excited!"

"Well, yes, I had twins," I said. "But, no, there is no husband. We're going through an ugly divorce."

"Oh, Michelle," she said. "I'm sorry to hear that."

"Don't be," I said. "It was the best decision of my life. It's a very long story and not a pretty one, but I have four amazing children and life is good. So tell me what you are into with Lindsey, and how do you know her."

Charley asked if I had time to meet with her, and we committed to breakfast the following morning at the Marmalade Cafe in Burbank.

We'd set aside an hour for breakfast, but three and a half hours later we were still talking. Charley was genuine and kind. I told her a bit about Sean and the marriage, and she told me that she and her wife, Maria, were also having problems. Charley had a daughter, Jaime, from a previous relationship who was grown and lived in Texas and they were very close. I could tell how much she loved Jaime. When we finally got down to business, she told me more about the music project and the singer that Chaka was grooming.

I asked, "If I invested in this, what would my rate of return be?"

She laughed out loud.

"Rate of return? This is the music industry. There is no rate of return!" I appreciated her honesty. "No," she said. "This isn't a good one for you."

It was lunchtime when we parted ways, and both of us had missed other appointments. I left with butterflies in my stomach. I felt like Charley was my new best friend. It felt good to connect with someone who wasn't a Scientologist.

By the time I got back to my office, she had already texted me.

"I really enjoyed our breakfast. Let's do it again soon."

◈

My mom was pestering me about returning to Flag to complete my divorce negotiations. "If you don't handle this divorce with the proper tech [auditing], then you will find yourself in a very bad place or, worse, very sick again," she said.

Sean had been acting up, so I decided it was time to finish what I'd started and return to Florida. Mary Mauser called Sean and convinced him to meet me there. If he refused, she said, she would no longer counsel him. Begrudgingly, he agreed to go.

I packed up the kids and my assistants and we flew to Florida. A limo was waiting at the airport to take us to the Fort Harrison Hotel. We were greeted at the hotel by our own personal butler and escorted to the fifth-floor penthouse. The penthouse was huge and breathtaking, with a grand piano in the living room and a private entrance for those who didn't want to be seen. I was told it was where Tom Cruise stayed when he was in town.

I hadn't even settled in when the butler announced that Charmaine was on her way up with a bouquet of flowers. I knew why she was there. She stayed four hours and left with another check. If it hastened my divorce, I was all for it.

Three days later, I returned home with a tentative divorce settlement. That same week, I closed the biggest deal of my career.

CHAPTER TEN

Deal Broker

◈

While I was at Flag, Charmaine had introduced me to a fellow Scientologist named Beth Linder. Beth was cofounder and chief executive of a large software company, and she was active in the church's human rights efforts. I knew the name, but hadn't met her before. She was one of the church's top donors. She'd been in Charmaine's office when I walked by one day. "Michelle!" Charmaine cried when she saw me pass. "Michelle, come in here! I want you to meet someone! Can you sit for a minute?"

No one said no to Charmaine. After the usual greetings, Charmaine explained that Beth was interested in moving up from a Gold to a Platinum Meritorious member, but she was $600,000 short of the $2.5 million minimum donation it took to

get to that level. Charmaine boasted about my success in the insurance business. She asked Beth if
she had a good estate plan and said I was very crea-
tive with insurance and had just closed a huge deal
with another very successful businessperson. Perhaps there was a way I could sell Beth an insurance
policy and give her a percentage of my commission, which she would then donate to the church
to qualify for the Platinum Meritorious.

As a tax-exempt religious organization, the
church was prohibited from brokering business
deals, but they always found ways around it. Charmaine was clear that the church could not be involved in the actual business transaction, on the
record, yet it would gladly be the beneficiary of
Beth's additional "donation." I explained that selling Beth a policy—if she even needed additional
insurance—would be a long process and I couldn't
just "give" a client my commission anyway. Beth
and I agreed that the unorthodox approach Charmaine had suggested wasn't something that either
of us was interested in. But that didn't stop Charmaine from pursuing her mission.

After I returned to my room, she called my
suite. She said she was with Flag's Commanding
Officer. They wanted to meet with me "for just a
minute." A few minutes later, the three of us were
sitting around the grand piano in my living room.
When the butler arrived with a pot of steeping tea
and a tray of cheese and crackers, I knew it wasn't

going to be the brief meeting that Charmaine had promised.

She began by complimenting me on always being such a good "team player." She quickly switched subjects to Beth Linder and how I could help her achieve that Platinum membership. My part, she explained, would be selling a policy to Beth and donating the bulk of my commission directly to the church. Wasn't that perfectly legal? The church would help Beth secure a short-term loan to cover what I would be donating over time. That way, we could close the deal that same week, the Commanding Officer said. I agreed to meet with Beth only if she truly needed a policy.

The next morning there was a knock at my door. When I opened it, the butler was standing there. He informed me that all the things I needed for work were on the way up to the suite. He had arranged for a laptop, a printer, a calculator, a fax machine and all the office supplies I might need.

We spoke to Beth's attorney and accountant and everyone agreed that the plan should be put in place. By the time I left for Los Angeles, Beth had signed all the necessary paperwork. In short order, Beth got her coverage (and her loan) and the church got its donation.

◆

My life now moved with a powerful momentum. My divorce settlement was in the hands of

Scientology lawyers, my insurance business was booming and Dror's regular reports to me indicated the **Not Forgotten** film project was right on track.

Charmaine soon contacted me with another opportunity. The actress Kirstie Alley had a business proposal she thought I might be interested in. As with Beth Linder, the church saw an opportunity that would benefit it as well as me. My big donations were paying off.

I was excited to meet Kirstie. I knew her from the television show **Cheers**, of course, and had met her in passing at the Celebrity Centre. I knew she was highly respected in the church. Charmaine and I arrived at her 1920s Mediterranean-style estate in Los Feliz on a warm weekday morning that spring for breakfast. The home was set atop a magnificent rolling lawn of green velvet grass and surrounded by an eight-foot-high wall covered in blooming bougainvillea. It screamed Old Hollywood, grand and mysterious. We announced ourselves at the gate and Kirstie's assistant, armed with a smartphone in each hand, clumsily opened the door to greet us. As she chatted on one phone, she motioned for us to follow. We passed four lemurs bouncing around in a cage the size of a Los Angeles apartment.

We wended our way through narrow hallways decorated with antiques and stepped into a warm, inviting kitchen that had been featured on **Oprah**.

Kirstie was seated at a small kitchen table with a woman named Peggy Crawford, a Sea Org member who had been given a leave of absence from her duties to help Kirstie launch the new business. I was surprised when I saw "KA," as everyone called her. She looked as if she had just rolled out of bed. A rumpled white cotton nightgown covered her considerable frame, her hair extensions were tangled in knots and she wasn't wearing a drop of makeup. Still, she was beautiful and intimidating. She exuded fierceness, a businesswoman who didn't care what anyone thought of her or her appearance. There was nothing inviting in her piercing green eyes, but she was captivating.

I listened as Kirstie launched into her sales pitch, with Peggy and Charmaine chiming in like minions. I was impressed with the thoroughness of her research and her presentation. The project was a weight-loss program and fat-burning supplements. She had financial projections, pictures of the products, ideas for a marketing campaign and a name: "Organic Liaisons." It was an interesting venture, and I was flattered that I was being asked to be a part of it, but it seemed risky to me, and not something I would recommend to my clients.

Scientology was a small world. Everyone knew everything about everyone else. So I wasn't surprised that Kirstie knew about my partnership with Dror. She asked how I'd raised the money for his movie. I explained that Dror had a lucrative international distribution deal in place, one that promised a generous return for investors once the movie was released overseas. She agreed that she wasn't in the position to make guarantees, but she was confident her product would sell. I said I'd have to think it over.

With that, Charmaine jumped in and asked Kirstie about her life insurance needs. I'd just assumed that someone with Kirstie's assets would be loaded with insurance, but if not I wanted the chance to persuade her that I was the best person to represent her. I pitched her my entire life insurance spiel, about how important it was that she protect her assets and her children's inheritance. She listened intently and asked, "Can you put something together for me?"

I spent the next few weeks putting together options for Kirstie. She was an extremely demanding client and she treated me like I was a subordinate, not the successful businesswoman I was. But I wasn't about to complain. I was honored that she wanted to work with me, and I stood to make millions on her policy.

Our next meeting took place at her insistence at her home in Clearwater. She'd invited me to stay in her guesthouse for the one night I'd be there. I arrived in Florida late in the evening, sometime between nine and nine thirty. I checked in at the main house and was surprised when the assistant said Kirstie wanted to see me. I hadn't expected to meet until the next day.

The house was different from the estate in LA. It was on the water and ultramodern—all white, boxy and open. The assistant led me to a back bedroom. She knocked, then pushed open the door. There was Kirstie, lying on a massage table buck naked. A masseuse was massaging her whole body using forks. Forks! As in the kind you have in your kitchen drawer. My first thought was that someone was going to pop out of the closet and tell me I was on **Candid Camera**. I didn't know where to look. I was so uncomfortable. Kirstie was completely at ease. She lifted her head to look at me.

"Hey, Michelle," she said. "Come on and sit down." **American Idol** was on the TV. "Do you watch **American Idol**?" she asked.

I said that I didn't. She went on to rave about her favorite contestant. I thought to myself, **Who is this person?** She was nothing like she'd been at our first meeting. She was so friendly, even jolly. Maybe I just needed to get to know her better, I thought.

Taking a seat on the white leather bench at the foot of Kirstie's bed, I tried to keep my eyes on the TV. After some small talk, I excused myself and told her I needed to get some rest to prepare for our meeting the following day.

It took time, but I ended up brokering an insurance deal for Kirstie that would pay millions in commission over the next few years. It was one of the most lucrative deals I had ever closed.

Between Beth and Kirstie, I had brokered tens of millions of insurance in a few months, which thrust me into the insurance world stratosphere. I decided to invest in Kirstie's weight-loss program. I would assume she made good on her promise to write a large check to the church in exchange for Charmaine's success in finding her an investor.

CHAPTER ELEVEN

Budding Friendship

❖

In the fall, Dror opened his production company, Windsor Pictures. My star continued to rise in the insurance industry. Between business meetings, insurance seminars, my kids and continuing discord in my relationship with Sean, there wasn't enough time for me to keep up with everything.

No matter what else was going on in my life, I always made time to meet with Charley. My friendship with her had begun to break down some of my Scientology beliefs. Charley hardly fit the profile of the homosexual I learned about from the church; in fact, she was the antithesis of it. And the idea that the church would deny me a friendship with such a sterling person simply because she wasn't heterosexual or a Scientologist had come to seem ludicrous to me.

Watching Charley "be" showed me what a successful person was. It wasn't just about how much money you made or projecting your best face. She didn't need to create a facade. She was authentic and real and highly accomplished. She had friends from all walks of life and of all religions. She didn't judge people, much less report them for breaching some arbitrary rule. My friendship with Charley made me begin to see that all my other relationships had nothing to do with genuine caring the ways ours did. Everyone else in my life was there because of our shared religion and because of my "good PR," which made me sought after by other Scientologists.

In the months since our meeting in February, Charley and I had regularly gotten together for coffee or lunch or an afternoon glass of wine. We had so much in common, so much to talk about. I looked forward to those meetings, hearing about her career and what she was working on, and she encouraged me to talk about mine.

I told Charley about **Not Forgotten**, which had premiered in the U.S. to positive trade reviews and was lined up for international distribution. Dror had suggested we keep the momentum of our success going by investing in new projects, which he was in the process of looking for.

During one of our conversations, Charley mentioned **Twist**, a musical she was working on with a famous actress, director and producer. Might a play be something Dror and I would be interested in producing?

She gave me the script, which I read on a flight from California to New York. The play was an African-American take on Dickens's **Oliver Twist**, and I fell in love with it. I shared the script with Dror. It wasn't a movie, I said, but Charley needed investors and this seemed like something we could get behind.

It took a bit of convincing on my part, but Dror agreed that by investing in **Twist** we could maintain the buzz about our partnership until he found a new film project.

Our shared interest in **Twist** gave Charley and me more reason to get together. I loved hearing her stories about growing up in rural Mississippi. Her family was wealthy and she had been raised by a black nanny named Vergie, whom she adored. It was Vergie, she told me, who'd helped her to develop her keen social conscience. Even as a little girl, she had taken a stand against racism. Defying her father's orders, she once stood up to a restaurant owner who didn't allow blacks by taking her dinner outside to the back steps to join Vergie.

By the end of the year, we were seeing each other almost every day. Our conversations had gotten more personal over time. Charley confided in me that she was contemplating leaving Maria. Tensions had been building between them for a long time and neither one was happy. The stories of their marriage reminded me of my own. Charley said Maria had a jealous streak and a nasty temper. She often lashed out, sometimes physically. Charley hadn't told anyone else about her marital problems. She was too embarrassed to admit another failed relationship. She had told Maria she wanted out and moved to the guest room with the intention of looking for her own place when she had time. Maria was in denial about the split, but Charley felt it would be best for both of them, so she was determined to see it through.

I lifted my water glass for a toast. "Amen!" I said. "Been there. Done that. And my life is so much better now. I'm here for you, Charley. I know this is hard."

Just before Christmas, Charley invited me to lunch at the tearoom at the Beverly Hills Montage Hotel. Her longtime entertainment attorney, Elaine Rogers, was coming to town from Boston, and Charley wanted me to meet her.

The Montage is a hip, swanky place in the middle of Beverly Hills. It was one of my favorite places to take clients. I walked in a few minutes late and joined Charley and Elaine at a window table overlooking the hotel courtyard. We settled into a comfortable conversation, talking and laughing and enjoying ourselves. At one point, I sensed someone watching us. I wondered if the person was looking at Charley. I'd noticed that sometimes people stared at her, even though it was 2009 and we were in freethinking Southern California. She was masculine in her dress and her demeanor, and sometimes I was self-conscious when I saw someone looking at her. Were they judging her? Judging me?

Charley excused herself to go to the restroom and I took the opportunity to look around. I glanced over my shoulder and saw a couple I knew from the church. Sarah and David Ehrlich were wealthy, high-level Scientologists from Beverly Hills. When Charley walked past their table, both made a point of looking her up and down, from her short man-nish haircut to her polished wing-tip shoes. Once she passed, they began nattering to each other. It didn't take much imagination to guess what they were saying. **Stay clear!**

When Charley returned, I took my turn to go to the restroom and made sure I stopped to greet the Ehrlichs.

"What are you doing here?" Sarah asked, as if she hadn't seen me.

"I'm here for a business meeting," I said.

"Oh!" she said. "Well, who are you meeting with?"

I knew why she was asking. At that moment, I felt so protective of Charley. Who were those smug, sorry-ass people to judge her?

"A friend in the music industry and her attorney."

"You really should be careful, Michelle," he said. A wave of righteous anger swept over me.

"Thank you, David, but I don't think I asked you for your opinion, did I?" With my voice steady and a smile plastered on my face, I added, "I don't think I need your opinion. I think I do pretty well on my own. Don't you?" With that, I returned to the table.

At that moment, something woke in me. The Ehrlichs believed it was their right—no, their obligation—to caution me against someone they knew absolutely nothing about, and for the sole reason that she was gay. They would never get to know someone like Charley because of their narrow-minded, church-sanctioned judgment of "people like her." I was sorry for them—and sorry for me that I had actually considered allowing my friendship with such a genuine, kindhearted person to slip through my fingers because of the same sanctimonious thinking. Let's see, I thought: the Ehrlichs versus Charley. They paid a great deal of money to be called good Scientologists. But Charley, who had done more for the greater good of humanity than anyone else I knew, donating so much of her time and money to women's issues and social causes, would be turned away from the church.

I didn't care what people thought of our friendship. Nothing was going to dissuade me from continuing. She was the most sincere and straightforward person I'd ever known.

When lunch was over, Charley said she had one more meeting at the hotel. If I waited, we could have a drink later and talk more about the play. I was so happy that she'd asked me to stay. We met again in the tearoom when her meeting was over. Over drinks, we discussed the music she was composing for **Twist** and plans for staging the production in Atlanta. If it hit big there, there was a chance it could run on Broadway. I was so excited to be a part of it, I said, however small my contribution ended up being.

Charley switched topics from the show to my divorce. I told her I'd thought it had been settled months ago, but then Sean decided he wanted more money and the proceedings stalled.

"It's frustrating," I said. "And very contentious."

I told her stories about the marriage and how difficult it had been for many years. She looked pained. "I'm just a checkbook to Maria too," she said. "Everyone told me that from day one, but I didn't listen."

Charley sipped her drink and went on. "She finds fault with everything about me. My shirt is too tight. My pants are too loose. Nothing I do is right and I'm losing my confidence." I had never seen Charley so vulnerable, and it made me sad.

"I can't imagine you allowing someone to push you around that way," I said.

"I thought the same about you," she replied. We both smiled. I wanted to comfort Charley. I looked at her and thought, **What a dear, dear friend you are**.

"You are one of the most wonderful people I've ever met," I said. "From the way you hold yourself, to what you've accomplished with your music, to your heart, I just think you're amazing."

I knew when I went home that evening that, after nearly a year of getting to know each other, Charley and I had entered a more intimate chapter of our friendship.

———⬦———

I spent the holidays alone at home with the kids. I often found myself looking at the house across the street, wondering about Charley and Maria. Were they fighting? Had they made a resolution to give their relationship another chance? Was the light on in the guest room? I had a knot in the pit of my stomach when I thought the next time I saw Charley she could tell me that things were better between them. Why would that bother me? I wondered. I decided the reason was that I didn't think Maria treated Charley the way she deserved to be treated and I wanted her to be happy.

Months passed and many meetings later, Charley invited me to the Montage for a meeting with a team of television producers. If I was going to be dabbling in the entertainment industry with Dror, she said, I needed to start learning the ropes. I promised I'd join them right after a meeting with

colleagues that I had scheduled at the same restaurant. I always wore pantsuits, but that day I
decided to slip into a blue Lanvin dress I'd bought
before I got pregnant and never wore. The dress
was beautiful and fit like a glove. I felt especially
confident in it.

While meeting with my colleagues, a handsome
man who was seated at the bar began flirting
with me. The people at my table teased me: "Jeez,
Michelle, that's a good-looking guy!" "Go to the
bar and talk to him!" "You have to start dating
again sometime!" I suppose I was flattered by the
attention, but the idea of striking something up
with a man made me shudder. I chalked up my
reaction to hormones. I had given birth to twins
and I'd nursed them until a few months earlier. I
had four kids under the age of nine and a company
to run. The last thing I was thinking about was
going on a date.

Just as my meeting was ending, Charley walked
into the tearoom. I loved how confidently she
strode across the restaurant floor. She was such an
attractive woman, I thought. I waved her over and
introduced her to my staff, then joined her at another table and waited for her guests to arrive. It
was about four p.m. and a glow in the room from
the setting winter sun was breathtaking. I found
myself wishing the television producers wouldn't
show. But they did.

They were two lesbians who were working on a

documentary about a well-known country singer who was coming out, and they wanted an on-camera interview with Charley about the challenges of being gay in the entertainment industry. As they went on about the project, I found myself getting defensive.

"Well, it doesn't sound all that interesting to me, but I'm not your demographic. I'm not gay!" About the third time I said it, I caught myself. **What am I doing?** I asked myself. **I need to stop this! Why do I feel like I need to make the point that I'm not gay?**

Eventually the four of us moved to a set of couches closer to the bar and switched from tea to wine. Charley and I were sitting opposite the pair of producers. At one point, I crossed my legs and caught Charley staring at them. She quickly looked away, but I was flooded with confusing emotions. Chills ran through my body and my hair stood up on the nape of my neck. My lips tingled and my heart rate took off. I took a big swig of wine and said I had to leave. Right then. Immediately. My children were waiting at home, I said. I couldn't stay out any longer. Charley, knowing that I had a babysitter with the kids, looked puzzled at my sudden need to bolt, but she graciously nodded and smiled.

She walked me out of the restaurant and asked if everything was okay.

"Yes! Of course!" I said. "Everything is fine! I'll talk to you tomorrow."

I rushed to my car and sped away. My emotions ran wild. One minute I felt as if I couldn't get a deep enough breath. The next minute I was giddy.

When I got home, I raced up the stairs to check on the kids. I went to my room, closed the door behind me and threw myself on the bed. Staring up at the ceiling, I didn't know whether to laugh or cry.

This woman is making me feel things I've never felt, I thought. **In my whole life I have never gotten chills like that. I am infatuated with her. Oh my God! I am a lesbian.**

A few nights later, Charley showed up at my door. She'd never been to my house before, even though we lived across the street from each other. I was getting the kids ready for bed, when the nanny came in to say that one of our neighbors wanted to speak to me. **That's odd,** I thought. I ran downstairs and found Charley waiting. She was a mess. Her hair was tousled, her face was scratched up and her shirt was splattered with blood.

"Oh my gosh! Charley! What happened?" I cried. I retrieved a warm washcloth and swabbed her bloody nose. "What happened?" I asked again.

Charley said she'd gotten home late from a

meeting with her **Twist** collaborator. They were working on the play and she'd lost track of the time. Maria had often made groundless accusations about Charley cheating and she'd become even more possessive when she sensed the relationship slipping away. This time, it was about her friend from **Twist**, which was absurd. Charley and the woman had been platonic friends for years, and she had been happily married to a former basketball star for nearly three decades. Charley tried to keep the peace by assuring Maria that nothing was going on except a working friendship, and then prepared herself for the worst. Strangely, Maria suddenly turned calm and asked Charley to sit down to dinner. Charley cautiously took her seat at the table and Maria put a plate of food in front of her. Just as Charley picked up her fork, Maria punched her so hard that Charley saw stars.

"I didn't know what to do, so I walked out," Charley said. "I didn't know where to go." I wiped more blood from her face and looked into her warm brown eyes.

"I'm glad you came here," I said.

The hour was late. Charley said she was sure Maria would be in bed asleep. "I need to go home and get some rest," she said. "I'm embarrassed that I came here."

We hugged and I asked Charley to text when she got home. I wanted to know she was safe. I watched out the window until I saw the light go on in the guest room. A while later, I received her message. "In bed," she wrote. "All is good. Sweet dreams."

———◆———

With spring break arriving, Charley mentioned that she wanted to go to Austin in April to visit her daughter, Jaime. Maria had put up a fuss about it, Charley said, but she hadn't seen Jaime for a while and she missed her. Charley was determined to go and I encouraged her to do so.

"Nothing is more important than your children," I said. She seemed grateful for the "support" and, against Maria's wishes, booked the flight.

She texted me from the Los Angeles airport while she waited for her flight, and then again when she landed in Texas. The second time surprised me.

"I miss you," she wrote. I thought it was so sweet.

"I miss you too," I responded.

Later in the day, she sent another text.

"Guess where I am. I'm sitting in Anthropologie while my daughter is shopping."

I texted right back that Dror's wife, Virginia, had designed a line of beautiful lingerie for the clothing retailer.

"It's called Bacini," I wrote. "It means 'little kisses.'"

She texted back, "Yours?"

I gasped when I read it. Had we just crossed some kind of threshold? I tried to think of something clever to text back, but I was in a dither. A moment passed and she texted again.

"Just kidding!" she wrote.

Was Charley really flirting with me? Or was she joking? It made me want to pull my hair out.

The flirty texts continued for the whole time Charley was away. I couldn't wait for the next one to arrive. I wasn't sure what was happening between us, but I knew Charley made me feel the way no one else had. I was certain she valued our friendship, but I wondered if the infatuation was more mine than hers. A month of flirty texts had passed and we knew it was time to address this newfound "something."

I met her at the Parkway Grill in Pasadena. We were seated at her regular table in front of the fireplace. I felt slightly awkward after our string of flirty texts. We both stared at the menu without speaking. The knot in my stomach tightened. Then Charley grabbed the arm of my chair and pulled it close to her. She leaned in to me and looked deeply into my eyes. "What are we doing?" she asked.

My words stuck in my throat. As Charley waited for a response, I went to another place. It was almost as if my spirit had left my body, the same way it had felt years earlier when my car was careening out of control and I surrendered to the inevitability of my fate, whatever that was supposed to be. Except now I had a choice. I literally saw myself approaching a fork in the road. One was a continuation of the route I'd been on and brought me back to a church that had taught me how to amass lots of money and collect prestigious awards, but didn't seem to value love. The other was a scary road with bumps and hairpin turns, but led to freedom and a place where I could be me. Standing at the fork, I didn't hesitate.

"I choose you," I said.

Coming out of my trancelike state, I saw that Charley looked bewildered. I explained my vision and said that the direction my life was about to take was crystal clear to me.

"I choose you," I said again. "I don't know what this means and I can't be responsible for breaking up your marriage."

Charley moved even closer. "Michelle, my marriage was over a long time ago," she said. "I don't know what all this means either—all I know is that I care deeply for you."

We had a lot to figure out. Would we have a secret love affair until she physically left Maria? Would I stay hidden in the closet? Could we stay in the friend zone until she divorced and then see what happened? What about the church? Neither of us had answers, but both of us knew there was no turning back from the feelings we had for each other.

I don't even remember the drive back to work or what I did for the rest of the day.

My cell phone rang at five the next morning. Charley said she hadn't been able to sleep. Could we meet at Starbucks before work? I hurriedly dressed and got the kids fed and ready for their day. I couldn't get to Charley fast enough.

She was already waiting when I pulled into the Starbucks parking lot. As soon as she spotted me, she jumped out of her car and into the passenger side of mine. This was all so new. I still had a difficult time looking her in the eye. I didn't know what to say, but I had never wanted anyone so much. She moved her hand to the back of my neck and slowly pulled me to her. Her lips pressed against mine and we shared the most passionate, loving kiss I had ever experienced. I didn't care who was watching. I was exactly where I was supposed to be. I reached up and touched my lips. It was as though they had been awakened.

CHAPTER TWELVE

Found Out

◈

Mary Mauser was becoming impatient. It had been months since I'd been active in the church, and she was losing credibility with the higher-ups. It was her job as my FSM, my guide, to reel me in, but she hadn't been successful. Every time she called to set up a meeting, I gave her an excuse. I was too busy with the kids. My business had taken me away. I had a new project that required so much of my time. The church was surely asking why I wasn't being "handled." Why hadn't she been able to get me back into auditing? When had I last signed on for my next step on the Bridge?

It was a Scientology tenet that members pulled away only when they had done something against the church and were loath to reveal their "overts" (harmful acts against the group) or confess their "withholds" (failure to disclose those overts). Mary and others would have assumed I was guilty of being "out ethics," breaking the church's punitive moral code in one way or another. As my FSM, she was in charge of getting me back "into ethics" and keeping me in line; the longer I resisted, the more money and credibility she lost.

I liked Mary and I understood her dilemma, but I wasn't ready to physically return to the church, at least not yet. I continued to consider myself a Scientologist and to make large donations, knowing it would ease some of the pressure to return. The alternative wasn't feasible. If I agreed to go to Ethics, I would be hooked up to the E-meter and "outed." At that point, my beautiful Charley would be declared a PTS (Potential Trouble Source), which meant that if I wanted to stay in good standing with the church, I would be forced to "disconnect" from her. If I challenged church rule, I myself would be labeled an SP (Suppressive Person). The consequences would be dire.

L. Ron Hubbard wrote extensively about misfortunes befalling SPs after leaving the church. I'd read his stories of people stricken with terrible illnesses, or going insane, even dying. The threat of expulsion both saddened and frightened me. How could it not? In **Introduction to Scientology Ethics**, Hubbard wrote, "You are threatening somebody with oblivion for eternity by expulsion from Scientology." I had lived in the Scientology world for so long that it was hard to imagine what my life would look like outside of it. I risked losing everything and everyone I'd known for twenty years. It was too big a sacrifice to take lightly. I knew I had to keep my new relationship under wraps, at least for the time being—until Charley moved out of her house and I could figure out something to pacify the church when we came out as a couple—but I was bursting to share my good news with someone.

I decided to take a chance with Dror and Virginia. They had proven to be good and loyal friends and had never reported me for all the times I complained about my marriage. I thought they could be trusted with my secret. Besides, Dror certainly wasn't going to betray his rainmaker. He had a brand-new production company and movies he wanted to make.

I told Charley that I was going to invite Dror and Virginia to dinner to tell them about us. She knew Dror from brief dealings with him on **Twist**, but she didn't know him very well. His company was receiving producer credit for the play, but I was the one who attended most of the auditions and rehearsals with Charley.

Charley was relieved I was "coming out," but she worried that it was too soon because she and Maria were not yet officially separated. She also questioned the wisdom of telling Dror and Virginia, who were both so heavily involved in Scientology.

From hanging out with me, Charley had seen enough to have serious doubts about the church, particularly the fact that so much of the religion seemed to revolve around money. She knew I was the money person in my partnership with Dror and, by extension, Virginia, and she'd been with me when Charmaine called, under the guise of checking in on the kids and me, to ask for yet another donation. I made excuses for them, telling Charley that Dror was only following the teachings of the church about how to succeed in business, as I had. And Charmaine was raising money to save the planet, so who could argue with that? I could tell she wasn't convinced, but she was reticent to criticize, and I was grateful for that. It was still my church.

Dinner was at Ago, an Italian restaurant off Melrose that was co-owned by Robert De Niro and popular with an A-list clientele. Dror and Virginia were all about the "in" LA restaurants. Spring was on the horizon and the night was warm. Dror and I arrived first and took a table in the crowded dining room. Earlier that day, I'd had a meeting with him at his Paramount Studios office and gave him the CliffsNotes version of the story. His reaction was guarded.

"Oh! Really? Charley?" Well"—he seemed to

be choosing his words carefully—"I'm glad that you're happy, Michelle."

Dror was a businessman before anything. He wasn't about to preach the word of Scientology to me when I had the potential to bring investments to his future film projects. I knew he lived for the acclaim and he wasn't about to jeopardize his business by alienating me; he would just look the other way. I didn't expect more than tepid acceptance from Dror—at least not at that point—but I was certain I could count on Virginia to be happy for me.

Virginia came in and the three of us settled into a conversation of small talk. I waited for the wine to be poured before I broke the news.

"The reason I invited you to dinner is that I really want to tell you something," I said. Virginia's eyes lit up.

"Oh my God!" she said. "You have a guy."

I looked at Dror, who nodded to urge me on.

"Well, not exactly," I said. Virginia didn't even hear me. She was as excited as I was.

"I knew something was up!" she said. "I just knew you were in love."

I didn't know if I had the courage to continue. Virginia looked at me, puzzled.

"I am in love," I said. "I have found the greatest love I have ever known. This person is not a Scientologist, but it doesn't matter to me."

Virginia narrowed her eyes and waited.

"It's Charley," I said plaintively.

Her mouth dropped and her eyes widened. "Charley?" she echoed.

The conversation wasn't going as planned. I could tell that Virginia was disappointed. She had heard about Charley and the play, but she'd never met her. She looked back and forth between Dror and me. Virginia was never at a loss for words, but she seemed unable to speak. My reaction was to fill in the awkward silence.

"Wait until you get to know her!" I cried. "Charley is the greatest person. She's kind and smart and very successful. You'll love her!"

"Charley," she said again. "I never would have expected this in a million years."

Scientology considers love a weakness and passion a "body thing" discussed only by people who were low on the Bridge. It had taken all my courage to break that code with Dror and Virginia.

Now, all hope of acceptance dashed, I tried to justify my feelings.

"Think of it this way," I said. "It's not that I'm in love with a woman. I am in love with this being. It has nothing to do with gender. It was her soul that attracted me, and souls have no gender. The church taught us that."

Dror nodded, but Virginia was unmoved. "I'm worried," she said. "Isn't there a big age difference?"

Yes, I said. There was a nineteen-year age gap.

"But Charley is a young soul and I am an old soul, so it kind of evens out," I said.

I felt like I had when I was a teenager trying to convince my mother that my best friend wasn't a bad influence on me, that she was a nice girl.

"I'm sorry, Michelle," Virginia said, backpedaling a bit. "I just didn't expect this. I'm worried. Look, I know Charley is successful, but I doubt she is as successful as you are. What does she want from you? Aren't you funding her musical? I'm concerned about her influence over you."

I laughed and assured her that Charley didn't need my money; she was quite well-off.

"Well, not as well-off as you," she said. "Wait a minute! Isn't she married?"

Yes, I said. Charley was married but they were headed toward a divorce.

I had been so sure that Virginia would be happy for me and this would be a celebration; instead I felt judged and embarrassed.

"Virginia, I can't help this," I said, hating the desperation in my voice. "I swear to God we're like magnets. I have never loved anyone more. This is just so right. There is nothing in the world I'm worried about or have concerns about." I waited for the inevitable question.

"What about the church?" she asked. "How do you think they will handle this?"

There it was. The question I had hoped she

wouldn't ask. My face flushed, and despite my own misgivings on this score I was overcome with feelings of anger.

"I don't give a fuck!" I lied. This was not the conversation I had hoped for. I was newly in love. I didn't want to be reminded—especially by one of my closest friends—that at some point the church would have to know I was with a woman. I wasn't prepared to deal with the ramifications of that yet. I just wanted to be happy. "My Bridge is my Bridge," I said. "My freedom is my freedom. No one is going to tell me who to love."

Virginia looked taken aback. "Well," she said, lifting her wineglass. "On that note, I guess we should toast. To love." She tried to seem cheerful, but I could see through the act. I was the woman who was funding her husband's career. What else could she do?

I left the restaurant feeling sad and dejected. I don't know why I expected a different outcome, except that perhaps love had made me delusional. Virginia and Dror were Scientologists first—just as I had been for most of my life. They weren't going to give me unconditional support for something the church—and therefore they—considered evil.

On the drive home, I thought back to the officiant's warning at my wedding, about how couples were expected to uphold their commitment even after love faded. "Know that life is stark and often somewhat grim, and tiredness and fret and pain and sickness do beget a state of mind where spring romance is far away and dead," he'd said. At the time, they were just words. Except that they weren't.

For years, the church had expected me to work things out with Sean—even if it meant subjecting myself to abuse and violence. It took threatening to cut off the stream of money spilling from my bank account into church coffers to finally be allowed to end the marriage with the church's blessing.

I knew the road to acceptance of my relationship with Charley would be long and difficult. In the eyes of the church, we were sexual deviants who threatened mankind by choosing a lifestyle that tended "toward the pollution and derangement of sex itself so as to make it as repulsive as possible to others and so to inhibit procreation." By choosing to love a woman, I would be considered a threat to the "well-ordered system for the creation and upbringing of children, by families," the master wrote.

But I had paid for ethics protection with large donations before. And I would do it again if it bought me a reprieve.

◈

Charley and I consummated our relationship in May. We'd held off mostly because of our shared guilt over her unfinished marriage. I didn't know what to expect. The only experience I'd had with a woman was my brief fling with my high school friend, Lacey, and this was an experienced, mature woman who had been "out" for most of her life. What if I didn't please her? I worried.

We met in the afternoon at the Langham Hotel at the foot of the San Gabriel Mountains in Pasadena. The hotel is from bygone Hollywood, majestic and grand. I had picked out my clothes the night before. I wanted to look beautiful for Charley.

I arrived first. The hotel room, which overlooked the lush hotel gardens, was romantic, with billowing silk curtains and a matching gold bedspread. Charley had arranged for champagne to be waiting for us—Veuve Clicquot.

Sitting nervously on the edge of the bed, I heard the click of the room key in the door and Charley walked in. She looked so handsome in her tailored suit and boyish haircut. "You still have your coat on," Charley said, laughing. Nervously, I pulled off my jacket while she popped the cork on the champagne. She filled two flutes and we held up our glasses to toast. "To our love," she said. "May this gift never end." We shared a kiss and talked for a while about trivial things. Charley poured us another glass of champagne. The second one did the trick. Any worries I'd had when I got there melted away. My cheeks flushed and my heart began to slow down. Charley took the empty glass from my hand and drew me close to her. She smelled heavenly. She unzipped my dress and pushed it to the floor, then pulled back and gazed at my body. "You are more beautiful than I could have ever imagined," she said. It was the first time in my life I felt so desired. Kissing had never been so passionate. When Charley ran her hands over my body, I marveled at the sensation. I had never been touched so tenderly. How had I been missing this my whole life? I wondered.

When our lovemaking was over, we lay entwined for a long time. "Miche, you were perfect," Charley said. "I could lie here with you forever. I'm in heaven."

The ice that had encased my heart for so many years was thawing. "Promise me this will never end," I whispered.

"I promise," she said.

The more time I spent with Charley, the less I had for Dror, and he wasn't happy about it. He complained I wasn't holding up my end of our business relationship. That I was always busy with my insurance company and **Twist**. My assistant, Monica, was overwhelmed and in over her head, and I needed to hire someone to coordinate the projects he and I were working on. "My bookkeeper has a friend who is available," Dror said. "She is LRH trained and very savvy with tech. I'd love for you to meet her." Eventually I got tired of Dror's nagging and hired Celeste as my office manager.

Celeste was different than the other young women who worked for me. She was a tough New Yorker with large breasts she liked to show off. That spring, she whirled in and took over the office. She was willing to take on any task, and her IT skills really were a plus. But she was ambitious and hard-driving, and in short order got under everyone's skin. I was too busy to notice, but even if I had been aware of the friction Celeste caused, I would have ignored it. That was my training as a Scientologist. All "nattering" was frowned upon. You were not to think ill of another Scientologist.

Celeste was always preaching about the benefits of Scientology and how much it had helped her to become the woman she was. She'd joined as a troubled teen, she said, and couldn't imagine how her life would have turned out if she hadn't kept up on the Bridge. She had met her husband in the church, and their twin daughters went to a Scientology school. "How long has it been since you've been on the Bridge?" she asked repeatedly.

I had tried to stay in the church's good graces with newsy e-mails to Mary Mauser about my busy life and promises to return as soon as I had a break in my hectic schedule, meanwhile writing big checks as a way to buy time. When I finally scheduled an auditing appointment and then missed it, I e-mailed Mary my apology. "I tried very hard to make it, but between kids and packing for a trip, I couldn't find the time to get down there," I wrote.

Perhaps as a way to elicit her sympathy, I mentioned that my friend Charley was dealing with some medical issues and I was worried about her. I asked Mary for her "postulates" (good thoughts that manifest into a positive outcome). I had mentioned Charley to her previously, although strictly in the context of working together on **Twist**, so she knew the name.

Mary responded a few hours later, but not with the compassion I expected: "On your partner in business ONLY [smiley face icon]: She is PTS, no question about it [translation: **If she's sick, it's because there is a "Potential Trouble Source" or "Suppressive Person" in her life**]. Disseminate [translation: **Tell her about Scientology**] and get her working with someone. Discovery [translation: **figuring out who the SP is**] and handle or disconnect [translation: **getting rid of them**] keeps people alive. Science of Survival and PTS tech [translation: **church policy for dealing with evil influences**] are very clear by LRH."

Charley's health turned out to be fine, but, rereading Mary's e-mail later, I was struck by the reference to her as my "partner in business ONLY." What had she meant by the capitalized "ONLY" and the smiley face? Charley and I had been intimate for only a couple of weeks at the time, and I hadn't told anyone except Virginia and Dror—and I was certain they wouldn't tell. What had Mary been implying? And why? Did she know about us, then? And if she did, how? Did she know about the tryst at the Langham? Was I being watched?

———◈———

Charley was scheduled to take a brief trip to New Orleans before we headed to New York for auditions for **Twist**. She suggested I meet her. We could spend time together and she would show me around her old stomping grounds. I was thrilled. I had never been to New Orleans, and the kids were scheduled to be with their father, so I was free to go.

I met Charley at the historic Roosevelt Hotel. After unpacking, we dressed for a romantic dinner at a quaint restaurant in town. We headed down the elevator, holding hands. When the door slid open, we were facing the bar. A group of well-dressed businessmen turned to look at us, and I dropped Charley's hand, suddenly embarrassed. I turned to Charley. "Honey," I said, "I have an idea. Why don't we order dinner in our room? Let's just spend the time alone together."

Charley looked confused at first, but then gave me a reassuring smile. "Maybe things are changing a little more slowly in the South. But let me ask you a question," she said. "Do you think a white woman with a black little girl wouldn't get stares if you walked into this hotel lobby?" Charley asked. "Would you look at your daughter, Savannah, and say, 'Baby, let's just have dinner back in the room tonight'?"

Tears stung my eyes. Of course she was right. If I couldn't be proud of who I was, then what was I teaching my children? "Absolutely not!" I said. "I would pull her closer and hold my head high and take her out to dinner!"

Charley smiled. I grabbed her hand and we walked out of the hotel and down the street to the restaurant. After that, there was no turning back for me. I was a lesbian and I would have to figure out how to deal with the church. Perhaps, because of my position, I could talk them into allowing me to be the catalyst for positive change. I could reason that L. Ron Hubbard's views about homosexuals and lesbians were archaic and the church could increase membership and donations by lifting its prohibition on homosexuality and coming into the present. I had always been good at making persuasive arguments about things I believed in. And I believed passionately in Charley and me. If I was able to convince the church to accept us as a couple, then others could live openly within our faith without fear of humiliation and punishment. Wasn't that a win for everyone?

Charley and I flew from New Orleans to New York for auditions for **Twist** in late June. I was becoming impatient that she was still living with Maria, but she assured me she was taking steps toward moving out.

The **Twist** team was waiting when we arrived at the small studio on Forty-Second Street where auditions were taking place. I had met Charley's actress friend and found her to be not just a talent and a serious businesswoman, but a comedian who had a nickname for everyone. Charley had confided in her about us. The two were as close as sisters. "Sparky, you're late!" she said, when we walked in. "You and Miss Universe need to stop fooling around in the backseat of cars and get your ass to work!"

We spent the weekend in auditions. Watching Charley at work was stirring. She was such a talented artist. Our evenings together were bliss. On Sunday evening, Charley received a text from Maria. She looked crestfallen as she read it. Maria planned a surprise visit, she said. "She'll be here tomorrow." I asked why Maria wanted to come when their relationship was on the rocks. She said Maria was still in denial about the split. She was probably coming to check out her suspicions about the actress. I had to trust that Charley was being straightforward with me. "If they're coming tomorrow, let's make the best of today," I said, squeezing her hand.

Auditions started early the next morning. I sat at the table with Charley. Two hours into the auditions, Maria strode into the theater. I felt suddenly insecure about my relationship with Charley. Seeing Maria brought home the reality that Charley was still someone's wife. Even if Maria was in denial, she was here and acting like she belonged. My heart dropped. **She's not mine,** I thought, looking at Charley. **I have no business being here**. I couldn't help myself, but as the young woman on the stage was auditioning, I was stealing glances at my rival.

Maria was a good-looking woman and well put together. She was younger than Charley, but probably a few years older than me. When Charley introduced us, I offered Maria my chair. It was an awkward moment—for me, because this woman was married to the person I loved; for Charley, because she was preparing to leave Maria and I knew how conflicted she was about it. Charley couldn't bear the thought of hurting anyone. In this case, not just Maria, whom she had been with for a dozen years. She feared her daughter would react badly. She worried about Maria's son, her stepson, whom she'd helped raise.

Maria gave me a half smile and took my place at the table. She had an arrogance about her that made her seem mean. I wondered what Charley saw in her. It was pretty obvious that Maria didn't appreciate Charley. She spoke to her in a dismissive way and rolled her eyes every time Charley made a joke. Between auditions, she grabbed Charley's notes and began reading them, then took the pencil out of her hand and doodled all over them.

"Maria, what are you doing?" Charley asked. "I need that paper."

Maria hid the pencil behind her back.

I couldn't believe Charley tolerated such childish behavior, but she sat back and said nothing. Maria tapped her shoe for the entire next performance, like a kid who was desperately trying to get attention.

Finally, Maria stood up and summoned Charley aside.

"You aren't paying attention to me, so why am I here?" she asked, raising her voice.

Charley looked embarrassed. "This isn't the place, Maria," she said.

"I'm going shopping!" Maria exclaimed. Charley always carried a wad of cash in her pocket. She pulled out the roll and started peeling off hundred-dollar bills. Maria grabbed the whole roll and stormed out.

At the end of the day, we all met for dinner at Nobu. The **Twist** team, my two personal assistants, and Charley and Maria sat around a large round table and ordered drinks. Charley was chewing gum and Maria took out a tissue and ordered her to dispose of it. I was humiliated for her. Charley's actress friend scolded Maria. "You need to chill out, woman!" she said. "You need to let Sparky be and you need to enjoy yourself. Life is too short!" Maria shot back, "I need to chill out? And who is 'Sparky' anyway?" When the evening was over, Charley put me in a cab and headed back to her hotel with her wife. I went back to my room, played classical music and moped. **God! What am I doing?** I asked myself. Why couldn't Charley be honest with Maria now instead of waiting for some "right" moment? **I can't do this anymore. I won't be someone's mistress. It's wrong. I love this person so much. Does she really love me?**

A knock came at the door.

"Miche! Open up! It's me!"

I pulled open the door and Charley was standing there. "How in the world? How did you manage this?" I asked.

Charley said she knew the moment she got to her hotel that Maria was waiting for her in the lobby. She was complaining about the day, the dinner, the people she had to be around. Everything. Then she started tearing Charley apart.

"I told her I was going to stay someplace else and I left," she said.

Charley stayed with me that night, never once answering her phone, which rang incessantly. We made love as if it could be our last time together. Afterward, I cried in Charley's arms. "I'm sorry," I said. "I'm so embarrassed. But I just can't bear the thought of you being with her anymore."

"Don't be embarrassed," she whispered. "I've never had anyone love me this much."

Maria flew home the following afternoon, convinced Charley was cheating with her **Twist** partner. I wasn't a threat. As far as she knew, I was a heterosexual mother of four who was just raising money for the play.

On our last day in Atlanta, Charley promised that when **Twist** debuted in September, the first thing she would do when she returned to California was find another place to live. After that, she would file for divorce.

I was okay with that. It gave me more time to figure out how I would break the news of our relationship to the church.

———◈———

We flew back to Los Angeles together on the Fourth of July. The summer heat was withering that day and I was drained from the long flight from New York and the time difference. With my bag still strapped over my shoulder, I rushed through my house and out to the backyard, where the kids were playing in the pool with Celeste and Monica. I never liked being away from my kids, and I ran toward them.

"Mommy's home! Mommmmeeeeeeee!" Sage and Savannah jumped out of the water and into my arms. I hadn't been home five minutes when, in the midst of wet hugs and happy squeals, my cell phone rang. As much as I didn't want to ruin the moment with my children, I saw that it was Mary Mauser—and you always took calls from church officials.

"Mary, hi!" I said, as my children clamored around me. "Listen, I literally just walked in from a trip and I'm with the kids. Can I call you back in a little while? Or is it something quick?"

Mary's voice was curt. She was always business-like, but now she was chilly. "This won't take long," she said. "I just have one question for you, Michelle."

I could tell from her tone that this wasn't a friendly call, or even a call to recruit me back "into ethics."

"What is it, Mary?" I asked.

"Are you having an affair with a married woman?" she asked bluntly.

At that moment, my world froze. Blood drained from my face. I couldn't breathe. I realized that, in a blink, my journey to happiness had hit a treacherous junction.

I walked away from the pool and out of earshot of the kids. I hadn't been ready to come out to the church. I was still trying to figure out how I could without having to choose between love and religion. But Mary ambushed me and I was trapped. I wanted to lie, but I couldn't bring myself to. What was the use? The truth would eventually come out. I just wished I'd had time to prepare.

"Mary," I stammered desperately, dabbing at the trickles of sweat dripping down my neck. "If your question is 'Am I in love with a woman?' the answer is yes. I was going to tell you, but this is very new to me and I wanted it to be on my time." Her silence was withering. I tried appealing to her sense of fairness. "Mary," I said, trying to collect myself. "This isn't what you think. There is a beautiful love story behind this and I want you to hear it."

With a sharp tongue, she cut me right off. "I don't care what your story is," she hissed.

"But, Mary, I don't think you understand!"

"Michelle! What have you done? You will never be able to go further on the Bridge. The church will never accept it. You will never have a normal life. Your kids will end up getting sick. Have you thought about your family and what this will do? And what about your business, Michelle? No one in your industry will come near you if they know this! What will happen when your business is gone?"

I felt fear creeping in. Was it true I would never be able to live a normal life as a lesbian? Would I regret choosing love? **No!** I thought. **I am living a normal life. What is** not **normal is this conversation.** Despite everything the church had tried to drum into me, I thought that everything Mary was saying was nonsense.

"You don't understand!" I said.

"Just how far have you taken this, Michelle?" Mary demanded. "Have you taken this from a friendship to a sexual relationship?" Her voice was raised now. "I need you to stop doing this and get back into session right now! Immediately!"

As I listened, my anxiety was replaced by feelings of power and conviction. I didn't care what Mary thought of my relationship. What I had with Charley was good and pure and loving and there was no reasonable argument for giving it up. Her bullying was really getting me angry.

I think what set me off the most was that Mary was making the beautiful love I felt for another person sound so wrong. What was more, this call was keeping me away from my children, who I hadn't seen in four days. **I have to put an end to this insanity,** I decided.

"I don't know who you think you are, but you have overstepped your bounds," I said. "I will not do anything other than love this woman and you will not make this dirty. I will have my Bridge to Total Freedom and I will have her by my side and no one will stop me!

"By the way, how did you know?" I added.

Mary paused and then stumbled over her words. "Um, someone saw you in Whole Foods and overheard you talking to a woman," she said.

I had been at Whole Foods that day. I'd shared a ride from the airport with Charley, and she'd asked the driver to stop briefly at the store. I never got out of the car, though. And no one could have seen me because the Town Car had blacked-out windows.

Oh my God, I thought. **Someone is following me and reporting to Mary—but who?** That's how she knew to call the minute I got home. Who had tipped her off about Charley and me? The only people I had told were Dror and Virginia.

"You're lying," I said. "No one overheard me talking to a woman in the store. I wasn't in the store. Now I am done with this conversation. You have crossed too many lines and you are wrong." With that, I hung up the phone. I had tried to put on a strong front with Mary, but I was shaking inside. My life was changing so quickly and I couldn't keep ahead of it. Now I would have to tell my friends, my mother, everyone! Where would I begin?

When I finally got to talk to Charley and tell her what had happened, I started to cry. I was conflicted. Part of me wanted the truth known. To be "out" for everyone to see. But I wanted it to be on my terms, not the church's. Charley had her own concerns. She didn't want Maria finding out about us until after they were separated. It seemed as if the church would stop at nothing when it wanted information. What kind of church followed people? she asked. "Miche, I'm really worried," she said. "This group is not right."

Part of me still wanted to defend the church, but I was preoccupied with worry about what Mary would do next.

I understood Charley's unease. I was concerned about Mary getting to church executives before I could, and Mom finding out about Charley before I had a chance to tell her.

It was time to contact the President's Office for a meeting.

The following morning, I was sitting with the vice president in his office at the Celebrity Centre. I'd known Greg LeClaire since my early Scientology days. Just as I'd suspected, Mary had already been there.

Greg was usually very warm to me, but he sat there expressionless as I told my side of the story. "Thank you very much for telling me, Michelle," he said. "I need to make it very clear to you that the Church of Scientology doesn't get involved when it comes to relationships, and your decisions are your own. What's important is that you are working on your Bridge and your programs. Scientology is your own progression. Your own journey."

That's certainly the way it should be, I thought, **but who are you kidding?** I almost laughed.

"C'mon, Greg," I said. "I got my ass kicked for thinking about a woman when I was nineteen, and now you're telling me the church won't get involved? You obviously don't want to upset a large donor, so you're acting like everything is fine, and then you'll write a report for my file so I have to be handled in session!"

"Now, Michelle," he said condescendingly. "You know it's not like that."

That's exactly how it is, I thought. I pressed the issue: "So if I invite Charley here and we hold hands and kiss in the rose garden, no one will have an issue? Is that what you're telling me?"

"I'm not saying that," he said. "I would suggest that if you want to hold hands, be prepared for people to react. But I don't know that I would necessarily kiss here."

"What you're saying is that Scientology is judgmental and discriminatory," I shot back. "If it isn't, where are the gay people?"

"There are gay people here."

"Really? Who? Where?"

"Well, I can't disclose who is handling what here, but there is a gay couple in session."

I was incredulous. He could think of a single gay couple in all of Scientology—besides, I was sure that they were in session to be cured.

"Greg, I am in love with a woman and I am a member of the church," I said. "I came here looking for support, but if you can't support me, just leave me alone, all of you."

Greg made no response, but at least I had put the church on notice, and I was still standing. I left his office relieved that I didn't have to hide anymore, and still foolishly confident that I could have both Charley and the church.

On July 14, Mary sent me an e-mail regarding our falling-out and backpedaled from our phone conversation. Writing in a conciliatory tone, she recommended I tell only my closest friends about my relationship with Charley and slowly introduce it to the kids, at least until we had a chance to figure things out. She insisted she wanted to continue to be my mentor and help guide me up the Bridge, and suggested I get to Flag to do some work there. Finally, she apologized for her brusqueness and asked for the chance to mend our relationship. She didn't want one unpleasant encounter to ruin what we had accomplished so far.

I presumed she had gotten orders to stand down. With a renewed sense of security and power, I responded the same day.

Mary,

I got your comm and I know you were blindsided but we really have to figure this out. I know you were not honest with me on how you found out or where you heard it and that's really not cool. I am also very aware that you have a lie on the line or at least a half-truth and it's sticking in the universe. . . . If it was a comm from someone then you should say who because obviously you were not given the data in the right way. . . .

I can't have an FSM that has any sort of problem with this. . . . I really thought I was this "tolerant" person, but over the last year having a best friend that is gay has really made me look at myself and my true tolerance and understanding of another. She has taught me so much and has made me a better person. I can't tell you how many times all the girls that work for me or my business partners have said how much nicer I have become or more understanding and compassionate. She brings that out in me. . . .

We get judged every day because we are Scientologists, but yet we have the right to judge a gay person? There are many that are successful and in long-term relationships, with children who are really doing amazing things for mankind. I'm not talking about the flamboyant, 1.1, pure body/sex people but that is also MANY straight people. . . .

Whether it is having a black daughter, being a single mom of four running many companies, being in love with a woman, or being a Scientologist, I'm always going to push the envelope. I'm always going to pick platforms that have controversy. That is me! I have been held back for way too long and now I found someone who is exactly like me! We flow each other with so much power, we calm each other, we make money together, we push each other to donate and most of all we make each other better people!

I know this is hard for you to think about, but I'm not asking for your approval or your advice on how to handle it. I know what to do and how to do it. I am happy to take on and confront whatever it takes and I can promise you that I will be on my OT levels with Charley! I have not one doubt that I can make that go right. . . .

Don't be my FSM if you can't accept me for all that I am because I assure you that this is not a fling or an experiment. . . .

I will approach this in the right way with my children; I will make sure they are cool. I have zero concern on my business. It has done nothing but flourish since I have been with her.

I'm not sure whether it was anger or a false sense of security driving me, but when I didn't hear back from Mary, I followed up with a second e-mail a few days later.

Mary—

I was surprised that I didn't hear from you on my last e-mail.

I found the definition of a friend that I think is awesome and might give you some insight to where my upset stemmed from:

"What a true friend does: For one thing they stand up for one, give him counsel, they help him in adversity, they safeguard his reputation, won't hear ill of him, share his triumphs and ignore his faults." —L. Ron Hubbard.

———◈———

I didn't want my mother to hear about Charley from someone else. I wanted to tell her about our relationship before the kids and I left for Atlanta to join Charley for rehearsals for **Twist**. I invited Mom to meet me at the Magnolia Café on Sunset Boulevard. So the church would give her a pass to leave her Sea Org base, I said I wanted to talk to her about getting back on the Bridge. It was off hours, between two and three o'clock, and the lunch crowd had emptied out. I led Mom to a round booth in a corner. We sat down next to each other and I got straight to the point.

"Mom," I said, "I have something I want to talk about."

My mother was not the person she had once been. Once she had been a liberal, freethinking, fun-loving, life-of-the-party type. But over the years, I'd watched her turn into a rigid thinker who had given up her values to adopt church values, as we all had. I was well aware she supported the church's stance on homosexuality, but I didn't believe that she believed those things, at least not deep down.

Still, I tiptoed.

"Mom," I said, "I know you've heard me talk about my friend Charley and the play we're working on together." I saw apprehension in my mother's expression. **Where is this going? What is this about?** "Mom," I said, "I love her. I'm in love with her." My mother's face turned a deep shade of red and she burst into tears. She couldn't stop crying.

My mother had bragged about me since I was a little girl. She was proud of everything I was and everything I did. She talked to her friends about how beautiful and kind and successful I was. I was the best mother, the best insurance agent, the best human rights advocate. Now she was embarrassed by me. It was heartbreaking. I could see it in her face. I told Mom about what had happened with Mary. She was crying too hard to speak. I knew she had to be worried about how having an openly gay child would affect her standing in the church. What would the people in the Sea Org say? Would she be ostracized? Would she be stripped of her post because of her daughter the lesbian?

While she cried, I tried to allay her fears by talking about Charley and all her wonderful qualities, including her business success. I reminded my mother about how unhappily married I'd been, and for how long. Sean had hurt me. He had done terrible things to me that the church did nothing about. "Are you with her because Sean hurt you?" she asked.

"No!" I said. "Mom, this is right, I promise. This is the first time in my life that I've felt this way. I've never been in love before and I am in love!"

How did I explain to my mother that I could not breathe without Charley? That my every thought included her? I ached to hear her voice, to feel her touch, to just be near her. I felt a magnetic pull that was indescribable; it was as if I had no control over what was happening to the two of us.

Those were all the things I really wanted to say to my mother, but I knew that day was not the day.

Lunch didn't last long. Mom said she had to get back to the church. It felt strange not being able to connect with my mom. After we parted, I thought about the church's disconnection policy, which pressured members to break ties with anyone who questioned church dogma. If she were one day told to abandon me, I wondered, would she do it?

CHAPTER THIRTEEN

Twist

The opening of **Twist** was set for September. Charley was trying to keep the peace with Maria until she could get back to Atlanta.

Right before she was supposed to leave, she told me there were housekeeping things she had to take care of at the cabin that she and Maria owned together in the San Bernardino Mountains. I worried about her being in such a remote location alone with Maria, who had become increasingly combative as their relationship deteriorated. What if she started a fight? What if she got physical? Who would be around to help Charley?

She assured me that she would be in the mountains for only a day. A crew was coming to repair the dock, which she wanted to oversee. She wouldn't even stay the night, she said. She'd pack things she needed for Atlanta, meet with the construction crew and drive back to LA. I was overcome with a foreboding and waited for word that she had arrived safely and everything was okay.

About halfway through the day, an e-mail from Charley popped up. "I am having the hardest time being here," she wrote. "Nothing is right without you near me. I miss you terribly. I cannot wait to see you." I was so relieved. Thinking it was safe to respond, I e-mailed back, "Only two days until freedom! Stay strong. You are amazing and I love you so much."

Some time passed and my cell phone rang. I didn't recognize the number but decided to answer anyway, just in case. I heard Charley's voice whispering frantically.

"Miche! Miche! She knows!"

"Oh my God!" I cried. "How?"

Charley said she had been outside with the contractors when she heard screaming and glass breaking inside. She ran back to the house, where she found Maria gripping her iPad. Glass shattered and liquid flew when Maria threw a flute of champagne at Charley, soaking her face and hair. Maria held up the iPad and screamed at her. "Two days until freedom? Two days until freedom?! What does that mean?!" She grabbed Charley's cell phone off the kitchen table and threw it and the iPad off the balcony and down the side of the mountain.

"Oh my God, Charley!" I said. "Are you okay? Where are you calling from? Whose phone is this?"

The phone went dead. A few very long minutes later, Charley called again. I could hear Maria screaming in the background.

"Miche," she whispered, her voice shaking, "I'm hiding in the bedroom. She has a knife. Call 911." The phone went dead again.

I was panic-stricken. I had finally found the love of my life and now she was going to die? Not if I had anything to say about it.

I dialed 911 and was patched in to the San Bernardino police. I explained a domestic violence incident was taking place and it was urgent that the police get there immediately.

"What is the name?" she asked.

"Charley Harper," I said.

"And what is the husband's name?"

"It's not a husband," I said, stammering. "She is married to a woman."

A pause.

"She's married to a **woman**?"

"Yes!" I cried. "What difference does that make? Get someone there! Right now!"

"Ma'am," she said dispassionately, "someone is already on the way . . . and who are you, by the way?"

"I am her friend," I said.

"Just her friend?" the dispatcher asked.

I was astonished. Charley was in grave danger and this woman was judging us. What was wrong with people?

"I don't think that's any of your business," I said, and hung up.

I had to get to Charley. I grabbed my purse and told my assistant that I was driving to the mountains. I gave her a brief synopsis of what was taking place. She knew that Charley and I were close friends and she looked concerned.

"It'll take you two hours to get there!" she said.

"I'm going!" I replied, grabbing my purse, and rushed out to my car.

When I got on the road, I called the CFO of Charley's company, Bob. He and Charley's **Twist** partner were the only people from her circle who knew about us.

"Bob!" I cried. "You are closer than I am. Can you get to the mountain house? Charley's life is in danger."

"Oh my God!" he said. "Why? What's wrong?"

I quickly explained about the fight with Maria. "I'm so scared," I said.

Bob promised to leave right away. "I'll call you when I get to her," he said.

The speedometer on my Bentley read 100 miles per hour as I passed cars on the I-5. Once I hit the 210, traffic was stopped dead. There's never traffic on the 210. I banged my hand on the steering wheel and tried to think. My love was going to die while I was sitting in traffic! **How will I get to her? A helicopter!** I thought. I picked up the phone and called my assistant. I was crying.

"Find me a helicopter," I said. "I don't care how you do it. Please find it and find it fast."

She called back within ten minutes with directions to the nearest helicopter hangar, near the airport in Van Nuys.

"It's ten minutes from where you are and the helicopter is waiting for you," she said.

As if in some kind of action movie, I ran several red lights and jumped out of my car as soon as I pulled up to the hangar, running to the copter as the rotors went **whoosh-whoosh-whoosh** over my head.

Flying over the San Bernardino Mountains, I had a moment of calm. It was almost as if God was with me and letting me know that everything would turn out okay.

"Where will I be landing?" I asked the pilot.

"We have to land on the other side of the mountains," he said.

"So how will I get to the house?" I asked.

"Uh, I don't know," he said. "Let me call ahead to see if someone can take you."

I closed my eyes and prayed. I loved this person so much and I would do anything for her. **Please, God, don't take her from me**.

As the helicopter hovered over what looked like

a farmer's field, Bob called. "Where are you?" he asked.

"I'm in a helicopter," I said.

"You're kidding me, right?" he asked.

"Where's Charley?"

"Charley's okay," Bob said. "She's beaten up, but she's okay. Don't come here. The police are here. Charley is refusing to press charges."

Bob told Charley that I was close by. "She's going to a hotel. She said to meet her there." He gave me directions.

"Okay," I replied. "Thank God she is safe."

The pilot announced that we were landing. I looked down and saw a farmhouse, but nothing that looked like an airport or a landing strip.

"This is it?" I asked. "This is where we're landing?"

"Yup, this is it!" he said.

Just as we touched down, I saw an old red pickup truck approaching. Inside were an older woman and a young man I assumed to be her son.

"Are you coming with me?" I asked the pilot.

"Oh no!" he said. "I have to get back before dark."

"Where to?" the woman asked.

I named the hotel.

She motioned me toward the back of the truck. I climbed up onto the dusty, muddy bed of the pickup and she took off on a winding mountain road. Bob was standing outside the lodge when we got there. I jumped off the back of the truck and dusted off my clothes, as my chauffeurs waved good-bye and screeched out of the parking lot. Bob just shook his head.

"Where is she?" I asked.

"She's inside," he said. "Just be calm."

I walked into the resort and saw Charley standing in the lobby. Her shirt was rumpled and ripped and she was soaked with champagne. She looked tired and defeated. I ran to her and wiped the bloody mascara from her cheek.

Right there in the lodge, in front of strangers, we held each other tightly and I didn't care who saw.

Charley cried quietly into my shoulder.

"I'm never going to let you go," I said.

CHAPTER FOURTEEN
Atlanta

During August and September, I spent long weekends in Atlanta with Charley. It was the place we could "play house" without anyone knowing about our pasts. The weeks leading up to the premiere of the play were bliss. Charley would attend rehearsals six days a week. When I was in town, I conducted my business from the theater. I delegated more to my staff than I probably should have, but I kept up with my clients and spoke every other day by phone with Dror about the production company.

I felt truly free in Atlanta. I didn't have to think about the church, and the people in the city were so progressive and accepting that I felt comfortable being "out."

I was hopelessly in love. Charley and I spent

every minute together and made love before falling asleep in each other's arms every night. **This is the person I want to be with for the rest of my life,** I thought. When I brought the kids to stay with us, we went to places like Piedmont Park or the aquarium and we scouted out our favorite Southern food. It felt like family.

Savy liked Charley from the start. She recognized her from walking the dog in our Valencia neighborhood and claimed credit for "finding her" for us. The twins were still too young to grasp what was happening. London seemed to adore Charley, but Jadon was generally more reticent and seemed to be keeping a close eye on her.

Sage was nine—old enough, I thought, to have "the conversation." I worried if I didn't tell him early, he'd eventually hear it from his father, and nothing positive would come of that.

I took Sage to a Mexican restaurant, just the two of us. As soon as we sat, I ordered a margarita, hoping it would give me courage. After a sip or two of my drink, I asked, "Sage, how do you feel about Charley?"

"I like her. Why?"

"Do you know what she does?"

"Something with music, right?"

Our meal came and Sage dove into his burrito. My stomach was in knots and I didn't touch my food.

"I want to have an adult conversation with you now, Sage," I said. "Are you up for it?"

He looked up from his burrito with a quizzical look on his face.

"I have something important to tell you and I want you to hear me," I said. "I want you to tell me how it makes you feel. Okay?"

Sage shrugged. "Okay," he said.

"I'm in love, honey," I said.

"Oh."

I took a deep breath. "I'm in love with Charley," I said, wincing.

My son paused midbite and stared into his plate. I waited for his reaction, which didn't seem to be coming. Finally, after what felt like an entire afternoon, he swallowed his food, threw his head back and giggled. "This is so embarrassing!" he cried. With that, we both laughed and the ice was broken.

"Look, Sage," I said. "I know this is different for you, but your dad and I made a mistake being together. The only good that came from our relationship was you and the other kids. Honey, I'm in love for the first time and she loves me too. There is nothing wrong with a woman loving a woman or a man loving a man. It's love."

"What will my friends say?" Sage asked sheepishly.

I thought for a moment and remembered when

I'd been uncomfortable holding hands with Charley at the hotel in New Orleans. "Honey, let me ask you something," I said. "Are you embarrassed that you have a brown sister?"

He sat straight up in his seat. "No! Of course not!" he said. "I love Savy!"

"Yes, you do," I said. "We all do. But there are people who think that us adopting her was wrong. But we weren't wrong, were we? We are the lucky ones because we understand that our differences make us more loving and compassionate and understanding toward others. Our differences make us better people. If your friends ask, hold your head high because all that matters is family and love, no matter who you love."

"Okay, Mom," my son said, sipping his drink. "Can we get dessert?"

———◈———

My divorce was final on September 10. Sometimes I couldn't believe my good luck. My kids were healthy and happy, I was in love and my life insurance business was thriving. We had more clients than we could handle. I left it to Dror to keep me updated on **Not Forgotten**, and he assured me that sales were on track.

By then, Dror was putting his energy into building up Windsor Pictures. We had **Twist** on our production roster and we'd met with some big hitters about future projects to invest in: Lee Daniels had a movie project called **Selma**, and Alicia Keys was looking for producing partners for the film **The Inevitable Defeat of Mister & Pete**, about a couple of kids growing up in the projects of Brooklyn.

Two days before **Twist** was set to debut at the Alliance Theatre in Atlanta, I flew in Celeste and Monica to help with the out-of-town guests who were coming for the opening. Celeste had pushed to be there. She said she didn't think Monica could handle the arrangements alone. I agreed that she should come along. I wanted everything to turn out perfectly.

From the moment Celeste landed, she began taking photographs with a camera I had purchased for the trip. It seemed excessive. At first, I thought it was just her excitement over being in a new place. But after a while I began to notice she was usually focusing the camera on Charley and me. When I asked her about it, Celeste said she just wanted to document everything about the opening. I didn't give it much thought. Until Charley expressed her concern.

"Miche," she said, one evening as we were preparing for bed. "Celeste is making me very uncomfortable. She is always in our face taking pictures, and it doesn't feel right. Something is up with that girl and I don't like it."

I told her I thought she was overreacting, but considering what had happened with Mary

Mauser, I wondered. I promised to talk to Celeste again.

At breakfast the following morning, Charley and I were sitting next to each other, each of us checking our e-mails, when I looked up and saw Celeste aiming her camera at us. **Click click**. **Click click**. **Click click**. Charley was furious. She put down her phone, slammed her reading glasses on the table and looked squarely at Celeste. "Get that camera out of my face," she insisted. "Why are you taking all these pictures of us? It's very strange. Now put it away."

I had never heard Charley raise her voice. It seemed to startle Celeste too.

"Oh! I'm sorry," she said, fiddling with the camera. "It's just, you two looked so cute!"

—◈—

Charley's family arrived the day before the opening. I hadn't met them and they didn't know about me. As far as they knew, Charley and Maria were still together.

I had heard so much about Charley's three sisters, and I was excited to meet them. Everyone gathered at the Four Seasons Hotel bar for a combined family reunion and preshow celebration. Charley had given me a heads-up that she'd be introducing me as one of the producers and a personal friend, which she did. The sisters were gracious and polite, asking the usual questions that strangers ask when they don't know anything about each other.

Charley's oldest sister, Katherine, examined me with laserlike eyes. She looked at me so deeply it seemed as if she were peering into my soul. I'd heard a lot about Katherine. She was the beauty queen of the Mississippi Harpers: married, well-off and unapologetic about all of her beautiful and sparkling things. Charley had compared Katherine to Suzanne Sugarbaker, the Delta Burke character in the 1980s television comedy **Designing Women**. She hadn't overstated it. Katherine was a clone of the character, movie star stunning, with a long, slow Southern drawl, a bawdy sense of humor and jewelry dripping from every extremity.

The sisters bantered and reminisced, and eventually Katherine stood up and said she was going to the restroom. She pointed at Charley and said, "You're coming with me!" Charley responded that she didn't need to go, but Katherine insisted. "Oh yes, you do!" she said. "Come with me!" I didn't think much of it, other than sisters being sisters.

Behind the closed doors of the ladies' lounge, Katherine confronted Charley. "Oh my God!" she cried. "You are dating that woman!" Charley tried skirting the issue, with little luck. "I don't know what you're talking about," she said, in that calm, direct way of hers. "Don't you dare lie to me, Rix!" Katherine warned. (Rix is Charley's middle name.) "I can see the way that woman looks at you. I have never seen anyone look at you that way. That woman is in love with you!" Charley confessed that Katherine was right. "She's in love with me and I'm in love with her," she said. Mustering her best Southern belle dramatics, Katherine tossed her Louis Vuitton handbag to the floor, threw up her perfectly manicured hands and exclaimed: "Thank God! I couldn't stand that other bitch!"

The sisters walked back to the bar, smiling like Cheshire cats. I was wondering what had happened when Katherine leaned in and whispered in my ear. "Welcome to the family, you old sneak!" she said.

I loved feeling like part of Charley's family. I imagined that one day they would be my family. They were good people with strong values who loved each other, and that really appealed to me.

I had become a better person since meeting Charley. She taught me about real love. That it wasn't critical or cruel or abusive, but kind and warm and breathtaking. If love was too human an emotion, well, I wanted to be human.

Charley was a role model. Watching her live her life, I realized that possessions didn't matter; people did. Understanding and acceptance prevailed over judgments. Love over ambition. Trust over suspicion. She was who I wanted to be. Kind. Patient. Empathic.

Someone who was a lot like I was before I was taught not to be.

———◆———

Twist premiered to a standing ovation and critical praise for Charley's musical score. I was so proud of her. It felt good to have a partner who outshined me.

Before Celeste's flight back to Los Angeles, I asked if she would leave the camera. Celeste said she had accidentally left it at the theater the night before. She would e-mail the stage manager to make sure I got it back, but it was never found.

Was I being paranoid? I wondered.

Or was Celeste a spy for the church?

CHAPTER FIFTEEN

Reality

◈

The beginning of October brought us all back to California and reality. Sage and Savy went back to school. Charley fought constantly with Maria and stressed about finding a new place to live. I worried that our relationship wouldn't survive the pressures in our lives.

We had been back home only a short time when I began hearing rumblings that Mary Mauser had been outing me to church members while I was away. Dror and Virginia had heard it from a mutual friend.

I struck back with a Knowledge Report on Mary in November:

Mary knew I had been in a very unhappy marriage for many years. Once my divorce was final I started a new 2D [relationship] with a woman. This was something that stemmed from falling in love with the being. This was not a sexual aberration. It is something I am extremely proud of. She is one of the leading music producers in the world and a huge contributor to mankind. . . .

Our story is very beautiful and because the relationship was new, I wanted to speak to Mary face-to-face but I'd been traveling so much that I didn't have the opportunity to do so.

I went on to explain about the July 4 phone call and the way Mary had handled herself when I'd admitted I was in love with a woman. I said that I had wanted to be the one to tell the church and my friends, but Mary had gossiped to everyone.

I recently found out that she told Sean, my X2D [ex-husband] . . . She told him I was "off Bridge" and this "aberration" would be handled.

[Another Scientologist] called my best friend Virginia Pereira-Soref and said she heard from a mutual friend who heard from Mary that I had outed myself as gay and this was not okay.

The part that is not okay is that my FSM is telling group members confidential data that I shared re: my 2D. It has now become rumor as something that is "wrong." I am very aware of the groupthink and I will handle in the proper PR [public relations] way.

As naive as I was, I felt untouchable. That year I had donated $2 million to the church. I convinced myself that as long as I kept writing checks, I would eventually triumph. I could be with Charley, and the church would look the other way and allow us to live in peace. I couldn't have been more misguided.

———◈———

Virginia and Dror threw a birthday party for their one-year-old daughter that same month. Virginia warned me that two high-level Scientologists declined the invitation because I would be there and that I had "come out as gay."

"Who?" I asked.

Reluctantly, she divulged the names. One was the Hollywood business mogul who had introduced me to Dror. The other was the wife of a Grammy-winning music producer. I was furious. I wondered how it would go over if word got out that they were homophobic bigots!

"Fuck 'em," Virginia said.

"Yes, screw them!" I added with a wry laugh. "I'm not missing my goddaughter's first birthday!"

By then, Charley had found a place of her own in Pasadena and we weren't hiding our relationship anymore.

Newly emboldened, I went to the party with my head held high. I immediately felt out of place. Some of the guests gave me the cold shoulder. I went outside and texted Charley. "I don't belong here anymore," I wrote. "I belong with you."

Just then, a woman I knew casually from our kids' Scientology school sat down next to me. She was a mother of four who lived in Beverly Hills with her much older wealthy husband.

"Can I talk to you for a minute?" she asked.

"Sure," I said, putting my phone away.

The woman had heard about Charley and me. "I just have to say that I'm so impressed with you," she said. "It takes courage to do what you did and forge the way for others."

I thanked her and she took a sip of her wine.

"I've always been in love with a woman," she whispered. "Don't get me wrong—I care about my husband. But you have given me such strength that I've decided I'm going to divorce him." She seemed almost giddy as she spoke. It was as if she were standing at the precipice of a cliff and had finally found the courage to jump. I was proud to be the conduit for her epiphany, but it didn't last long.

A few weeks later, Virginia told me that the woman had retreated to Flag in Clearwater sometime after the birthday party. She'd undergone rigorous "handling" in auditing and ethics and was now working her way back up from Lower Conditions. Part of her penance had been to "strike a blow to the enemy." She chose me, writing in a report that I had promoted homosexuality at the party. I felt sorry for her in a way. I was certain she'd been "persuaded" to rethink her sexuality and drop her plans for divorce. Part of the process was getting me, a PTS, "off her lines" (out of her life). But I was still angry that she'd thrown me under the bus after I'd been so supportive of her.

It was no coincidence that I was summoned to the Celebrity Centre for an important meeting with the top ethics officer from Flag. I agreed to go because there was still a part of me that wasn't ready to sever ties with the church.

The meeting began friendly enough. I was asked if I planned to get back into session and return to my work on the Bridge. I said I was committed to coming back but had no immediate plans.

I was then told that others had written reports for my file. A young woman who had turned to me for support after she'd come out to the church, and was later ordered to go to Flag to be "cured," had filed a report saying I'd persuaded her to experiment with women, which was a total lie.

A Scientologist I knew only casually claimed to have seen me being "inappropriately affectionate" with a woman in public. I remembered seeing him at a restaurant where Charley and I were having lunch one day. We had been holding hands, but as soon as I'd spotted him I dropped Charley's hand. This was what he called "inappropriately affectionate," holding hands? Yes, because, he wrote, "Per the chart of human evaluation, homosexuality is 1.1 on the tone scale and perverted."

At that point, things became perfectly clear to me. I would never be free to be me and be a member of the Church of Scientology.

I left the Celebrity Centre that day, vowing never to return.

CHAPTER SIXTEEN

The Office
of Special Affairs

❖

My friend Ken Wright called and said he needed
to see me. Would I meet him for lunch? When I
walked into the restaurant, I could see he was not
his usual jovial self. It didn't take long for me to
realize that he'd heard about my "confession." Sure
enough, he'd heard from Mary Mauser. He urged
me to get back into auditing to "fix the homosexual thing." Ken was a good person, but I knew the
church was pulling his strings and I was tired of
them trying to control me.

"Ken, I love Charley with every part of me," I
said. "I'm not giving her up. I'm not going in session to fix something that isn't broken and I sure
as hell won't have a group of people who are sup-

posed to be my friends inserting themselves into my relationship."

Suddenly, his manner changed. His fear for me was real. I could feel it.

"You have to listen to me," Ken said. "This is getting serious and I want to help you. I shouldn't tell you this, but you are a good person and I care about you. Stop being defensive and listen to me."

As I sat quietly across from him, Ken leaned forward, looked around.

"I received a phone call yesterday from OSA and they were asking me very specific questions about you," he said, his voice nearly a whisper. "They wanted to know if I had ever done business with you. They wanted to know if I had invested with you or bought life insurance from you. They wanted to know what I thought about you personally and professionally. I told them all the business we've done together has been impeccable. I told them that you were a smart businesswoman. They asked about your integrity and I told them it was first-class, but I did tell them that I felt you needed to be in session more. I asked them why they were calling me. The woman on the phone said they had 'an unofficial investigation' going on. They were poking around."

Ken was worried. He tried to get across the seriousness of what was happening, but I was sure the "investigation" would go nowhere. This wasn't about my business, I said. It was all about me being a lesbian. What were they going to do, arrest me? Let them call people, I said. I had nothing to hide.

He wouldn't be put off.

"I asked them if they were talking to anyone else and they said they were," he said, sounding desperate. "They've talked to a lot of people. You have to take this seriously, Michelle. I've seen investigations spin out of control in the past, and I don't want to see that happen to you. Promise me that you will look at going in session? Please."

———— ◈ ————

Mom was transferred from Los Angeles to Clearwater for a few months, and she frequently called asking me to purchase sets of L. Ron Hubbard books. As the leader of a sales team at Flag, she was responsible for making sure her group made its daily sales quota. Every time she was in a pinch, I bought a set. The leather-bound books retailed for between $3,000 and $4,000 a set, and I'd purchased a storage unit full of them. But what was a few thousand dollars here and there when I was taking in millions—especially if it meant helping my mom?

Even though Sea Org members were secretive about life inside the organization, I'd gotten a glimpse of what it was like when I'd joined for that brief period in my teens. Since then, I'd heard the same leaked stories that everyone else had. Being in the Sea Org was a tough gig—as rigorous as it was prestigious. Members worked fourteen-plus-hour days with only a few hours off each week, and most were much younger than my mother. I worried about the strain it was putting on her both physically and psychologically. She always claimed she was happy, insisting it was a privilege to serve in the Sea Org. As with everything else, there were consequences when you didn't meet expectations, she said—for instance, when you didn't sell enough books. She never offered what those consequences were, and I never asked. I just wrote checks to cover her.

I was angry, though, when I discovered she'd charged books to the credit card I'd loaned her for the incidentals she couldn't afford on her meager Sea Org salary of fifty dollars a week. Why would she do that? I wondered. It wasn't like I'd ever turned her down for anything.

"I'm sorry," she said when I confronted her about the credit card bill. She stuttered and stammered and began to cry. She'd been desperate when she charged the books to my card, she said. Her supervisor had forbidden her to leave until she made a sale. She'd done everything she could before using my card, even calling people in different time zones—Australia and Europe—trying to make a sale. Frantic, she had finally used my card.

What I didn't know, and what my mother would never tell me, was the abuse she suffered when she didn't make her quota. Her twenty-five-year-old supervisor berated her by screaming at the top of her lungs that Mom was "a fat pig . . . a shithead . . . a screwup." She was ordered to do demeaning tasks like scrubbing filthy toilets, cleaning out Dumpsters and cleaning sets of stairs using a rag.

The worst was the night her supervisor announced that she and her team were "going to the bilges." In the pitch dark, Mom and the others were marched down to Clearwater Bay. As waves crashed up against the seawall, they were ordered to roll up their pants, take off their shoes and jump into the black water. The supervisor tossed scrub brushes into the bay and commanded them to scour the barnacles off the seawall. This was the consequence, they were told, of caring so little about the souls they weren't saving by not selling enough books.

The humiliation was punishment enough for Mom. But when she grumbled about it, she was reported by a team member and subsequently banished for weeks to "Pigs Berthing," a filthy, run-down efficiency apartment on church property with no electricity or running water.

It was no wonder she sounded so frightened when faced with losing her best customer.

———◈———

Mom had always gotten on me when I strayed from the church. She was insistent now I come back. The Ethics Department had been urging her to do what she could to convince me to return. They hadn't mentioned my relationship with Charley. They had said only that they were concerned that I'd been away for too long. They'd asked questions, she said. "What is Michelle doing with her life? Is she working? Does she need assistance? She is such a hard worker and she's done so much for the church. We want to help her. We need to get her in here to talk to her." I was pretty sure they were missing my money more than they were missing me.

Mom didn't know the details about what was going on, just that people in the church were worried about my well-being because I hadn't been around. She was worried too. I had too many pressures—raising my kids, managing my business, the continuing battle with Sean over alimony and visitation rights, and taking constant calls from Dror about potential movie projects. How could I be expected to cope without the weight of the church behind me? I needed to come back, my mother said, or I would collapse.

"We need you back so you can handle your life," she said. "The church is the only solution."

At that point, I couldn't have been dragged back, not even with a tow truck. I did, though, want to escape the cloud of suspicion enveloping me.

❖

On December 29, 2010, I wrote my own "Things That Shouldn't Be" report, hoping to nip whatever investigation there was in the bud. I sent it to the top ethics officer at Flag in Clearwater and Chairman of the Board David Miscavige in Los Angeles.

"It is absolutely NOT okay that any rumor is being forwarded about me. I am not being confronted by my accusers, nor am I being backed up or protected by the Ethics Department."

I said I'd been told, "There were many reports recently coming out on me having financial irregs. I paid no attention to this, as it was absolutely false and natter [gossip]."

My closest friends were being punished for my alleged crime, I wrote.

"In the past few weeks, my business partner, Dror Soref, and his wife, Virginia Soref, have been put on Sec Checks" and stopped from pursuing the next level on the Bridge "because they were told by their ethics officers that I was under 'investigation' re: financial irregs and because Dror was my business partner, he was being checked. . . .

"Whatever is happening with me or NOT happening is my personal ethics and Bridge and not up for discussion or rumor."

The church didn't respond, but the rumors about me—some of them insane—continued to fly! I felt like no one would come out and say that it was my relationship that was the problem, so they were trying to cook up a financial scandal. It was one thing for the church to try to control my personal life. But digging into my business dealings could only mean one thing: I had become the target of a Black Propaganda campaign.

If I had any doubt at all, my suspicions were confirmed in an e-mail from my now ex-husband, who was still active in the church. Sean warned that I had no idea how bad things were about to get for me. He said that he'd been asked by the ethics officer at Flag to write reports on me and that reports from others about me were flying around. "Your clients will sue you and you will lose everything very soon," he wrote. "But it will all stop if you just leave that SP"—I knew he was referring to Charley—"and get back into the church."

Only when I got "back on lines," he said, would the noise stop.

CHAPTER SEVENTEEN

Trouble Ahead

❖

Dror phoned in March 2011 asking for a meeting. I headed to his office at Paramount. He looked anxious but greeted me warmly. I sat on a couch and looked at him expectantly. He said he had recently been summoned to Flag in Clearwater for a Sec Check. While he was there, he'd made admissions that needed to be "handled." His next step in the process was making a confession to me, he said. I swallowed hard. What in the world was he about to say? Dror held up a sheet of paper. "I want to read you something, but I'm not going to give it to you," he said. "My ethics officer said that once I have read it, it needs to be put back in my file." I thought it odd, but I nodded in agreement.

First of all, he read, he should have told me

earlier, but the international distributor of **Not Forgotten** had breached its commitment to get the movie proper marketing and distribution overseas.

Dror had said from the beginning that it would take around two years for the movie to show a profit and we were only just nearing that mark, so I hadn't really been focused on it. As far as I knew—as Dror had consistently told me—everything was going as planned. He hadn't given me any indication that there was a problem that could affect our profit margin. My heart was pumping furiously. I was headed toward panic. **My clients!** "You promised, Dror. I saw the contracts. You said there was no risk, that it was a guaranteed investment. What does this mean for my clients?"

Dror quickly backpedaled. I was getting upset over nothing, he said. It was a setback, that was all. He was working with the distributor to work things out. Everything would be fine. I recognized that he was using the Scientology mind-set: "There are no problems; only situations and solutions."

I believed Dror when he said he was on top of things. Still, I called a meeting with members of my staff whose clients had invested with Dror to warn them that there might be a problem. I said, honestly, that I was consulting with an attorney to make sure our clients' interests were protected, but I believed we were okay.

Two weeks later, I was at the Beverly Wilshire

Hotel for an event with Charley when my assistant Monica called.

"I'm sorry to bother you, but this is urgent," Monica said. "A guy came knocking on the door and you just got a subpoena."

"Okay," I said. "Will you open it, please?"

I could hear Monica ripping open the envelope.

The subpoena was from the State of California, Monica said. "They want financial records for **Not Forgotten**."

"What? A subpoena for financial records? Oh my God. What does that mean?"

My heart leapt to my throat.

I called Dror immediately and told him about being served. He sounded surprised, but said he wasn't worried. If it was something serious, he would have received a subpoena too, he said.

Standing there alone, I felt the walls closing in on me. I was certain the church had something to do with the government subpoena. It wasn't a coincidence that Dror had made whatever "admissions" he did while he was being interrogated at Flag—and now the government was knocking. What in the world had he said? I had seen how the church deflected attention from itself by coercing others to do its dirty work—even when others didn't know that that was what they were doing. In this case, we were talking about the State of California. What in the world did they think they knew?

My friend Ken had warned me. The drumbeat had begun.

Dror was served with a subpoena after me. I persuaded him to join me in a meeting with corporate attorneys that Charley recommended. He balked at first, but I insisted. "You own the company," I said. "You handle the money. You make the decisions. I am the sales agent. Our deal was that you provide all paperwork and handle the productions and the finances. What I told clients about the movie deal came directly from you. So do I expect you to be there? Yes, I do."

Dror finally gave in. During the two-hour meeting, he said he was close to getting the distribution deal back on course. Once that happened, **Not Forgotten** would have an international release and we would be able to pay back our investors. He didn't know what the government was looking for, but he was confident that everything would check out. The lawyers seemed satisfied with Dror's explanation. Before we left, they requested he submit to them all contracts relating to the film, as well as a certified financial audit from the distributor. "Anything you need," Dror said. I agreed to put up $1 million to cover attorney fees and any past-due interest that our clients were owed.

When I left the meeting, I felt relief. If the lawyers weren't too concerned and Dror was willing to get them whatever they needed to satisfy the state, there didn't seem to be any need to worry. What-

ever the government thought it had would be resolved and we could all move on.

———◆———

In May, with just weeks until **Twist**'s Pasadena premiere, Dror dropped a bombshell. Windsor wasn't
in a position to honor its $2 million commitment
to the play, he said. I was stunned. We had to keep
our commitment, I cried. We had Broadway producers coming to the opening. The future of the
play was at stake. Dror said the problem was in
the timing. Windsor's money was tied up in the
movie projects he had in preproduction. He'd just
sunk $1 million plus into **Selma** alone, he said.
I was frustrated and angry with him—and with
myself. The numbers weren't adding up and there
were too many red flags.

Dror couldn't explain the discrepancy except to
say that once the other projects he had going got
off the ground, we would be on firm footing again.

I was tired of his excuses.

I called our attorneys. In poring over copies of the early documents that Dror had turned
over, they discovered he had been paying himself a $50,000-a-month salary out of the Wind-
sor account—more than twice the $20,800 we'd
agreed upon and a hefty sum to be taking from a
fledgling company that wasn't yet making a profit.
Dror had not yet delivered the certified financial
audit he'd promised, the lawyers said, so it was

impossible to tell if there were other discrepancies. We would have to wait for the certified financial audit to be completed.

I met with Dror and asked about the salary. He insisted that I had approved the increase. Nice try, but I had done no such thing, I said, nor had we even discussed it.

"I'm okay with you being paid as a producer on a project," I said. "But to be paid that much as an executive of a company that isn't making money yet isn't practical. I would never have approved something like that and I certainly would remember if I had."

After a heated discussion, Dror agreed to cut his salary to match what we'd agreed upon initially. He then suggested we bring in an experienced film industry executive to manage the business so he could focus solely on what he did best, which was directing and producing. He seemed surprised when I agreed, but I was comforted by the idea of having someone else run the business side of Windsor.

Charley was troubled by my conversation with Dror. "I pray to God he's not stringing you along for money the way the church has," she said.

If what she was suggesting was true, it would mean that I had been duped, and the thought of that was too terrifying to acknowledge even to myself.

Instead, I reacted defensively, responding to Charley with what I had learned by rote in the church. "It is not up to me or you to determine what is a good religion and what is not," I said. "Just because Scientology may not be working for me right now, it is working for many others."

As for Dror, I said, "He just wants to make films. He's handling the international distribution problem. **Selma** is moving along. We have other projects in preproduction. Our lawyers are looking over everything and soon we'll have someone with experience running the business side of things. I appreciate your concern, but everything will be fine."

If Charley was surprised at my reaction, she didn't show it, but she was unconvinced. "I don't know," she said warily, "but I hope you're right."

————◆————

We began interviewing candidates for the Windsor job immediately. One was a highly respected film producer named Leah Cummings. Leah had been Steven Spielberg's producing partner and had to her credit big hits, including **Saving Private Ryan**, **Jurassic Park** and **Minority Report**. The three of us met in Dror's office on the Paramount lot.

I liked Leah right away. She was a lesbian and a Southerner. She asked all the right questions and it was obvious that she really knew her stuff.

After the meeting, when Leah and I walked

to our cars together, she turned to me and asked, "Michelle, how did you meet Dror?"

I told her that we'd met at a Scientology fund-raiser and that Dror had relentlessly pursued me as a financial backer.

"I hope I'm not overstepping my bounds, but may I ask how much you raised for him?" she asked.

"Well, between the first movie and the projects he has on deck, maybe $18 to $20 million," I said.

Leah shook her head. Her expression was incredulous.

"I could have made five pictures with that by now!" she said. "I have to be honest. I'm worried about you."

Alarm bells sounded. First Charley and now Leah, both of them experienced businesswomen who knew the entertainment business. I felt as if my legs might buckle under me. How could I continue to ignore what seemed obvious to two very smart businesswomen whose judgment I trusted?

I told Leah not to worry; my hope was that she would join our team and together we could figure everything out. "I'll be in touch," I said.

Sitting in my car in the parking lot, I thought back to the beginning of my relationship with Dror. About how he'd dominated my time at the Scientology fund-raiser. How he'd happened to be at the same party with me the following week.

How he and Virginia had both courted me the way a smitten lover would.

If Dror had set me up—had Virginia known from the beginning? I wondered. Had our friendship been a sham?

I never had the chance to ask.

———⬥———

With the state subpoena hanging over our heads, Dror took Virginia on a vacation to Europe in late June. I was afraid he wouldn't return. He said he'd be gone for ten days, but instead traveled from Europe to Israel—to make a short film, he said. In his absence, I was left to fund Windsor's overhead and find the extra money needed to keep **Twist** on schedule. My main concern was my clients. They had entrusted me with their savings and I was prepared to do whatever it took to keep **Twist** and Windsor afloat so that their investments would pay off the way Dror had promised.

He finally returned to the States at the end of July and immediately asked for more money for Windsor's expenses. I didn't understand, I said. I had covered all the expenses with my own money while he was gone. Why not pay the bills from his Windsor account? He reiterated what he had said two months earlier: Everything was tied up in projects. I put my foot down. I understood how important it was to keep the production roster moving forward, I said, but I wasn't going to contribute another cent to Windsor until he submitted the certified audit he'd promised the attorneys, and until we brought on Leah Cummings or someone else with experience in the film industry to help get our financial ducks in a row.

In mid-August, while I was watching rehearsals for **Twist** with Charley, I received a call from Mitch Lampert, one of my attorneys.

"Michelle, have you seen the e-mail we just received from Dror's personal attorney?" he asked, his voice hollow.

I walked outside the theater to continue the call.

"I haven't seen it," I said. "What does it say?"

"Dror is filing for bankruptcy on both Windsor and **Not Forgotten**—unless you want to take over and assume all liabilities."

It took a moment for what he had said to sink in.

"What do you mean, bankruptcy?" I cried. "How can he bankrupt a company with assets?"

"Well," Mitch said haltingly, "according to this letter, it doesn't look like there are any assets."

Dror was claiming that **Not Forgotten** had not earned any revenue and there was no expectation of future returns. Windsor was $10 million in debt "with no income and no potential for income in the immediate or near future," the letter said.

"No assets? No potential for income?" What about the other projects he had in the works?

My hands were shaking uncontrollably. I was in disbelief, but at the same time I wasn't totally shocked. I hadn't allowed myself to listen to my instincts whenever I felt something wasn't right with Dror. During those moments of doubt, I had reverted back to Scientology—the rule that said you never question a fellow Scientologist—rather than face my fears. Charley had warned me and I'd defended Dror. I'd never imagined, not for a single moment, that he was capable of deception of this magnitude.

Mitch's voice brought me back from my thoughts. He sounded angry. "From reading this, it looks like he is trying to place the burden on you," he said.

"Me?"

Mitch promised to phone Dror's lawyer immediately to figure out what was happening and what could be done. When we hung up, I stood outside the Pasadena Playhouse and, for a moment, glanced up at the banner for **Twist. What does this mean for the play?** I wondered. **For** Selma **and the other projects that are on the runway? What does this mean for my clients? Oh my God—what about the subpoena?** Did the state know something I didn't?

The following week I called a meeting with all my insurance agents and staff, some of whom had also invested their clients' money in Dror's ventures. Everyone was seated around the large conference table. The room was silent when I walked in. Everyone knew that, whatever was about to happen, it was serious. I pulled out the black leather chair at the head of the table and sat down.

"Some of you may know what this is about and some of you may have heard rumors," I said. "Dror Soref has declared bankruptcy and walked away from **Not Forgotten** and Windsor Pictures." The statement was met with a collective gasp.

I was working with my team of lawyers to get on top of the situation, I said. Our clients who had invested in Dror's projects were about to be notified. I was doing everything possible to gain control of whatever assets were available from **Not Forgotten** and Windsor. We did not yet have a complete financial picture because Dror had never delivered on the financial audit he'd promised, but I felt confident we could recover a good portion of Windsor's assets. I didn't know what all of this meant for our investors, or me, or my company, I said. But the insurance business was strong, with millions of dollars in underwriting, and I would personally make good on any losses suffered by our clients.

Most important, I said, was that each of them be available to take questions from investors. The lawyers were drawing up a letter and we needed to prepare them for what was coming. Everyone was handed a list of clients to call and a script of what to say, and I adjourned the meeting.

Returning to my office, I closed the door, rested my head on my desk and fought back tears. How could he do this? I asked myself. How could Dror be so callous as to walk away from the good people who had trusted him—trusted me—with their financial futures? Some of those people were my friends. My own father had invested!

There was a soft knock on my door. I patted my eyes dry. "Yes, come in!" I said. My assistant Monica walked in and took a seat facing me. Her sister had invested in Windsor and I knew how concerned Monica had to be, but, at that moment, she was there for me.

"Are you okay?" she asked.

I smiled at her. In many ways, Monica was more like a daughter to me than an assistant. "Thank you. I'm okay," I said. "I'm in shock, but I'm going to figure this out. I just have to get a handle on it all."

"I have faith in you. Everyone does," she said, smiling sweetly. "Just let me know what I need to do to help."

"Well, you can start by getting me a list of the clients you think need to be called first," I said, buoyed by her faith in me.

"I'm on it! We can do this, Michelle," she said, bouncing out of the office.

I prayed she was right.

◆

I didn't anticipate hearing from Dror, but he called and asked that I meet him for lunch. I didn't know what to expect, but I wanted answers. Dror was already at the restaurant when I arrived. He looked disheveled and nervous. I felt no compassion for him, just anger. There was no way this man, who had pretended to be my friend, was going to get away without answering questions, not if I had anything to say about it.

Over lunch, I fired away. What happened to the distribution deal for **Not Forgotten**? I asked. Where were the contracts? What was the status of the bank loans I'd guaranteed? Why hadn't he provided the financial audit he'd promised? What had happened to the other projects he said we had?

Beads of sweat formed on Dror's face. Shifting in his seat, he began stuttering and stammering. He seemed to be having trouble forming words. I looked him dead in the eye, determined to make him tell me what he knew. When he finally collected himself enough to speak, he reiterated what was in the letter from his attorney. **Not Forgotten** was a dead issue, he stammered. There was no contract with a distributor. They had backed out long ago and he was sorry that he had not told me the truth back then. Whatever money the investors had already gotten back—which, for most, wasn't even half of their original investment—was all there was. There would be nothing forthcoming.

As for future projects for Windsor, he said, there were none. Any association we had with **Selma** or Alicia Keys had ended. Lee Daniels, who had been our connection to **Selma**, was no longer associated with the movie. Keys had found another producing partner for her project. The only project left was **Twist**. "And you can have that," he said, as if giving me a gift.

In typical Scientology style, he then turned the tables on me.

"Look, Michelle," he said. "I never knew how you were selling this project. I'm just the director. I never offered any guarantees."

I was incredulous. Was this new, concocted story supposed to make what he had done wrong my problem? I wasn't having it.

"Dror, you aren't fooling me," I said. "You can sit here and tell me your made-up story, but I know exactly what happened. You handled the business. You were the sole signer on all bank accounts. You provided me with the distribution contracts and all of the financials. You met with my clients. You gave me the guarantees. You must have lied about everything. The only thing I did wrong was trust you!"

I stood to leave.

"Michelle, please sit down. There have been too many people that have come between us and filled you with information that is incorrect. You and I just need to talk and get back together as partners. We can work everything out together," Dror wheedled.

At that moment, I could see through this evil man. I was no longer swayed by Scientology or his facade. He was trying to set me up for his crimes and I was not having it!

"You can take care of the check," I said, grabbing my briefcase. "That's the least you can do. You'll hear from my attorney."

A week or so later, Dror came back to me again with a proposal.

"I want to work with you," he said, seeming contrite. "Let's do a WISE arbitration. I've already spoken to them."

WISE is an acronym for World Institute of Scientology Enterprises. Its mission is to share L. Ron Hubbard's management philosophy for "strict standards of ethical conduct in the workplace." At a price, of course. The organization claims to be independent from the church, but it is staffed entirely by Scientologists, and the mediators are ethics officers who base their decisions on L. Ron Hubbard "technology." The way it works is that the mediators review the evidence presented to them by both sides and then make a finding, which is final. The settlements are usually predicated upon both parties agreeing to get back in the church for auditing, courses or Sec Checks.

"Let's get back on church lines," he said. "Then

I'll provide the rest of the paperwork you need to take over Windsor."

"Have WISE call me," I said.

I had about as much intention of turning myself over to WISE—aka the church—as I did of marrying another man.

Later that month I took a call from Scott Foulk, a former business partner and one of my top life insurance agents. Scott hadn't been supportive of my relationship with Charley. We'd had our ups and downs over the course of our twelve-year business relationship, but we deeply respected each other.

"Michelle, do you know a Mark Loweree?" he asked.

I'd met Mark Loweree through Mary Mauser. He was a high-ranking Scientologist and a good friend of hers. He had been Beth Linder's life insurance agent, and after she started working with me instead, he had spitefully submitted a Knowledge Report accusing me of insurance fraud. Ironically, back then, Dror had written a Knowledge Report defending me against Loweree's slanderous accusation: "Let me put it simply," he wrote. "Loweree's accusations of fraud (or any other inappropriate behavior, for that matter) have no basis in reality. And I know, and he doesn't."

"Yes, I know Mark Loweree," I said. "Why?"

Scott sounded worried. "He called me last night and wanted a list of all our clients," he said. "He told me that he and Mary Mauser and Dror and other Scientologists were doing a formal investigation of you and writing reports and he wanted to know if I would like to join them.

"I told them no and hung up."

More than a year had passed since my confrontation with Mary Mauser about my sexuality. I should have known her righteous vengeance wouldn't end there. I was about to learn that only six days after my final e-mail on July 14, 2010, dismissing her as my church counselor, her husband, Steve Mauser, submitted a "Things That Shouldn't Be" report on me to the church's Office of Special Affairs implicating me as "out ethics" in my insurance business. Mark Loweree followed up a week later with a second report charging that I was running an insurance scam and possible Ponzi scheme for a movie "and it must be investigated now." Loweree followed up with a request to the Office of Special Affairs that the allegations be turned over to the state. In his report, he wrote, "Unhandled, Michelle's activities are going to turn up front-page news. The headline is going to say 'Scientology Defrauds Insurance Company of Millions.'"

"I thought you needed to know this," Scott said.

I thanked Scott for his loyalty and hung up.

It had been months since my last large donation to the Church of Scientology. Since I'd cut it off completely, there was nothing to protect me from the wrath of the thetans anymore. The full weight of the Black Propaganda campaign was bearing down on me.

Suddenly, what was happening to me was crystal clear. My coming out had set in motion a predictable series of steps that we were taught in the church. As a lesbian with no intention of seeking a cure within the church, I was in violation of L. Ron Hubbard's Second Dynamic of human survival, which promotes procreation and "is the urge toward existence as a future generation." That automatically put me at a 1.1 on the Tone Scale and meant I was "perverted," "covertly hostile" and "a danger to society." Tolerance of such perversion was as actionable as the "crime" of homosexuality itself, Hubbard wrote. Failing to strike a blow against the enemy was itself a crime.

Hubbard wrote that all of the Eight Dynamics of human survival are so closely connected that if someone is "out ethics" on one, he or she is likely "out ethics" on all the others; therefore, as Scientologists, we were encouraged to investigate any suspect's Third Dynamic, or work, to find out what he or she was hiding there. Mary would have had no choice but to report me for being gay, and she then would have been asked in session what she was doing to "handle" me, this "out-ethics" person. The only correct response she could have given was that she was digging for dirt on what other "crimes" I had committed.

In October I received notification that I was under investigation by two separate state agencies: the Department of Corporations and the Department of Insurance.

It was pretty clear what had prompted the government probe. If I had been reluctant to purge myself completely of the church and anyone associated with it, I wasn't now.

———◈———

Charley and I were lying in bed one night when she asked, "Honey, are you sure Celeste isn't working for the church? I've always thought that she was the person who told Mary about us."

Everything Charley said to me was out of love and truth and I trusted her judgment. I realized with a jolt that she was right. Celeste had come to me three months before the Mary Mauser call, and at Dror's behest. She handled all my travel arrangements and had the passwords to all my e-mail accounts. I felt sure she was working with Mary and Mark and Dror and whoever else was on the team to take me down.

The next morning, I called Monica into my office.

"Do you have any reason to believe that Celeste may be working with Dror directly and the church?" I asked her.

"Michelle, we have all felt like something has been off with Celeste. She's very secretive. She works late with Dror. She's constantly asking for information that doesn't pertain to her job. I constantly have to do her work as well as mine. I never wanted to bring this up to you because you had so much on your plate. What should we do?" Monica asked.

"Give me thirty minutes and call everyone into the boardroom." I said.

I called my attorney and informed him of my conversation with Monica. He advised me on my next steps.

I walked into the boardroom and explained that at nine a.m. the following morning a forensics specialist would be in the office to copy everyone's work computers and laptops. This was purely a precaution to make sure that our computers and servers had not been hacked.

I watched the blood drain out of Celeste's face. I believed at that moment that she was guilty of something, and my intuition was confirmed when she left work early that day and took her laptop with her.

I fired Celeste the next day.

After Celeste left, the attorneys sent in an IT person, a computer whiz named Julian, to ensure that my computer network was secure. He informed me that he had been unable to remove Celeste as the administrator because my company didn't own the server, and without her password, which she refused to give us, he wasn't able to ac-

cess any of our computer files or e-mails. I had always been under the impression that my company
hosted our computer network. When I found out
who did, I googled the name. Celeste had switched
to a tech firm in Clearwater, Florida—near the
church's Flag compound—that was owned by a
Scientologist.

I needed to dig deeper, but didn't know where
to start.

I remembered a man I'd met several years earlier at a city council meeting. I was appealing for
funds to help tsunami victims in Thailand. He approached me afterward with the names of contacts
he had in Asia. Our meeting led to a philanthropic
partnership to get schools built in Sri Lanka. We
ended up getting three schools and a day care center built, and the rest of the money was put in trust
to fund scholarships for Sri Lankan orphans.

I hadn't seen Jonathan Kraut in years, but I
knew that he was a private investigator with years
of experience. More importantly, he had no affilia-
tion with the Church of Scientology. I reached out
to him and explained as briefly as I could my problems with the church and told him I was concerned
that my computer had been illegally breached.

Jonathan didn't hesitate. He said he had a friend
who was a forensic analyst for the government
and he was certain they could help.

He and the forensic analyst culled through all
the data on my hard drive. After more than two

hundred hours of probing, they were able to follow
a trail of virtual evidence that led back to Celeste.

While she was still in my employ, she had
downloaded everything from my office hard drive—
e-mails, confidential client information, my divorce documents—and sent over nineteen hundred
e-mails to her personal e-mail address, as well as to
an e-mail address listed to her husband, who was
also a Scientologist.

I would later discover an invoice in my bookkeeper's files showing that Celeste had instructed
her to pay a different IT specialist whose name I
also didn't recognize. I did some investigating of
my own and discovered he was an administrator
for the church's computer network.

My company was paying him to handle my
server—which gave him admittance to all my personal correspondence and client information—and
I didn't know it.

My entire digital life was in my computer, and
all these Scientologists had access to it.

"To me, this looks clearly like a coordinated effort," Jonathan said. "I firmly believe Celeste is operating in concert with the church. I am concerned
for you, Michelle, and I will do everything I can to
help you." I was beyond grateful for Jonathan's help
because I was starting to feel like I was crazy or some
conspiracy theorist.

It was one thing to have suspicions, but an investigator with twenty-plus years of experience and

no score to settle with the church confirmed what I'd been fearing all along.

If I couldn't say definitively that the church was directing my downfall, I strongly believed that was the case.

CHAPTER EIGHTEEN
Paul Haggis

◈

In January 2012, I reached out to Paul Haggis for advice about how to gain control of what was becoming an out-of-control situation. I was grateful when he agreed to meet with Charley and me for lunch. Paul is one of the church's most famous defectors. An Oscar-winning screenwriter and film director, he had broken with the church three years earlier, in part because of its cruel treatment of his daughter when she came out as a lesbian. He'd told his story to Lawrence Wright, who went on to publish a long exposé in **The New Yorker**, after which the church excoriated both him and the writer. I admired his grit. We arrived at the restaurant after Paul. He was obviously a regular.

"Oh, yes!" the hostess said. "Yes! Of course! He's right over there."

Paul was unshaven and dressed in jeans and scuffed boots, the embodiment of what I thought a laid-back director type should look like. For the first few minutes, Paul and Charley talked about people they knew in common and projects each of them was working on. I found Paul to be warm and easy to talk to, but I was anxious about raising the subject of the church. Even though he had left Scientology behind in defense of his gay daughter, I wondered how much, if any, of the "group-think" lingered.

The church had launched a full-fledged smear campaign against Paul after the **New Yorker** piece. In a rebuttal published in the church's magazine, his own sister, a Scientologist, was quoted, calling him "a chronic liar" and "a born con artist." In an accompanying video on the church magazine website, she said his avarice drove him to step over anyone who got in his way.

"He can't do this," she cried. "He has to know it's not okay to destroy the reputations of good and decent people on the altar of his ambitions."

I wondered if the tears she shed were even vaguely about betraying her own brother. Or had she, like the rest of us, been programmed to defend the church at all cost? Even at the expense of our own families.

Watching Paul's interaction with Charley, I decided to trust him with my story. I found him to be compassionate and genuinely concerned about the state investigations and the flurry of damning reports that had been written about me by my fellow Scientologists.

"This is a lot of crazy shit," Charley said, looking between Paul and me. "And what kind of religion has people write reports on each other?"

"This is not a religion," he said. "This is a cult that has brainwashed you, Michelle. I know how difficult it is to realize what you were a part of and how hard it is to get out."

I assured Paul that my eyes were wide-open. Over the past several years, I'd recognized the lunacy and distanced myself from the church. My worry was, how could I stop the runaway train that I was certain had been engineered by the church?

Paul didn't mince words. There was more trouble ahead, he said. He could almost guarantee it. The church considered me an enemy and that meant one thing: No matter what it took or how long, I had to be discredited and destroyed. If they couldn't accomplish it by feeding the state with their bullshit, he said, they would find another way. "They will go through your trash, they will follow you, they will do whatever they have to do to destroy you, the same way they did to me," he said.

Paul was steadfast with his advice that I go public with my story. He said if I hadn't already, I needed to come clean with everything in my past that the church could—and would—use against me. He had been open with Lawrence Wright about having done drugs and stolen as a kid because he knew the church would cull the contents of his ethics file and make hay with whatever was there.

The book Wright was writing would be a perfect platform for me to tell my story, Paul said. Transparency was the only way.

"Let me get him in touch with you," he said.

———◈———

I consulted my attorneys and they advised against going public with my story. It was too soon, they said. While the state was still conducting its investigation, I could incriminate myself without even knowing it. But I hadn't done anything wrong except trust the wrong person, I said. I was a victim as much as anyone in the case. Why couldn't I just go to the state and tell them what I knew? The attorneys said it was too risky. The state could take whatever I said and twist it to their advantage. Government agencies worked together, they said. Depending on the outcome of investigations by the Department of Corporations and the Department of Insurance, I was still subject to criminal charges.

I couldn't shake the feeling that Paul was right when he predicted more trouble ahead, but I had to believe the government would do right by me once they realized that whatever information they had been fed to start them on this path came from people with agendas from the Church of Scientology.

I hired a law firm to develop a trust to pay back my clients whatever they had lost from investing in Dror's productions. I was determined to do whatever was needed to make sure they were compensated. I knew my clients were fearful for their financial futures, yet they couldn't have been more supportive and I was humbled by their willingness to stand by me. Most of us had enjoyed long and trusting relationships. They knew my character, and that I never would have intentionally risked their hard-earned savings. It was all because of my blind trust in a fellow Scientologist. But that didn't dull the pain and guilt I felt for their anguish. They had lost money—in some cases, their life savings—because they had taken **my** advice. How could I live with that knowledge? How could I make them see that I would rather go broke myself than watch them suffer? If it took the rest of my life, I would pay back everything they had lost.

That April, the kids and I moved from our gated community in Valencia to a smaller home in Pasadena to be closer to Charley. Charley and Maria were legally separated and working out the terms of their divorce, and our relationship was in full bloom.

Within a week of the move, I began noticing cars I didn't recognize parked outside the house. It was usually the same scenario: a man in the driver's seat passing the time reading a newspaper. I tried not to think the worst, but by then I'd read a lot about the church's longtime use of private investigators to gather "intelligence" on its enemies.

One day, the same car appeared on and off all day outside my house, then came back at night and parked at the curb. In the shadow of darkness, I could see a person get out, look around and get back in again. I was frightened and called my attorney and friend, Pam Johnson, who was a formidable woman. I told her the same car had been there a day earlier. Pam lived a short distance from me. She drove to my home and confronted the man.

"What are you doing here?" she asked.

"I need to get a few things to Michelle," he said. At nine o'clock at night?

"You can give whatever you have to me," Pam said. The man put his car in gear and drove off.

After that, I didn't go anywhere without checking my surroundings. Cars were always parked outside. I was often followed when I drove anywhere—to the grocery store, to the bank, to the kids' schools. On one particular afternoon, I circled around and got behind the car following me. It had a Scientology symbol on the bumper.

A short time later, my dad was visiting from Nevada. One night he noticed someone sitting in a car outside for a long time. We turned out the lights and sat on the couch, watching as the car drove slowly back and forth in front of the house. The car stopped at the curb. We saw someone get out, then in again, and continue sitting there, watching. Dad wanted to go outside to confront him, but I wouldn't let him. I leaned my head on his shoulder. "I'm scared," I said.

"I'm scared for you," he replied.

———◈———

In August, my clients and I agreed on the terms of the trust: Their losses amounted to $11.8 million. An independent accounting firm determined that by liquidating most of my assets and promising 35 percent of my future income, I could contribute $8.5 million. I decided to subsidize the remainder using outstanding residuals from insurance deals that were coming due. It would take some time to get the trust finalized, but everyone was satisfied with the proposal. Dror was nowhere to be found.

Things seemed like they might be turning around.

For the first time in months, I saw hope on the horizon.

Once my clients were paid off, I would get back on my feet and begin life anew. I wasn't afraid of hard work and I could earn back whatever I'd lost. Somehow I would convince my mother to leave the church. My children were thriving. And I had Charley, the love of my life.

With the state's investigation looming over me, Charley decided to take me away to New York for a long weekend. New York was a blissful place for us. We'd spent many wonderful days and nights in the city and we loved it there. Charley booked a room at the Ritz with a view of Central Park. On our second night, we had dinner at our favorite restaurant in the Meatpacking District. In the dim, candlelit room, I stared at Charley as she studied the menu. I admired her sophisticated good looks and I loved it when she wore her sexy glasses.

"What are you staring at?" she asked.

"You! The love of my life! The sexy love of my life!" I answered.

"Mmm, I love that! Maybe we need to cut this dinner short!" she said.

"Maybe so."

Charley and I. We were perfect together in so many ways. Even if it was just eating dinner together, she could make me forget all of my problems.

With encouragement from Charley, I began putting myself out in the real world. I made new friends and we made friends together. One was Pat Mitchell, the media mogul who once headed PBS and was now chief executive of the Paley Center for Media.

Charley and I met Pat and her husband, Scott

Seydel, at an annual "think tank" retreat that Norman Lear hosts every year at his southern Vermont farm, formerly the home of the poet Robert Frost. I was forty years old and in the presence of media icons Norman Lear and Bill Moyers and Pat Mitchell. It might have been an intimidating experience—especially since I'd only recently begun to take an interest in the great big world outside of Scientology—but everyone was warm and welcoming.

Pat is all about empowering women, and she took me under her wing. I'd told her about my struggle transitioning out of the church, how my whole adult life had been lived around it and how everything I'd done and everyone I'd known was in some way related to it. I wasn't sure how to begin rebuilding my life outside of Scientology.

In September, one month after my clients and I had come to an agreement on the trust, and I felt freer than I had since my troubles began back in July 2010, Pat invited me to New York City for a women's conference where she was a guest speaker. It was a three-day summit focused on investing in initiatives that benefited women and girls around the globe. I was so excited to go. I missed my charitable work and was champing at the possibility of getting involved again.

The conference began on Thursday, September 20, with an inspiring keynote speech by Gloria Steinem. For the first time in a long time, I felt a sense of purpose I hadn't had since my human rights work for the church. I felt as if I belonged.

Pat's speech was Friday morning. She had just begun speaking when I felt my cell phone vibrating. I ignored it, but the vibrating went on and on, so finally I took the phone out of my purse to see who was trying so frantically to reach me. Of course, my first thought was always the kids. The missed calls had been followed by a stream of text messages from my friend Simon.

"OMG!" the first message said. "Have you seen the **Hollywood Reporter**?" It was followed by a headline: "State of California Sues Movie Producers over Alleged Ponzi Scheme."

Then: "Michelle! This is about you and Dror!"

My face went white.

I quickly googled the story.

The Department of Corporations had filed a lawsuit against Dror and me.

"The suit claims a 2009 movie starring Simon Baker and Paz Vega cheated investors, many of them senior citizens, out of millions of dollars," the subtitle read.

I continued to read in disbelief:

According to a lawsuit filed Thursday in Los Angeles Superior Court and obtained by **The Hollywood Reporter**, the defendants used the money raised to pay large commissions, skim money to various interrelated companies and distribute divi-

dends to investors until that abruptly stopped. . . .
"Defendants specifically targeted unsophisticated
senior investors," says the suit, filed by the state's
corporations commissioner. . . . "Many investors
face significant hardships," says the suit, "including an inability to pay for basic necessities such as
housing and medical care."

I was stunned. Where had this come from? Why
didn't I know? Barely able to keep my balance, I
stood up, fled from the summit and caught a flight
home. Before I could get there, the **Los Angeles
Times** had come out with its own story.

Seward . . . allegedly convinced her clients to
invest their life savings in a film directed by Soref
called **Not Forgotten**. . . . Seward convinced
clients to cash in their annuities early—causing
them to pay steep penalties—by promising returns of 10% to 18% on their investment in **Not
Forgotten**, according to investigators.

After the film's completion, Seward and
Soref solicited more funds from investors to
produce several films through a company called
Windsor Pictures LLC. However, money used
to form Windsor Pictures was instead used to
pay back investors in the production of **Not
Forgotten**.

More than 140 people were victims of the
scheme, which operated between 2007 and 2010.

Most were retirees living in Los Angeles and Kern counties, according to investigators.

The alleged scheme is thought to be among the most elaborate film investment frauds the department has investigated.

How many of my clients had already read the reports before I had the chance to tell them? I wondered. **What must they be thinking?**

The lawsuit undid the settlement agreement my clients and I had spent months negotiating. It was now the state's job to determine a fair resolution. My good name was mud. My company was bleeding clients and my assets were depleting faster than I could earn money.

I was hit from all sides after that. Sean was granted temporary custody of our children during a simple court hearing about where they would attend school. Sean attached the state filing in his court brief and the judge ruled in his favor. I was devastated and couldn't even walk out of the courtroom on my own.

Two of my most profitable accounts, Beth Linder and Kirstie Alley, pulled their business. It was the death knell for my company. Beth wrote me a "disconnection" e-mail and backed out of her policy deal a year early, with a penalty to me of $1.5 million.

I knew where it was all coming from. **Kick 'em when they're down**—I'd learned it during the briefing on the Black Propaganda campaign against the BBC reporter.

I remembered something L. Ron Hubbard wrote: "The purpose of the suit is to harass and discourage rather than to win. The law can be used very easily to harass, and enough harassment on somebody who is simply on the thin edge anyway, well knowing that he is not authorized, will generally be sufficient to cause his professional decease. If possible, of course, ruin him utterly."

The fog in my brain had finally completely lifted. I finally understood, completely and without a doubt, that my so-called religion was a cult. For the first time in years, emotions I had been taught to ignore spilled over. Sometimes I felt like a fool for having been so blind, and for so long. I was furious over the church's betrayal—of me and so many other believers—and fearful of what lay ahead. I was overwhelmed by remorse about people I had hurt along the way because of my twisted religious beliefs. Sometimes my regrets hung over me like a storm cloud and I couldn't see the light that another day could bring, but then I would remind myself that I was a victim, like so many others, of a calculated scam called Scientology.

Along with that knowledge came a certain freedom. I would reteach myself how to be the person I was before the church infiltrated the mind of a vulnerable young girl and then systematically and subliminally indoctrinated her into the warped imaginings of L. Ron Hubbard. **They can take away all of my belongings,** I told myself. **They can ruin my business. But they cannot destroy who I am. Or whom I love.**

It was time for me to regain my strength and my children! I knew that Sean was only interested in money, so I sold the little bit that I had left and negotiated his price. For $25,000 up front and $2500 in monthly payments, I would have my children back the following day. I could not fight this cult or the state without them safe and by my side.

The next day, seeing their scared little faces as they ran into my arms, I felt I was receiving the greatest gift on earth! My older son, Sage, looked so sad and confused that I knew this was taking a much bigger toll on him than I had imagined.

Once my children were back, I had to deal with the collateral damage of my former belief system.

CHAPTER NINETEEN

Defection

◈

I repeatedly begged my mother to leave the church, to see that all my misfortune began when I came out as gay, that the church was persecuting me for it. For more than two years, she had repeatedly appealed to the church for ways to help me, but all she'd received were more probing questions about me and my life. What was I doing? Who was I with? How was my business? What kind of income was I bringing in? Could she get me to make another donation? Tell us more about this woman she's with. She had always answered their questions, trusting the church's word that they were only asking so they could help me. Whenever my mother tried convincing me that they were asking out of concern, I pleaded with her to open her eyes. The church had no intention of helping me. My fellow Scientologists—the people I had been taught to trust blindly—were trolling for information to hurt me.

Mom had doubted me for the longest time, but then she began asking herself: Might she be blind to what was happening? She had been with the church for twenty-six years. Was everything she thought colored by her bubblelike existence? Perhaps she didn't even know how to think for herself anymore. But the idea that she could be so wrong frightened her, so she wavered for a while.

That September the Ethics Department sent my mother to visit me in a last-ditch attempt to bring me back to the church. I unloaded all the things I'd learned and all my suspicions about the church's role in my misfortune of the last few years. About the strange cars sitting outside, always someone watching. All the lies told about me. The shadowy behavior by church members. The chaos that had been thrust upon my personal and professional life had left me angry and disillusioned, I said.

That day, I'd given my mother a smartphone. At first she said no—as a Sea Org member, she was forbidden to have her own phone—but she finally accepted it. She kept the phone hidden, but every chance she got she used it to search the Internet for information about the things I'd been telling her. Reading the claims of ex-communicants about vendettas by the church, she recognized a pattern.

Their stories were chillingly similar to what was happening to me.

After Mom returned from her visit with me, she was ordered to meet with an ethics officer daily. She was told that since I was doing so poorly in my life, it was affecting her performance in the Sea Org. She was taken off her post, the ethics officer told her, on the orders of "those senior to him." Her every move was monitored. She was not permitted to talk to anyone except for the ethics officer, who assigned her to read articles by L. Ron Hubbard every day and night.

After a month of this, my sixty-year-old mother was confined to her room at the Los Angeles "berthing" and ordered not to leave unless an ethics officer accompanied her. She was under house arrest.

An ethics officer brought her a copy of the church's "Disconnection Policy" (which it claims doesn't exist). She already knew what it said: Members who associate with "enemies" of the church risk being declared enemies themselves unless they "disconnected."

The ethics officer told my mother that if she stayed connected to me, she would be banished from the church and lose her chance for immortality. She started to cry and told the auditor that she needed the church, but she didn't want to sever her ties with me. He listened intently and prescribed a series of auditing sessions to help her make the right decision. He said it would take two weeks to set it up and the actual program would take two to four weeks.

She called me that night from the bathroom.

"I have to make my escape this week," she whispered. She told me about the meeting with the ethics officer and said they planned to have her call me the following afternoon to explain that she would be off the grid for a while and I shouldn't worry. The ethics officer had coached her about what to say. He would be listening in. She had seen fellow church members "disappear" under similar circumstances. She had heard whispers about Sea Org members banished to prison-like camps and not seen again for months or years. Sometimes not ever. She was determined it was not going to happen to her.

We hatched a plan: When Mom told me she would be going away for a while, I would vehemently object. She would assure me she was fine, but I would insist she was being held against her will and threaten to make a lot of noise in the press.

"Whatever I say, know I don't mean it—and fight back," my mother said before hanging up the phone.

The call was scheduled for one p.m. the next day. I worried there was time for my mother to change her mind. Or that the church would whisk her away first and I wouldn't know where she was.

The morning seemed endless. Mom called a minute after one p.m.

"Hey, Michelle!" she said, sounding breezy.

"Hey, Mom," I replied. "How's it going? It sounds like you're on speakerphone."

"Yes. I'm with the ethics officer."

"What's going on?" I asked.

As planned, Mom explained she was going away for a while for auditing and wouldn't be in touch.

"Mother, you listen to me!" I cried. "And Dave the ethics officer, you listen too," I demanded. "Let me be clear. I am not messing around. I am not scared of you and my mother is getting out of there today. If you don't have her in front of the Hollywood Guaranty Building, I will contact the police and tell them you are holding her against her will. And when I come there, I will bring the press with me. Don't doubt me. This is not an idle threat. My mother is getting out of there today."

Mom tried to object. "Honey, I'm fine," she said. "This is something I want to do."

"Mother! I don't want to hear it!" I said. "You are to get back to me by three p.m. If I don't hear from you, I will show up with the police and the press."

"Okay, honey," she said. "I'll call you back."

I was shaking when I hung up the phone. **Holy shit!** I thought. **I just threatened to call the police on the Church of Scientology!**

Waiting for a call back from my mother was dreadful. Finally, at two thirty p.m., she called.

"Michelle," she said calmly, "I have my things. They want you to meet me in Denny's parking lot on Sunset Boulevard at three."

"Denny's?" I said. The pancake house? If the situation hadn't been so serious, I would have laughed. "I'll be there," I said.

In exchange for being let go, Mom was ordered to sign a waiver stating that she understood if she ever spoke out against the church she would be fined $25,000 for each offense. They told her that if she didn't sign it, they would not let her go. She signed it and asked for a copy. They refused. A security guard watched her pack her things. Sweet notes she had written to her roommates were confiscated. Her bags were searched and her iPad was wiped clean. She had hidden the cell phone between her underwear and her pants.

I pulled into Denny's at three p.m. and saw Mom standing there with three boxes containing all her worldly possessions. A white van idled at the other end of the parking lot.

"Security?" I asked. Mom nodded.

I loaded her three boxes into the trunk of my car and started to pull away.

It was a perfect October afternoon. The sky was pastel blue, the sun was golden and a slight breeze blew.

As the ethics officers watched from the van, I

opened my window, pumped my fist in the air
and shouted at the top of my lungs: "FUCK YOU,
SCIENTOLOGY!"

Freeeeeeeeeeeeedom!

◈

My mom and I had been through so much together over the years and I wasn't about to leave
without her with me. I had nothing, but everything. I couldn't afford to support my family any
longer, but I was in love and we were happy. In
November, Charley found a home for all of us
in the mountainous La Cañada section of Pasadena. It was a Spanish-style cottage surrounded
by tall ponderosa pines and wisteria. The house
was small enough to feel intimate and cozy
but large enough to accommodate the kids,
Mom, Charley and me. We became a real family
there. Charley and I loved to cook dinner together
and have the kids sit down at our long French farm
table to eat and talk. Nothing was better than
when Charley's daughter, who was in vet school
at UGA, came to visit. We felt complete. We had
friends over. New friends. Our friends.

I began to feel some balance in my life. Savannah and the twins were thriving.

Mom was rediscovering such simple pleasures as
watching TV and reading magazines. Sometimes
she just stood on the patio behind the house and
seemed to be drinking in her freedom.

My oldest son, Sage, who was by now a teenager, chose to live part-time with his father in Valencia. The influence of school and friends won out, so I had to settle for visitations every other weekend. I picked him up on Friday after school and dropped him back off on Monday mornings. We shared a special mother-son dinner once a week. It was hardly ideal, but it was what my son wanted. There was still a lot of bitterness between Sean and me, and that was hard on all of us, but especially on Sage. I felt like I had failed him and I lived in fear that Sean would get him involved in the church. Nothing I said could change his mind and I didn't want to lose him, so we made the best of every moment we were together.

The days of multiple nannies and personal shoppers and fancy cars were behind me, but I didn't care. Except for the situation with Sage, I was happier than I had ever been. I loved being home to make lunches for the kids and walk them to school in the morning. I listened to music as I ran along the winding streets of our neighborhood. Charley and I sat at the fireside in our study and read passages from a book by Mark Nepo, **Finding Inner Courage**. In many ways, I felt as if I had recaptured the girl I was when I used to sit at my grandparents' cabin, admiring the simple things in life. The blooming flowers. The chirping birds. Things I had taken for granted for too long while

I chased the superficial dreams I had been taught by the church.

All that fall I had been involved in mediation talks with the Department of Corporations. A judge had ruled that the word "fraud" be taken out of the equation and ordered the mediation to determine restitution for the movie investors. The talks led to a settlement, five days before Christmas, of $17.4 million, the portion of the $23 million in investments that investors had yet to recover. Only half of the seventy-eight investors were my clients. Dror and Scott Foulk, the former vice president of my insurance firm, had brought the others in.

I learned that Dror had filed for bankruptcy— for the third time. That meant his creditors were prohibited from going after his personal assets, so he was effectively off the hook.

"The agreement resolves the department's civil action alleging the offer and sale of unqualified securities in violation of state law," the Department of Corporations wrote in a press release. I breathed a sigh of relief. All I had ever wanted was that my clients be reimbursed for their losses.

I rang in the year 2014 with a toast to the future. I had so much to be thankful for. My beautiful children, my loyal partner, my mom's safety. I vowed to put the nightmare behind me and work day and night to restore my insurance business and repay my clients in full. It was not to be.

That same month, the state Department of Insurance filed a sixty-four-page accusation against me to revoke my insurance license.

Shortly after my attorneys informed me, I got a call from my friend Michael, who said he'd been contacted by the state investigator in charge of both the Department of Corporations and the Department of Insurance cases.

The investigator told Michael that he had in his possession a copy of a recent e-mail exchange between Michael and me, and he had a few questions about it. Michael asked the investigator how he'd gotten access to my private e-mail account. With a subpoena? If so, for what? he asked. The investigator told Michael there was no subpoena; he'd received the e-mail in an unmarked envelope delivered to his office.

The e-mail exchange, which was innocuous, had happened two years after Celeste left my company—and both my server and e-mail accounts had been changed since then. Obviously, my new account had been breached. I contacted my attorneys and they agreed that something wasn't right. Hacking was illegal, whether it was by the church, an individual or the investigator for the State of California.

My attorney's IT experts went back to work. They discovered that three of the last five IP addresses that had accessed my e-mail account were not mine.

When is this going to end?

The investigator also contacted some of my former clients who had remained loyal friends. They informed me that he seemed to have a peculiar interest in keeping the heat on me. He'd called me a "beautiful psychopath" and told some of them I had money hidden in a Swiss bank account. Hardly.

Most disturbing, he told my clients he'd received information in an unmarked white envelope that proved I was a criminal. He said he was personally going to see to it that I went to jail.

———◈———

In March, my mom came upstairs holding my old cell phone, which I'd given her when I changed my number. She had just received a text from the carrier noting that my contact information had been changed.

"I didn't do that. Did you?" Mom asked.

"I didn't change anything," I said.

I immediately called the carrier to ask for an explanation. They told me a woman claiming to be me had called earlier that morning to "update my billing address" to a post office box number. To do that, she needed my birth date and social security number, which she did indeed have. She gave my former home telephone number as a contact number, and she knew the names of my children, whose phones were also on my account.

That narrowed the list of suspects to a handful of people who knew me intimately, and all were Scientologists.

I remembered that, a few months back, when I hadn't received a bill, I'd checked with the carrier and was told the bill had been sent to a different address, a post office box. I had just assumed it was their mistake and changed the address back to mine. Now I wondered.

"Can you check your records to see if the new box number is the same as it was that time?" I asked.

"Of course," the representative said.

I heard the clicking of her keyboard, and then a sigh.

"I'm afraid it is," she said.

"Why would someone do that?" I asked.

But in truth I already knew. The bill showed the numbers of everyone I called and texted during the month.

"The church," Mom said.

"Yes," I said. "The church."

At first I was angry, but then I felt the same sense of satisfaction I did each time I found a link to the church that confirmed my suspicions. I **wasn't** crazy. Given all the pieces, I came to the only conclusion that made sense: They **were** following me. They **had** stolen my digital profile. My client information. My e-mails. And they had obviously attempted to steal my phone records. They

were trying to destroy me. "The law can be used very easily to harass, and enough harassment on somebody who is simply on the thin edge anyway, well knowing that he is not authorized, will generally be sufficient to cause his professional decease. If possible, of course, ruin him utterly."

What I didn't understand was how the government of the State of California allowed itself to be influenced by an organization that was known for being corrupt and vindictive.

That was terrifying.

CHAPTER TWENTY

Criminal Charges

I couldn't afford to fight the Department of Insurance's case in court, so I was forced to agree to give up my license to practice for five years. As relieved as I felt to have my legal problems behind me—as far as I knew, anyway—losing my license meant I could never recover my business. Insurance was all I'd ever known. I didn't have a college degree. I didn't have the money to start a new business. How would I ever repay my clients if I couldn't collect the insurance residuals I'd been counting on when we'd agreed to the trust? How would I support my children and my mom?

Charley tried to comfort me by saying she would always take care of us, but I couldn't possibly ask her to do more than she already was. I felt like a total failure. Everything I'd worked my whole life for was gone.

I tried to remind myself that I still had Charley and the kids, so what else mattered? But I constantly fought feelings of worthlessness. What did I have to offer anyone anymore?

I spent my time trying to be the best mother and partner I could be. I cooked and cleaned and saw to it that nothing in the house was out of place. I pasted on a fake smile, but inside I was seething. I hated my life. I hated Dror and Sean and Celeste and the state's investigator. I hated the church. I became difficult to live with. Charley couldn't leave a sock on the floor without me making a comment, and the children's manners at dinner had better be perfect or else. I ran in the mornings to try to work off some of the smoldering resentment I felt, but it didn't do much.

Charley said I was becoming mean. She begged me to see someone. She said everyone was walking on eggshells and our home was no longer happy. I needed professional help.

I finally gave in and took her advice. I made an appointment with a psychologist and committed to regular appointments. Over time, I started to allow myself hope for a brighter future.

I'd had nine more months of relative peace— except for the strange cars that still idled outside our home, but I had grown accustomed to that.

Then our home was raided on that October morning in 2014. I still didn't know what they expected to find in my house that day, but I remembered all too well how the agents had sneaked up onto my property under the cover of a gray dawn and terrorized my children, my mother and me.

After tearing my house apart, all they could say was the state had been "informed" that I had property in my possession proving I'd committed a felony. Informed by whom? And what property exactly? The state's investigator had been there that day. I didn't want him in my house and asked that he be made to wait outside while the officers did their search. I wanted to scream at him. **Enough! What do you think you know?** What was in my possession that pointed to a crime? Nothing. Because I had not committed a crime. I have never committed a crime!

———◈———

I had to get away from Los Angeles. I felt like the place had eaten me alive. Everywhere I turned there was a reminder of Scientology. The buildings are everywhere. The light blue tops and dark blue bottoms that make up the Sea Org uniforms. Billboards recruiting members. Eight-pointed Scientology crosses (representing Hubbard's "Eight Dynamics" of life). Bumper stickers, some of which actually made me laugh—"Lord Xenu is my home-

boy" or "Scientology: Out of This World" . . . I
didn't have a business to keep me in California anymore, and the house in La Cañada, which all of us
had once adored, didn't seem safe after the police
invasion. I was tired of being watched and hacked
and followed. I just wanted to live peacefully with
my family.

Atlanta had become like a second home during the time we'd spent there for **Twist**. Our best
friends, Pat and Scott, had a home there. The
kids loved it and Charley had kept an office there.
When the lease was up on the house, we moved to
Georgia. Mom had an apartment within walking
distance of us, the first time in thirty years she had
a place of her own. Charley and I joined the local
Episcopal church, a place where there was no judgment or ridicule. People didn't write one another
up or instigate hate campaigns.

Our new environment was rustic, with lush
trees, tall grass, walking paths and horse farms.
There were no eight-pointed Scientology crosses to
be found. I loved being surrounded by nature. I
finally felt at peace. The only drawback was that
Sage had decided to stay in Los Angeles with his
father. He was old enough to make his own decision, so I agreed. But I vowed to see him every
other weekend, whether that meant me going to
him or him coming to us.

It was during one of those trips to Los Angeles to
see Sage, in September 2015, two months after the

move, eleven months after the raid on my house, that I learned I was going to be arrested. I had settled with the Department of Corporations. Given up my license to the Department of Insurance. It still wasn't enough. What the investigator had vowed would happen—what he'd told my friends he was determined to accomplish—was coming true. The Los Angeles County District Attorney was charging me criminally. The search of my home for "proof I had committed a felony" had yielded nothing, but apparently the state felt as if it had enough damning evidence to charge me with a crime.

I had just landed at LAX and was parking my rental car in a hotel parking lot when I got the call from Dan Nixon, the criminal attorney Steve Cooley had recommended when my house was searched. Dan told me that both Dror and I were being charged with fraud in connection with what the government insisted was a Ponzi scheme. Both he and Steve were caught off guard by the criminal charges, he said. I burst into tears.

"I'm sorry," Dan said. "Please try to stay calm. You have to stay focused. We'll figure this out."

I couldn't calm down. I hated him at that moment, and I heaped all my misguided anger on him. "I thought you told me this was all going away!" I cried. "I agreed to a settlement for something I didn't do because you told me to agree to it! I gave up my professional license. My whole career!" I screamed, ending the call.

For one fleeting moment, I thought about going to my hotel room and ending my life.

Instead, I checked in, went to my room and collapsed on the bed. I wondered if I had any fight left in me. I was tired of fighting. Tired of trying to do right and being accused of terrible wrongs.

I called Charley and wept some more.

"What about my children?" I cried. "They will grow up knowing their mother was arrested. That monster will get custody. What about their futures? This is so unfair!"

She tried to calm me, but it was no use.

I thought about how Charley had taken care of us so well and so selflessly after I'd lost everything. She had given up so much to protect me. To protect us. She had done more than I could imagine almost anyone doing. But would she be able to get through this now with me? Could I expect our love to survive?

What about my former clients, the people who had trusted me, believed in me? I wondered. How would I ever repay them if I went to jail? Hundreds of people had been hurt, and for what? Because the Church of Scientology decided I was an enemy and spread lies about me? The government had even used the same words that my fellow Scientologists used in their reports to the church.

The criminal case made headlines. A spokeswoman for the district attorney was quoted as saying, "It's certainly one of the largest Ponzi schemes that I can recall."

My life was at its lowest point. It was hard for me to get out of bed or even eat. My family would tell me that everything was going to be okay, but it was not okay. Charley knew that I was not pulling out of my depression, so she called my sister and asked her to fly in to see me.

When Jess arrived, I collapsed into her arms and cried harder than I had ever cried. I was able to tell Jess things that I couldn't say to anyone else because everyone else wanted to solve the problem for me. Charley wanted me to buck up and fight. My mom was angry and overwhelmed with guilt. My attorneys didn't want to hear the crying. I knew Jess couldn't fix my problems, but she listened. I was able to be honest with her. I was able to tell her that I didn't want my children visiting me in jail or that I didn't have the strength to fight anymore. I was able to say what I was holding so close to my heart. Everyone was better off with me dead. That brutal honesty was my first step up. Saying it out loud made me hear how low I had actually gone.

Jess looked at me, held my hand and said, "Chell, if you choose to leave us, you will let them win. You will let the truth be buried, you will let your children fall into the grip of Scientology and you will show Charley that love did not prevail. **Do not let them win.**"

Those words stung like ice and woke me up. I felt the fire in my core reignite. I had truth on my side! I would not let them win or take my children from me, and I sure as hell would not let Charley ever believe that our love was not worth the fight to me!

After that, I spent my days combing through legal documents, check registers, e-mails—anything to help my attorneys prove my innocence. I started my mornings with long walks in the wildflower meadow near our home waiting for some kind of message or epiphany. Why was this happening? What was I supposed to be seeing? One day, I stopped and sat on a stone with my legs crossed, my face to the sun, and closed my eyes. I saw my grandmother and she was smiling. I heard her speaking. **Be open, Michelle. Be who you are. Be kind. You will be fine**. When I opened my eyes, I felt an urge to take a selfie. When I got home and looked at the picture, I saw what looked like an angel standing over my shoulder. I knew I wasn't in this alone. It reminded me of the daily calls from Charley's second oldest sister wanting to know that I was okay or the constant messages of inspiration that Kathy Ridenour sent my way. I could feel something happening in the universe. It was almost like a quiet hum of prayer, almost out of range, but I could feel it. It was that hum of love that kept me going when days clouded over.

During the discovery process for my case, I finally learned that the state's interest in me had indeed begun with an anonymous letter. It was written in March 2011, eight months after Mary Mauser had confronted me about being gay, three months after the birthday party where the other Scientology woman came out to me, two months after one of them wrote the report at Flag in Florida accusing me of promoting homosexuality, one month after Dror had returned from Flag, where he'd been summoned for a Sec Check.

The letter, dated March 8, 2011, read:

> We wish to remain anonymous as we fear retribution from the parties involved in this multimillion-dollar Ponzi scheme which has bilked investors out of millions of dollars! Most of these investors are retired seniors and have no idea their money has been squandered away to support the lifestyles and business ventures of these guilty parties. Investor money was spent on expensive cars, living in expensive homes and having lavish offices at Paramount Studios.
>
> The scheme dates back to 2007, maybe longer, whereby these parties sold unregistered securities under the guise of production loans to try and skate regulations and give the appearance these investments were 100 percent secure. Investors were promised returns of 10 percent up to 12 percent annually and were provided with unsecured promissory notes which the issuing

parties knowingly could not pay and didn't have assets to back. They convinced earlier investors to roll their original production loans or investments over into future movie and live stage projects and paid interest using newer investor money to older investors, which now numbers well over 100 investors.

What frightened me was that what had started with an anonymous letter from someone I firmly believed was a Scientologist had carried through, almost with the same wording, to the day's headlines.

How did this vendetta get so far? I asked myself. I thought the justice system would protect me. Far from it. It had victimized me just as the church had.

Over the next year, I provided the State of California with definitive proof that I had done nothing wrong. I offered up bank statements I'd found in discovery, showing how Dror had transferred millions of my clients' money from the intended movie investment account to his own personal and business accounts. I volunteered to be interviewed by the DA and answered every question asked of me. I learned that the state's investigator had not turned over anything that had been confiscated from my home. As it turned out, much of it would have helped my case. In finally going through the boxes, we discovered he'd held back evidence that would have proved my innocence. What was his motive? Was he somehow connected to the church? Was he being paid to incriminate me? Was he under pressure from his bosses to get me charged? Whatever the reason, the damage was done and, as far as I know, without consequences for him.

On September 21, 2016, the Los Angeles County District Attorney offered me immunity in exchange for my testimony against Dror. I accepted the offer.

My friend Jonathan has a theory, and it wasn't lost on me in the midst of all this. He said that during his many years of working with prosecutors, he'd known many who were interested only in getting at the truth. But he also knew others who would do anything to save face and protect their reputations, even if it meant sacrificing the innocent.

It sounded a lot like a church I knew.

On March 30, 2017, the state dismissed seventy of the seventy-two charges against Dror based on the statute of limitations. The other two were dropped for lack of proof of intent to defraud. He got off scot-free because of a technicality . . . but he will have to live with his guilt.

My charges were dropped—not on a technicality but, in the words of the court, "in the interest of justice." It took six years, and in the end truth prevailed. I was innocent.

Finally, I am free. Free for my children. Free to love the person I do. Free to start over.

Meanwhile, revelations about the church and its powerful influence, even over institutions that are meant to protect us, continue to emerge. What happened to me is over, but I worry about other victims—people who may not have the stamina, the support or the resources that I had for the fight of my life. Just recently I was reading about the lagging investigation of four women who claim they were sexually assaulted by the actor and longtime Scientologist Danny Masterson. One of the women, a Scientologist herself, filed a police report with the LAPD in 2004, but the case was derailed after dozens of Scientologists filed affidavits refuting the story. Masterson has denied any allegations of rape and claims the encounters in question were consensual. What sent chills down my spine was an excerpt from a letter that one of Masterson's alleged victims sent to LAPD chief Charlie Beck, which was published in the Underground Bunker, a blog by investigative journalist Tony Ortega. The victim wrote that an investigator handling the case admitted to her that she was worried about the investigation because "some LAPD officers are very friendly with the church of Scientology."

The Masterson case has since been sent up for further investigation to the Los Angeles District Attorney's Office—the same office that charged me.

The Underground Bunker reported that the victims have told their stories to Leah Remini—the actress who so boldly left the church, then bravely wrote a book about her experience—for her A&E series, **Leah Remini: Scientology and the Aftermath.** But the district attorney stepped in and requested that the episode be held until the investigation is complete and they decide whether to charge Masterson. I'm not holding my breath, but I hope the women get the chance to tell their stories publicly. Every person who steps up takes power away from the omnipotent church and makes it that much more difficult for them to hurt the next person. And the next.

<hr>

On April 7, 2017, I was on a plane from New York to Los Angeles. The ride was bumpy and I prayed to God to keep me safe. When I opened my eyes again, I looked to my left and saw Leah Remini.

I'd met Leah through the years at church functions, and we had both been part of the Black Propaganda campaign against the BBC reporter years earlier, but we didn't really know each other. I'd followed her very public break with the church and knew about her successful television show showcasing other victims of Scientology. I admired her.

I got up all my courage and approached her,

fearful she might reject me. She couldn't have been nicer. She had lost the hard edge she'd learned (as I had) in the church and her eyes were soft and warm. I quickly told her my story and she listened intently. We hugged and vowed to talk again. I hope we do. In the name of truth. And justice.

AFTERWORD

Sunshine pours through my window this morning, brightening a bowl of oranges on the kitchen table. Quiet has settled over the house. In a little while, I'll head to the park with Charley and the kids, but I am enjoying this brief stillness after the quagmire of legal problems and uncertainty that had become my life.

For so many years, I was afraid of silence and all it connoted. A dearth of noise meant inaction, lack of progress, failure, laziness. What I never understood, until now, was the real reason silence was so challenging.

"We cannot see our reflection in running water," according to an ancient Chinese proverb. "It is only in still water that we can see."

In the quiet, you must confront your thoughts. Silence requires the maintenance of an inner life. You are alone with yourself. Appearances matter little. Professional success is irrelevant. What bubbles up are your memories and feelings, specifically how you feel about yourself and your loved ones. And sometimes you think about your place in the universe.

I lost nearly everything after I left the Church of Scientology. As I set out to leave, people in the church warned me that my business and personal reputation were already under siege and I should expect the worst.

And the furies did pounce. Even now, when I have proven myself to be innocent of any wrongdoing, I still read comments on the Internet by Scientologists who want me, in the words of L. Ron Hubbard, "utterly destroyed."

Within the swirl of darkness that enveloped me, however, my faith in humankind remained intact. I could not have made it through the degrading days in court without my two priests, Reverend Ed Bacon and Reverend Zelda Kennedy, who held me tight within their loving embrace. Friends like Martie and Simon, who sat by my side and entwined their warm and calming hands with my shaking ones. I have been extremely heartened by the actions of my clients. Before the charges against me were dropped, they refused to testify against me and banded together to petition the state to leave me alone and allow me to rebuild my shattered life. They attended my court hearings, and wrote letters of support, and signed sworn affidavits testifying to my honesty and integrity. They continued to believe in me when it must have been hard to do so. Out of all the people that I knew in the insurance industry, only two never walked away. Tracey Carragher and Sam Watson were constantly looking for ways to support me, and when I finally asked for support, Tracey and Sam were right by my side. I became witness to this amazing energy of love that not only transformed my heart but also guided me through the roughest of days.

In a letter to the district attorney, my former client Kathy Ridenour, who is a spokesperson for the group, wrote: "The vast majority of people involved with this case are fully supportive of Ms. Seward. There may be 5 percent who want some sort of revenge, but should we allow this small of a group to dictate this case? We certainly hope not. That would be a travesty and a tragedy." She has been one of the angels who sustained me over these torturous months and years.

The playwrights of ancient Greece well understood the elements of tragedy. To learn, Aeschylus said, one must suffer. The legal assaults sullied my professional reputation. The news media accounts of these investigations humiliated me.

The days of driving Bentleys and renting helicopters on a whim are far behind me. I am broke now. I have used every last asset to reimburse clients. I am far from being able to say they have been repaid. But my loyalty to them will remain unbroken until every penny of what they lost has been recovered.

My greatest loss, however, has nothing to do with my pride or fortune. By walking away from the church, I turned my back on an entire life—friendships and associations that were decades old. In doing so, I also rejected the ethical foundation that had guided my life. I was a ship unmoored. My entire adult existence was founded on the guidelines of Scientology. I thought I was progressing toward a higher state of being. I believed that the church was a righteous force in society. We were going to save the world! Then it was gone. All of it. My beliefs. My values. My purpose. I had to figure out which parts of me were my brainwashed self and what was authentic. Who was I? And who did I want to be? The questions both excited and angered me. Excited because I could finally explore thoughts and feelings that had been asleep for more than twenty years. Angry because I had allowed myself to be conned by a so-called religion based on science fiction, absurdities and deception.

I left when I no longer felt that the church played any positive role, when I realized its doctrines—such as rejecting gay people and others following lifestyles it would not recognize—were destructive and exploitative. But what was my plan B? What was I supposed to believe in afterward?

I spy flowers—bluebells? hosta?—through my window and ponder growth. The Chinese philosopher Lao-tzu conjectured that you cannot grow until you confront the void within.

"Become totally empty," he wrote. "Quiet the restlessness of the mind. Only then will you witness everything unfolding from emptiness."

That was what I discovered. I was empty.

After so many years of following Scientology's rules with the goal of reaching enlightenment, I experienced a realization so difficult to swallow that it was staggering. I was nothing but a shell—a brittle, hard shell—of a person. Appearances can be so deceiving. From the outside, I looked pretty good. I worked hard. I was financially successful. I devoted myself to the church. I sold my religion to anyone who was willing to bite. **It will fulfill you like nothing else you have ever known!** I would say. Yet there was nothing inside of me. Nothing. I was taught to feel nothing. By conforming, by doing what others did merely because they did it, I had paved the way, in the words of Virginia Woolf, for a lethargy that "steals over all the finer nerves and faculties of the soul." I had become "all outer show and inward emptiness; dull, callous, and indifferent."

But there's something to be said for emptiness. Once it becomes obvious to you, all the important matters become apparent too.

Truth has empowered me. Truth. Verity. Certainty. I know who I am now. I know what I did and didn't do. I am not afraid of the truth. I have come a long way and paid the price for knowing the truth about myself. I will never lose my way again. I am determined to "speak out the whole truth," as Mahatma Gandhi often put it. Silence is a form of cowardice.

I am finding my way in my new spirituality. I have promised myself never to put all my beliefs under one heading. I find solace in reading the Bible and quotes from Buddha and Mark Nepo's book **Finding Inner Courage**. My practice of meditation and prayer has brought me to God.

Grace has saved me too. When I think of grace, I think of the simple elegance, the refinement of movement, of my own children when they race across the lawn. I've come to believe in another kind of grace too. Life bestows gifts upon us, often unmerited. The key is to recognize and appreciate them. My children and Charley are my greatest gifts. When I reflect upon how each came into my life, "grace" is the only description that fits.

For too long, I sped through my days, rushing through breakfast with my children, often leaving them with caregivers while I worked. I loved my children fiercely as any mother would. As a single mother, I was preoccupied with providing the best life for them. It may sound obvious, but what has changed for me is that my children are no longer part of my to-do list. **Drive this one**

to practice. Check this one's homework. How's that art project coming? I am much more focused now on savoring moments with them. They can be small, like when we laugh and act silly together. They can be important, such as the first time one of them learned to ride a bike.

By appreciating how incredibly beautiful and wonderful my children are, I have learned to notice and take in other gifts. Nature means more to me than it used to. And I don't have to go to Yellowstone National Park either. I open the window, feel the breeze, embrace the sun.

I struggle to explain the importance of romantic love in my life. I want to do it justice. I want to say that a person in love is consumed with the other and possesses a need for her or him as raw as hunger. I was not prepared for how much love has changed me. It came to me late but came to me just the same. I have never been so happy, so balanced, so free. The idea that Charley feels the same about me is intoxicating.

Charley is beautiful, brilliant, vivacious and the love of my life. Not a minute goes by without me thinking of her or being aware of her in some way, even if she is not around. When you are loved and appreciated and understood, it changes the way you look at life. I wish this gift for everyone. There is a happy momentum; you live in the present and you are confident in the future because you will be there for each other. You are bound to each other.

This overwhelming sense of union, to me, is the central characteristic of love.

There are still times when I feel angry and defeated and scared, but not very often. Mostly, I am grateful. I know I went through all of this for a reason. I needed to be humbled. I needed to be reminded of how it felt to be marginalized and small and without hope, which led me back to empathy. I am emotionally free from the vicious, judgmental restraints of Scientology. My children are healthy and happy. My mom is safe and we can finally have a real life together. And my relationship with Charley is stronger than ever. I feel like I have tapped into a real energy that flows in this world, which is love. I have a lot of repair ahead of me but this time I'm doing it differently!

My message is this: Love allows you to see the truth clearly. Grace, truth and love will always prevail.

I gaze outside once again. The sky is cloudless, the wind soft. I head out to enjoy another beautiful day.

April 22, 2015
Renee Smith Cartaya
Deputy District Attorney
201 North Figueroa St. Suite 1600
Los Angeles, Calif. 90012

Dear Ms. Cartaya,

On January 19, 2015, I wrote a letter to you pleading for you to drop the case against Michelle Seward. I am again writing to you on behalf of the vast majority of clients in the Michelle Seward Trust. See the attached list.

As members of the trust we are getting extremely frustrated, stressed to the limit, with some members experiencing physical ailments of many kinds because of this non-ending investigation. We want it to end. The insurance investigator keeps calling and pushing our members to turn against Ms. Seward. This we will not do. There has been no evidence of any wrongdoing on the part of Michelle Seward, and yet the investigation continues to try to prove that she did something wrong. When will this end?

The investigator is repeatedly calling clients trying to get them to interview with him with the end result of ultimately testifying against Ms. Seward. He is using scare tactics, telling people that Michelle is a sociopath who deliberately set up this investment as a Ponzi scheme; she never had any intention of paying anyone back. One client, Mr. Tedrow, was interviewed with a tape recorder recording the interview. The agent then turned off the tape recorder and told Mr. Tedrow that he wanted to tell him some things off the record. He then proceeded to tell him personal things about Michelle concerning how much she used to pay for her house payment, and what kind of luxury car she drove. This appears to be a pattern with this investigator.

My own personal experience with this investigator during an interview was very frightening. He informed my husband and me that we would never see any of our money back because Ms. Seward is the worst kind of sociopath there is, a person who cares about no one but herself. He stated that she went after senior citizens because she knew we were more vulnerable. He seemed obsessed with her, even at one point mentioning how extraordinarily beautiful Ms. Seward is.

This type of so-called investigation work is causing many people to suffer. I would like to tell you about just a few of the people that have experienced stress due to this ongoing investigation. It is only a sampling of the hurt that is being caused by this endless investigation, but it will give you an idea of how people's health is being affected.

For myself, as a trustee who is in contact with the trust members, the stress of this non-stop investigation, which is beginning to feel like a witch hunt, has really taken a toll on my health. At one point my doctor could not figure out what was wrong with me. I could barely get out of bed for weeks. After doing tests, the doctors discovered that my inflammation level was off the chart. The final conclusion, however, was that the stress I am under was causing me serious problems. I also ended up in the hospital for a week because they thought I was having heart problems. The cause again was stress. The stress, which other members are also experiencing, is coming from this ongoing, ruthless investigation.

Another client, Michael Turnipseed, has experienced similar problems. He was taken to the emergency room with a blood pressure rating of 196 over 138. His wife told me that an investigator calls them daily wanting an interview. She said the stress is overwhelming and that she believes this ongoing investigation is causing her husband's problems.

Mr. and Mrs. Brown are two other clients that have had serious health problems brought on by the stress of what is happening. Mr. Brown was in the hospital for an extended period of time with heart problems. They have been called repeatedly by an investigator as well. They cannot handle the stress of what is happening and refuse to talk to any agent that calls them.

Lloyd Dickey is another client that I'm going to tell you about. I had talked to him on many occasions. He had told me that he could not handle everything that was going on and that his health was in serious jeopardy. Mr. Dickey died before this case could be resolved. I believe that the stress of the ongoing investigation, along with the many scare tactics that were being used to get people to testify against Ms. Seward, certainly hastened his death.

There are many more clients that have told me that they are stressed and have experienced health problems because of the ongoing investigation. Everyone wants it to end. I have been in contact with at least 90 to 95% of the clients, and everyone is standing behind Ms. Seward. They all want investigators to stop the constant pressuring for interviews and the scare tactics to try to get them to testify against Michelle. They want the District Attorney to drop this case. They want to get on with their lives and to have this constant continued stress on their lives stopped!

I think it is important for you to know that

people in the trust don't want to cooperate with this investigation because the few times that people have cooperated their statements have been changed, taken out of context, or the good things that were said about Michelle Seward were deleted.

The vast majority of people involved with this case are fully supportive of Ms. Seward. There may be 5% who want some sort of revenge, but should we allow this small of a group to dictate this case? I certainly hope not. That would be a travesty and a tragedy.

Those of us who are in the Michelle Seward Trust are suffering with all kinds of ailments because of the ongoing investigation. We know that Ms. Seward has done nothing wrong, and it pains us to see an innocent person continually being persecuted. We want this persecution to stop!

Attached are the names of the members of this trust who support this letter and urge you to drop this case. If you have any questions, I would be happy to speak with you.

On behalf of the clients in the Michelle Seward Trust,

Respectfully,
Kathy Ridenour

ACKNOWLEDGMENTS

When I started writing my acknowledgments and gratitude, I realized that there were so many people who not only stood steadfast by my side, but who actually helped to save my life. My words of gratitude don't do justice to the depth of love I feel for you. I would not be free, or even be here, to love my family without every single one of you.

Mom, thank you for choosing me. Thank you for allowing love to guide you back and thank you for being by my side through it all. We have a second chance at getting it right as mother and daughter. I am grateful that you are here with me to raise my children and experience all the gifts that life has brought us! Freedom has been a mountain to climb for us both, but we have done it together. I love you!

Dad and Sue, you have always stood by my side—allowing me to grow, to run and to fall, but you have always been there. I am forever grateful for your compassion, your kindness and your love. Dad, I know how hard you worked at being a great father, a great teacher, and an amazing human being. I didn't get enough time in this book to say how thankful I am for you!

To my sister, my best friend, you have given so much of your adult life to be by my side! In my darkest moment, you were there to hold my hand and tell me I was going to be okay. You have given me the gifts of love, trust, friendship and my sweet nephew and nieces, Riley, Keira and Baby Charlie! I know that my tragedy also affected your life, and for that, I am sorry! Now I am thrilled that we can share the best of times together. I am so proud of the woman you have become and I love you so much.

To my brother, Jeremy, you were able to see through the facade before I did. You were able to protect yourself and your family and stay steadfast, no matter what came in your direction. You have also been wrongly attacked by this chaos. I am sorry, and I admire your strength, your intelligence and your unwavering support. I love you and your amazing and beautiful wife, Diana, and my sweet niece, Baya!

Martie, you have shared the greatest times and the worst of times with us. You have been there for us and the children in more ways than I can count. You have provided refuge, sanctuary, love and support when we needed it most. You are more than a friend—you are family, and you will hold a special place in my heart forever.

Cody and Josh, thank you for loving me and believing in me enough to know that I would make it through this storm. Thank you for giving me the space to love such an amazing woman. I'm so happy to have you in my life! Your constant encouragement and love helped me along the way.

To my spiritual guides and armor, Reverend Ed Bacon and Reverend Zelda Kennedy from All Saints Episcopal, from the moment I walked through your door, you accepted all of me—my doubts, my fears, my questions—but most of all you saw only the good in me. You held my hand during the worst of times and shined the light for me to find my way out of darkness. Thank you, my dear friends.

Ginger, Jimmy, Sherry, Charlie, Suzanne and Jessica, you have always welcomed me with open arms into your family, even with all the turmoil that surrounded me. You always provided us a place to breathe and a place for my children to run and experience their love of nature. You taught me the true importance of love and family, and Ginger, Your daily calls helped keep us going! Thank you.

Kathy and Rik Ridenour, I would not be on the other side of hell without you helping guide me on my way to freedom. You are two of the most selfless people I know and your kindness pulled me up when I needed it the most. You are spiritual warriors for truth and justice, and this world is a better place because you are in it. Kathy, there could be a whole book just on your unwavering love and support!

Pat Mitchell and Scott Seydel, the word "friend" doesn't come close to describing my love and gratitude for you. From the moment we met in Vermont, we knew that you would be our best friends! You have been our shoulders to cry on, the ears to listen to our fears and the souls who have mended our broken hearts. I look forward to more travels, lots of great wine and storytelling around the fire with our two best friends!

Tracey Carragher, it is rare to find a person who embodies your strength, conviction, empathy, compassion and love! You have always believed in my innocence, the truth and my abilities, even when I did not. You helped to save my life, and for that I will always be grateful! I hope to grow into the person that you have become.

Simon, Carla and Lily Baitler, thank you for helping me see the truth. Thank you for loving me and always being my biggest cheerleaders!

Jerald Welch, thank you for riding out the storm as long as you could and for always lending an open ear when I needed it.

To the 127 clients who worked diligently to protect and support me, I am here today because of you! Your constant support, letters, petitions and caring e-mails got me through each day! You stood by my side and I will always stand by yours.

Gene O'Brien, thank you for taking on a trust that few people believed in and thank you for the opportunity to prove myself to you and my clients!

Cindy and Trisha, it is difficult to put into words my gratefulness for the two of you. You never left my side. You put yourselves in jeopardy to help me and you never wavered in your belief of my innocence. You will always be in my heart and I will always be here for you.

Trisha, Courtney, Vanessa, Chrissy, Kelli and Deco, your love for my children wrapped them in a protective blanket when I could not. You gave up your lives for our lives and I will never forget your sacrifices. I love you all and you must know that my children are wonderful little human beings because of your love and influence!

Ana, you made our lives beautiful with your talent and your love. We are so grateful!

My amazing attorneys whose hearts always stayed in the fight—Steve Cooley, Daniel Nixon, Jennifer Derwin, Pam Johnston, Bob Hogeboom, Mark Seelig, Mitch Lampert, Elaine Rodgers, Eddie Garland, Diane Goodman, Vince Chieffo and Jay Cooper! Thank you for believing in me. Thank you for never giving up and thank you for saving my life!

To our friends who never wavered in their support and their love: Jackie and Bob Kosocoff and their daughter, Davida; Kay and Billy Koplovitz; Norman and Lynn Lear; Kevin and Gina Gore; Edie Fraser and Joe Oppenheimer; the DMI team, Ken, Kevin G., Kevin C., Brian, Laura, Steve, Nicole and everyone who gave great hugs and encouraging smiles! You always made me feel welcome, loved and supported! You are kind souls and I thank you for believing in me!

Debbie Allen, AKA Ms. Galaxy, thank you for always protecting the love that you witnessed between "Charlie" and me, no matter how crazy it was! You have believed in us, you have given us refuge, laughter and now an outlet for our story! You are a sister and a friend to us both, and I will be forever orbiting your galaxy!

Lynn Shanahan, thank you for believing in my vision and mission to help other women feel beautiful! Your guidance, expertise and friendship mean the world to me, and I cannot wait to see what the future has in store for us!

BJ Bernstein, thank you for welcoming us with open arms and giving me a place to be as open as I needed in a place that no one knew the truth! Your friendship is dear to us and always will be!

Jonathan Kraut, thank you for uncovering the truth and doing it so selflessly! Your talent, your confidence in me and your steadfast belief in uncovering the lie helped save my life! I am forever grateful!

Robin Gaby Fisher, thank you for choosing to write my story, for believing in me, for living this hell with me and for experiencing the joy of love and freedom together! You are the conduit for a very complicated story and I am so grateful that you stuck it out with me.

Thanks to my agent, Anthony Mattero of Foundry, for believing in my story and never giving up on me when things continued to get worse. You gave me hope when all was lost. Tracy Bernstein of Penguin, you gave me my voice back, a way to work through my pain and a light at the end of a very long and dark tunnel! Your own personal strength and perseverance were a reminder to me that I could not give up! I am more grateful than I have words to express to the both of you!

Hope, you were my monthly respite, my monthly psychological session, a dear friend, an ear when I needed it and, most of all, the best damn hair-stylist ever! You helped me feel good on the outside when I felt horrible on the inside! Thank you, my friend!

I could have dedicated entire chapters to some of the angels who have touched my life, but sadly I wasn't able to do so. My parents, our best friends and our family, these pages do not come close to explaining how much you mean to me!